MAXIM HEALTH

How to follow God's will 719-635 1/1/
$75.00

How to Live a Longer, Healthier Life as You Safeguard Yourself and Your Loved Ones from the **H1N1 Virus**

God's will Package

DR. TED BROER

Bookmark
PUBLISHING
DALLAS, TEXAS

Mosses missed God's calling

MAXIMUM HEALTH

Published by
Bookmark Publishing
Dallas, Texas

Details in some anecdotes and stories have been changed to protect the identities of the persons involved.

ISBN: 1-59024-405-2

Printed in the United States of America

CONTENTS

INTRODUCTION

Like you, I began hearing the term "pandemic" applied to the influenza A virus subtype H1N1 (also known as swine flu) at the beginning of 2009. During April of that year, the World Health Organization (WHO) raised its pandemic alert level on H1N1 from a three to a five. Then on June 11, 2009, with nearly thirty thousand confirmed cases around the globe, that pandemic level was pushed up to level six, WHO's highest level, and it became the world's first full-blown pandemic since 1968.[1]

More than ever, people took notice. After all, a pandemic is nothing to be ignored, right?

In case you are wondering, a pandemic is an epidemic of infectious disease that spreads through humans across a large region, such as a continent or even worldwide. A disease is not labeled a pandemic just because it is widespread or because a large number of people die from it; it must also be infectious and contagious.

PANDEMICS IN HISTORY

According to WHO, a pandemic can start when three conditions are met:

1. the emergence of a disease new to a population
2. humans are infected, causing serious illness

3. the infection spreads easily and over a sustained period of time[2]

There have been a number of pandemics throughout history, including such highly destructive ones as:

- **Plague of Athens**, 430 BC: Typhoid fever killed a quarter of the Athenian population and lasted over four years, eventually reducing the dominance of Athens as a world power.[3]

- **Antonine Plague** in Italy, AD 165–180: The plague killed a quarter of all who were infected, perhaps as many as five million. During a second outbreak, called the Plague of Cyprian (AD 251–266), five thousand people died daily in Rome alone.[4]

- **Plague of Justinian**, AD 541–750: This was the first recorded outbreak of bubonic plague. It spread from Egypt to Constantinople, killing 25–50 percent of the population of the known world.[5]

- **Black Death**, 1348–1600s: One of the deadliest pandemics in human history, widely thought to have been an outbreak of bubonic plague, the first of many two- to five-year cycles of more than one hundred plagues that swept through Europe, eventually killing an estimated seventy-five million people worldwide.[6]

- **Third Pandemic**, 1800–present: This plague was spread through the bacillus that causes bubonic plague and ranged from China throughout the world, eventually killing ten million people in India alone. According to WHO, the pandemic was considered active until 1959, but as many as two hundred cases are reported each year, largely in the western United States.[7]

• **Smallpox Pandemic**, 1157 BC–present: Small-pox kills at least one-third of all it infects. It spread from Egypt to India then to China and around the world. Half the native population of Hispaniola in 1518 was killed by this pandemic, which also ravaged Mexico in the 1520s, killing 150,000 in Tenochtitlán alone.[8] In 1618–19, smallpox wiped out 90 percent of the native tribes of Massachusetts Bay, and during the 1770s smallpox killed at least 30 percent of the native peoples of the Pacific Northwest. Smallpox epidemics in 1780–82 and 1837–38 brought devastation and drastic depopulation among the tribes of the Great Plains. Smallpox also devastated the native population of Australia, killing around 50 percent of indigenous Australians in the early years of British colonization. An estimated three hundred million people around the world died from smallpox in the twentieth century.[9]

The list of historical pandemics goes on and on, including leprosy (which has plagued mankind since ancient times, and even today as many as 750,000 new cases are detected worldwide each year), malaria (once common throughout Europe and North America, it continues to be widespread mostly in the tropical areas of the Americas, Asia, and Africa, with 350–500 million new cases each year), measles (200 million people worldwide have died from this highly contagious disease over the past 150 years, and there are still approximately 40 million cases globally each year), tuberculosis (each year 8 million people around the world become ill with this disease and 2 million die), typhus (this disease emerged in the 1400s; it is often called camp fever, gaol [jail] fever, and ship fever for its pattern of sweeping through soldiers, prisoners of war, and sailors during times of conflict; it has afflicted millions through the years), and yellow fever (a virus transmitted by mosquitoes, yellow fever was deemed one of the most dangerous infectious diseases during the 1900s, and since the number of cases of yellow fever has been increasing during recent decades, yellow fever is considered a reemerging disease).

One of the most recent pandemics to emerge is HIV/AIDS, first noticed on a growing scale in 1969. Acquired immunodeficiency syndrome (AIDS) is a disease of the human immune system caused by the human immunodeficiency virus (HIV). HIV is a condition in which the immune system begins to fail. The disease spreads through the transfer of blood, semen, vaginal fluid, preejaculate, and breast milk.[10] HIV infection in humans is considered pandemic by WHO. Since the late 1970s, AIDS has killed more than 25 million people, and HIV currently infects about .6 percent of the world's population.[11] As I type these words, 33.2 million people have AIDS, an estimated 2.4–3.3 million lives will be lost this year, of which more than 570,000 will be children, with a third of all HIV/AIDS-related deaths occurring in sub-Saharan Africa.[12]

INFLUENZA PANDEMICS

Influenza, first described in 412 BC by Hippocrates, the Greek physician and father of medicine, has caused more than its share of pandemics, dating back to the first recorded outbreak in 1580 and continuing since then on an average of every ten to thirty years.[13] Influenza pandemics have included the **Asiatic Flu** (1889–90, possibly caused by the H2N8 type of flu virus, resulting in as many as one million deaths), the **Spanish Flu** (1918–19, which became a worldwide pandemic on all continents, with an estimated fifty million to one hundred million deaths, eventually infected an estimated one-third of the world's population, and it has since been identified as a type of the H1N1 virus), the **Asian Flu** (1957–58, an H2N2 virus first identified in China then spread to the United States, causing about seventy thousand deaths and eventually causing approximately two million deaths globally), and the **Hong Kong Flu** (1968–69, an H3N2 virus that was first detected in Hong Kong and spread to the United States, where it caused about thirty-four thousand deaths, and to the world, where it killed approximately one million people.

The bird flu or aviary flu scare of a few years ago, although still around and dangerous, never reached pandemic levels. However, that changed.

Emergence of H1N1 Flu

Although flu pandemics are hardly new, the H1N1 virus that emerged in Mexico in April 2009 was the first truly novel flu virus seen for more than forty years. Since flu pandemics exclude seasonal influenzas, for the H1N1 flu to reach pandemic levels, it was obviously more than a typical outbreak.

It was originally (and erroneously) called swine flu because laboratory testing showed that many of the genes in this new virus were very similar to influenza viruses that normally occur in pigs in North America. However, studies quickly showed that the new H1N1 virus was very different from what normally circulates in North American swine.

What happened next was a worldwide roller coaster of dire predictions, unsavory solutions, and much misinformation. Headlines around the world trumpeted, "Swine Flu Pandemic Is Not Just Another Health Scare." We were told by experts on the Presidential Advisory Panel that the H1N1 virus could infect 50 percent of the U.S. population, possibly killing as many as one hundred thousand people. The World Health Organization estimated that this pandemic could infect one-third of all people before it finished its course. Worse, no one seemed to know if the H1N1 vaccine would be effective or harmful or if there would be enough for the people who desired to be immunized.

Most people who became ill with this new virus recovered without requiring medical treatment. However, the infection quickly began spreading around the world, ranging in impact from mild to severe, and often requiring hospitalization.

Statistics have been difficult to gather, but in the United States alone, somewhere between 1,200 and 4,000 deaths occurred during 2009 (depending upon whose statistics you believe). Regardless, after all the buildup, it was a small fraction of the yearly average of the 41,400 people who die each year in the United States from influenza.[14]

The total number of cases worldwide confirmed to have H1N1 symptoms is just over 500,000.

Influenza spreads around the world in seasonal epidemics, resulting in the deaths of hundreds of thousands worldwide annually and millions in pandemic years.

What Direction Now?

What is a person supposed to do? Ignore or heed the dire warnings? Refuse or receive the vaccination?

I strongly suggest that you stay aware of the news, realizing that statistics can prove anything and understanding that government agencies, educational institutions, healthcare providers, and other experts often have a less-than-pure agenda.

Heed the warning from your parents: it's okay to listen to the people trying to do wonderful things for you, but keep your hand on your wallet!

There is an old Russian proverb: *Doveryai, no proveryai.* It means "trust but verify."

That, in a nutshell, is what I recommend to people who respond to anything that could hurt their families, including diseases du jour.

For starters, know the symptoms and the risks.

Symptoms and Risks

The symptoms of most seasonal influenzas may include the following:

- fever
- cough
- sore throat
- runny or stuffy nose
- body aches
- chills
- vomiting
- diarrhea

In adults, emergency warning signs that need urgent medical attention include:

- difficulty breathing or shortness of breath
- pain or pressure in the chest or abdomen
- sudden dizziness

- confusion
- severe or persistent vomiting
- flu-like symptoms improve but then return with fever and a worse cough

Among children, emergency warning signs that need urgent medical attention include:

- fast breathing or trouble breathing
- bluish or gray skin color
- not drinking enough fluids
- severe or persistent vomiting
- not waking up or not interacting
- being so irritable that the child does not want to be held
- flu-like symptoms improve but then return with fever and a worse cough

It is important to realize that, as with seasonal flu, certain people are at high risk of serious complications, including people sixty-five years and older, children younger than five years old, pregnant women, and people of any age with certain chronic medical conditions. In fact, approximately 70 percent of people who have been hospitalized with the H1N1 virus have experienced one or more medical conditions, such as pregnancy, diabetes, heart disease, asthma, and kidney ailments.

Young children are also at a high risk of serious complications from the H1N1 virus, just as they are from seasonal flu. And while people sixty-five and older are the least likely to be infected with the H1N1 flu, if they get sick, they are also at a high risk of developing serious complications from their illness.

BASIC TIPS FOR KEEPING HEALTHY DURING INFLUENZA OUTBREAKS

In addition to knowing the symptoms and risks of seasonal flu outbreaks, there are ten basic guidelines that anyone can follow to stay healthier:

1. **Wash your hands frequently** with soap and water for twenty seconds or use an alcohol-based hand sanitizer if soap and water are not available.
2. **Avoid touching your nose, mouth, and eyes.** These are infection hot spots.
3. **Keep frequently touched common surfaces clean.** This includes telephones, cell phones, doorknobs, computer keyboards, and sink faucets.
4. **Cover your coughs and sneezes with a tissue, or cough and sneeze into your upper sleeve.** Dispose of tissues in no-touch trash receptacles, then wash your hands or use an alcohol-based hand sanitizer afterward.
5. **Stay home** if you are sick with an influenza-like illness; for example, fever or chills and cough or sore throat. In addition, flu symptoms can include a runny nose, body aches, headache, fatigue, diarrhea, or vomiting. The Centers for Disease Control

recommends that people stay home if they are ill with influenza-like illness until they have been free of a fever (100°F [37.8°C] or greater) at least twenty-four hours or until they have no sign of a fever without the use of fever-reducing medications. In most cases, this would require staying home for three to five days in order to meet the recommended waiting period whether or not antiviral medications are used.

6. **Avoid using other people's phones, desks, offices, work tools, or other equipment.** If absolutely necessary, clean the item first with a disinfectant.

7. **Maintain a healthy lifestyle** with attention to rest diet, exercise, and relaxation. This also helps to maintain physical and emotional health.

8. **Use the best immune support vitamins and supplements.** We make available the finest, most effective products for you at Health Masters (contact www.HealthMasters.com or 1-800-726-1834 for more information or to purchase these supplements from my office).

9. **Take vitamin C to build your immune system.** I recommend our excellent C product (which is highly effective with calcium ascorbate, magnesium ascorbate, and potassium ascorbate).

10. Also, be sure to **take natural lanolin-based D3 vitamins.** I recommend 500 IUs daily.

Actually, these are great guidelines for everyday life. They are the primary steps toward safeguarding yourself and your loved ones from diseases such as the H1N1 virus.

MAXIMUM HEALTH

But what else should you do to have great health, year in and year out, regardless of the latest diseases, epidemics, and pandemics?

I have spent decades developing my Eat, Drink, and Be Healthy! program. Again and again, people's lives have been changed as they have learned to develop great habits and eliminate bad ones. Armed with decades of research and development, I have written this book specifically to offer the very best strategies that I have gleaned and utilized by offering twenty steps to a power-packed immune system to safeguard you and your loved ones. Each of the following twenty chapters is filled with proven, practical principles, beginning at the top by maximizing your brain.

One note: Since what I teach is a multifaceted approach toward health—body, mind, and spirit—across a variety of leading-edge nutrition and fitness strategies, there will be some overlapping of principles throughout the book. This is done on purpose to reinforce the steps toward a power-packed immune system.

I have devoted my career to blasting away the barriers that tend to keep people of all ages and backgrounds from achieving their goals, and this book was born from my overwhelming desire to motivate people toward maximum health, energy, and fitness. You can have a life of adventure and wellness, no matter what happens around you or how others respond to always-present challenges. But everything depends upon how you take responsibility for yourself!

SELF-RESPONSIBILITY

You have heard the old adage, "Life is God's gift to you; what you do with it is your gift back to Him."

He gave quite a gift. The psalmist wrote, "I will praise You, for I am fearfully and wonderfully made; marvelous are Your works, and that my soul knows very well" (Psalm 139:14).

You have probably also read this Bible verse: "Each of you should know how to possess his own vessel in sanctification and honor" (1 Thessalonians 4:4). Another translation of that verse says, "Learn to appreciate and give dignity to your body, not abusing it, as is so common among those who know nothing of God" (4:4–5, MSG).

Self-responsibility lies at the center of health and wellness. Your life and health depend upon factors largely under your own control. You hold the key to tomorrow's doors. Your actions and decisions affect all the next steps.

Winston Churchill once said, "The price of greatness is responsibility." More specifically, for the sake of this book and your life, I would paraphrase that as, "The price of maximum health is self-responsibility."

You are the key! Therefore, this book can be a journal of your own journey. Read and reread the chapters. If it is your copy, write in it and dog-ear things that are especially important to you. Make it your own even as you internalize what you learn.

Maximum health is up to you as you receive wisdom to use the tools and principles available to you. What better time than right now to get started?

1

MAXIMIZE YOUR BRAIN

Recently I was privileged to be invited by Joel Osteen to be with him at Lakewood Church in Houston. He had used my Eat, Drink, and Be Healthy! program to teach three Sunday mornings on the subject of health.

What a phenomenal church! They hold services in the old Compaq Center where the Houston Rockets won so many exciting games. I remember speaking there twice back in the 1990s on the Success Circuit. It was at those events where I had the privilege to share the platform with President George H. W. Bush, Barbara Bush, Colin Powell, Bill Cosby, Larry King, and so many more of my heroes. So while I was there with Joel and Victoria Osteen, it was great to see the renovation and how beautiful the facility had become.

The first words out of Joel's mouth to me—"I love your stuff!"—referred to my books, CDs, DVDs, and supplements.

"I love your stuff too!" I said. My words to him were equally heartfelt.

We really hit it off, and I was able to spend quite a bit of time with him after the service. Interestingly enough, a group of Christian reporters was there from Germany. They were shocked when I started speaking German to them.

My first language is German. What I noticed immediately was that these Germans wanted what Joel had. They wanted the joy of the Lord. During the television interview they had with him, they were enamored with the power, joy, and love of God that flows so freely through him.

So, you may be thinking, what does this have to do in a book titled *Maximum Health* in a chapter about maximizing your brain?

I'm glad you asked!

The Importance of Your Brain

To live a longer, healthier life, one of the best places to start is at the top! The brain, whether we are speaking a foreign language, remembering scriptures, or recalling where we placed our car keys, is critical to maintaining a healthy, happy, and productive life. Everything you do to have great brain health will affect your life and wellness.

Until recently the standard medical belief was that we were born with a certain number of brain cells that slowly died off and were never replaced, resulting in a gradual mental decline that usually ended in senility. In fact, "benign forgetfulness of old age" remained a formal diagnosis.

Well, let me tell you, you can forget all of that. Advances in brain imaging, genetics, and neuroscience now show that our body continues to create new brain cells throughout our life. Also the neurons in our brains continue to change, develop, and forge new connections even as we age. We actually have physical changes in our brain every time we learn something new. This evoking adaptability is called neuroplasticity.

Some scientists believe that dementia and Alzheimer's occurs when the brain loses this ability to grow and change. I think other causes include aluminum, lead, and aspartame (NutraSweet) poisoning. In fact, I wrote a book titled *Maximum Memory* (available by calling 1-800-726-1834 or online at www.HealthMasters.com).

The sad reality of Alzheimer's is that 50 percent of all baby boomers will develop the disease. I am so glad that is not going to happen to any of you who read my newsletters and follow my simple advice.

FOUR QUICK ACTION ITEMS TO MAXIMIZE YOUR BRAIN

Probably the biggest falsehood based on all this new information is that growing old has to lead to the deterioration of our mental ability. Here are four tips that I have used for years to keep my brain and memory sharp.

1. **Exercise your brain daily.** The brain is similar to your muscles. If you don't use it, you lose it. Crossword puzzles are another great brain exercise. But remember, crossword puzzles and number puzzles have to challenge you. They can't be simple. Go through old photo albums on a regular basis. Remember your friends and vacations long forgotten. Force your brain to recall positive, happy thoughts from your childhood. Engage in activities that involve multiple senses, such as learning dance steps or a new form of aerobics or, for those of you who are capable or inclined, karate. Also excellent are goals such as learning to play a guitar or keyboard. Remember, any time you challenge your brain, it renews itself, forming new dendrites and synapses. That in turn prompts the brain to produce growth molecules.

2. **Focus on what you are doing.** Try not to multi-task too much. Focus, focus, focus. For example, I have four children plus a lot of employees. When I write, I go to a backroom of my office and close the door. I don't bring my phone, and I don't take calls unless it is an emergency. Remember, I am over fifty years old and I feel great. My mental acuity is as good as ever.

3. **Stay social. Interact.** Don't be a hermit. Older

adults who stay social after retirement have been shown to score much better on IQ tests. Socialization requires memory, logical function, interactive skills, communication, reasoning, and thinking. Keeping active is so important.

4. **Eat right.** You knew I would get to this sooner or later. Refer to chapter 2. What you eat directly affects your brain, and your brain health affects your entire body.

NINE KEY STRATEGIES FOR BRAIN HEALTH

In addition to these four action items, let me offer nine of the best guidelines I have found for developing your brain:

1. **Take cod liver oil daily.** Take one to two teaspoons daily. The brain has to have omega-3 fatty acid to function. The brand that we carry and I personally take is simply the best. The right kind of omega-3 fatty acid also helps to burn body fat, fight depression (actually better than Prozac), increase IQ scores in children and adults, reduce inflammation, and relieve joint pain.

   By the way, postpartum depression in most cases is caused by a lack of omega-3 fatty acid in the brain of the mother. During the last trimester of pregnancy, the fetus requires large amounts of omega-3 fatty acid for proper brain development. If the mother isn't taking an omega-3 supplement (like cod liver oil), the fetus literally sucks the omega-3 fatty acid from the mother's brain. This can cause severe mood swings and postpartum depression.

I am partial to our Health Masters Cod Liver Oil (available at www.HealthMasters.com), since it offers more vitamin A and D than any other product on the market. It is fermented cod liver oil, twice as potent with half the dosage! Fermentation of the raw liver yields oil rich in enzymes, making the fermented oil uniquely strengthening. Our fermented oil contains ten times more quinones than unfermented. Quinones include vitamins K and E, coenzyme Q_{10}, and other important biological molecules.

2. **Avoid alcohol.** I mention this in the eating healthy chapter. Alcohol kills brain cells. Enough said!

3. **Avoid aspartame.** I also mention this in the eating healthy chapter. Aspartame kills brain cells. Again, enough said.

4. **Avoid MSG.** It also kills brain cells. There are plenty of healthy alternatives (order my wife's *Maximum Energy Cookbook* and *Healthy Country Cooking* for suggestions).

5. **Avoid hydrogenated oils and trans fats.** They plug up your arteries and reduce oxygen flow to the brain, thereby killing brain cells.

6. **Don't use aluminum anything.** The brain and our bodies are both based on bioelectrical development.

Our brain literally sends a bioelectrical charge through our spine and nerves for us to move. Thoughts are real things that can be measured. When we put metals in our brain that conduct electricity, they affect neurological functions in a very negative way.

Aluminum, lead, and mercury can pass through the blood-brain barrier. It gets into the brain. Aluminum, lead, and mercury are incredibly toxic and also conduct electricity.

The brain literally short circuits. It can no longer function the way God made it. Hence we are diagnosed with Alzheimer's or senile dementia.

7. **Exercise is always critical.** See chapter 7. Exercise increases blood flow to the brain. Walking with a good pair of shoes or using an elliptical running machine are great blood-pumping exercises.

    In one American Academy of Neurology study, for every extra mile a woman walked per week, her risk of cognitive decline dropped by 13 percent. In a study of more than seventeen hundred seniors, those who exercised three or more times a week had the lowest risk of Alzheimer's; see the January 2006 *Annals of Internal Medicine.*

8. **Manage your stress.** See chapter 9. Stress increases cortisol, a stress hormone. Cortisol kills brain cells.

    Don't get mad. Be happy. Rejoice in all things.

Don't let the little things bug you. Remember, stress erodes the brain. Researchers have found that one of the contributors to dementia is chronic stress. Just a side note, coffee also elevates cortisol.

9. **Get eight to ten hours of sleep a night.** See chapter 9. Before Thomas Edison developed the light bulb, people slept an average of ten hours a night. A lack of sleep has been shown clinically to reduce neural plasticity. The brain can't grow new cells and rebuild itself. Remember, on the seventh day even God rested.

Eight Critical Supplements

Even though I spend all of chapter 12 on building your health with supplements, I would be remiss if I failed to mention supplements that specifically help with brain health. I recommend the following:

1. **Take a multiple vitamin every day.** I recommend Health Masters Ultimate Multiple (available at www.HealthMasters.com or 1-800-726-1834). This is an easily absorbed, biologically assimilated multiple vitamin that everyone can use. I believe this is the best multiple vitamin on the planet, period! If you want a product that will make you feel better and feed your cells, this is it. From personal experience, I know that you will feel better in thirty days.

I always try to provide people with the best products possible. They are the same products that my family and I use every day.

Remember these facts: Never use tablet vitamins if at all possible. There is so much glue and heat used in producing these products that it is impossible for your body to break them down. They pass unused right through your body. Don't use gelatin capsules either. Use only cellulose fiber capsules. Gelatin capsules are probably a pork byproduct. Less than 1 percent of all products use cellulose fiber capsules because of the cost. They are much more expensive than tablets or gelatin capsules. All of my Health Masters products use only cellulose capsules.

Plus my multiple vitamin uses only activated B vitamins. Most cheap vitamins use cyancobal amine. This is a cyanide B_{12} vitamin and is very toxic. The body cannot use it. It is poison. Our B_{12} is methyl cobal amine, which is highly absorbable. A lot of cheap products list their B_{12} as cobal amine, but they won't tell you whether it's methyl cobal amine or cyancobal amine. Guess why. It's because they use cheap cyancobal amine, and they don't want you to know this.

2. **Take at least a teaspoon of cod liver oil.** I mentioned cod liver oil earlier. It is so important that I want to repeat it in this list. Our Health Masters Cod

Liver Oil is produced in Norway to our exact specifications. The cod is seasonally fished and exclusively harvested from the icy blue waters of the Arctic Ocean to ensure a premium quality, natural high-vitamin cod liver oil.

3. **Take a vitamin formulated specifically for your memory and brain.** Ours is Health Masters Memory Support. It is a nutrient and botanical blend for optimum cognitive function and memory enhancement.

4. **Take vitamin E.** I am partial to Health Masters Super Potent E. This is a mixed tocopherol product, which is high in gamma E. This is the most potent E to protect against LDL cholesterol breakdown.

When you oxidize or break down LDL cholesterol, it is like turning little razor blades loose in your arteries. This oxidized LDL cholesterol actually creates lesions (little cuts) in the blood vessels. These little cuts then form scars, which can cause blockages in the arteries, heart disease, and heart attacks.

I recommend 1600 IU for men and 800 IU for women daily. I have been taking 1600 IU for twenty-five years.

Just in case you are worried about the study several years ago that concluded vitamin E was bad for you, you should know that the study used chemically produced, cheap, synthetic vitamin E. By contrast, no study has ever shown that natural, mixed tocopherol E (like we use in Health Masters Super Potent E) does anything but good. Best of all, it helps boost brainpower.

5. **Take magnesium and malate acid.** Our brand includes Health Masters Magnesium and Malate Acid. These are natural muscle relaxants, which help to lower blood pressure. We use patented Albion chelate minerals, which are absorbed by the body as food.

   Remember that metallic minerals are essentially rocks and are absorbed very poorly by the body. Magnesium also helps to lower blood pressure and allows more oxygen to be delivered to the brain and heart.

6. **Use a supplement that boosts your immune system.** Our product is Health Masters Ultimate Immune Booster. This one is important since xeno-estrogens cause cancer. They come from chemicals and pesticides in our environment. They get into our liver and become carcinogens.

   Our immunity booster has been clinically proven to reverse and neutralize environmental carcinogens. It has also been shown to kill lung cancer cells in vitro. This is one of the only substances known to man that is not toxic and will kill lung cancer cells (our product is made from broccoli). It has five U.S. patents from Johns Hopkins University. Always remember: cancer is a continuum, the cells are always forming. This product is incredible for your lungs, colon, breast tissue, and ultimately your brain!

7. **Take vitamin C.** Ours is Health Masters Excellent C, a functional vitamin C formula. It has an added 7.5 mg of BioPerine per capsule. BioPerine is a proprietary, patented piperine extract that has been shown in clinical studies to increase the bioavailability of vitamin C by up to 40 percent.

Vitamin C provides valuable antioxidant protection and supports the production of collagen and healthy connective tissue. Excellent C is buffered to prevent potential stomach upset often found with high-dietary ascorbic acid intake.

8. **Add a vitamin B complex supplement.** Ours is called Health Masters B Complex. This supplement supplies significant amounts of water-soluble B vitamins.

A vitamin B complex is important for the support of the adrenal hormone production, regulation, and the body's own production of energy through its enhancement of coenzyme A production. Activated B vitamins are utilized in our formula for optimal effectiveness.

All of these high-quality supplements can be purchased by calling my office at 1-800-726-1834 or by ordering online at www.HealthMasters.com.

Remember, as your brain goes, so goes your health. Safeguard yourself and your loved ones by starting at the top. Maximize your brain!

2

EAT FOR MAXIMUM HEALTH

Everyone wants to be healthy and happy, right? Yet our society has failed miserably at the most important things any of us can do at any age: avoiding the wrong foods while feasting responsibly on the best foods. As a result, most modern diets have an overemphasis on the wrong things, which are starchy, sweet, and oozing with fat.

How bad is it?

As our country approached the year 2000, the U.S. Department of Health and Human Services set health goals for the nation to reach by 2010. How did we do? Not so well. Today, there are more overweight (67 percent) and obese (34 percent) American adults than a decade ago, not fewer. More of us have high blood pressure (29 percent, compared with the goal of 16 percent). In fact, the analysis found that just 18 percent of the 2000 goals for 2010 were met.[1]

One of the main culprits in this deficiency is a food industry with a vested interest in producing foods that appeal to modern lifestyles and tastes. Quite frankly, they have provided a tempting and tasty assortment of foods that have helped us become addicted to the worst things.

As a result, the average American consumes 150 to 170 pounds of sugar each year![2] Americans spend $21 billion on candy alone.[3] Perhaps the greatest surprise is that only 67 percent of American adults are overweight, with at least forty million Americans obese and three million morbidly obese. And this trend continues to explode among children and young people. In 1982, only 4 percent of the nation's youngsters were considered overweight. By 1994 that number had risen to 16 percent. By 2001, the figure had soared to over 25 percent.[4] Obesity is rampant and also linked to many chronic diseases, illnesses, and symptoms.

We all know that Americans are overeating in staggering numbers. But you might not know that obesity is linked to disease. Researchers say that losing weight, for example, could prevent one of every six cancer deaths in the United States, more than ninety thousand each year. According to a study by the American Cancer Society, 30 percent of breast cancer deaths can be linked to obesity.

Unless something changes quickly, if adult statistics are an indication, the number of overweight children and young people will likely bulge to 50 percent or more during the next few years.

To safeguard yourself and your loved ones from disease, you must avoid the worst offenders.

TOP TEN FOODS NOT TO EAT

Let me quickly offer a list of foods to avoid that I have used over and over in speeches and broadcasts:

1. **Pork**: This includes high-fat luncheon meats, ham, pepperoni, hot dogs, bacon, and sausage meat.
2. **Shellfish**: Scavengers such as oysters, scallops, clams, crabs, and lobster feed at the bottom of the ocean, where high levels of mercury are a special risk.
3. **Aspartame**: This is sold as Nutrasweet and Equal. Instead, try barley malt sweetener, an all-natural product that is inexpensive and available at quality health food stores.
4. **Hydrogenated or partially hydrogenated oils**: This includes margarine, shortening, and thousands of products such as peanut butter that contain these oils. Read the label. If the ingredients say hydrogenated or partly hydrogenated oil, leave it on the shelf.
5. **Junk food**: Generally this includes foods with zero nutritional value, such as snack cakes, candy, and sugary soft drinks. I often say, "If it comes in a cellophane wrapper, throw it away!"

6. **Soy products:** I spend an entire chapter on these dangerous products. We have become a nation obsessed with soy: soy drinks, tofu, soy milk, soy protein, soy burgers, and even soy pet food. Only in the past few years have we discovered that soy can sometimes damage the thyroid gland and cause a decrease in energy. Soy can damage the pancreas and cause an increase in diabetes. Soy interferes with calcium absorption. And there is much more, as you will read in chapter 13.

7. **Caffeine:** This taps our emergency energy reserve system by overstimulating the adrenal system, leaving you without energy, at risk for certain diseases, and often addicted.

8. **High-fat dairy products:** Up to 60 percent of allergies afflicting people throughout the United States are directly attributed to the consumption of dairy products. Cow's milk isn't necessary for human health, which is why I recommend raw goat's milk. Avoid cheese, ice cream, and yogurt.

9. **Chlorine and fluoride in water:** Use a filter or be a filter. Chlorination of drinking water has been linked to bladder and rectal cancer, as well as destroying cells as it destroys the cells of other living organisms. See chapter 15.

10. **Alcohol:** Just one ounce of alcohol reduces the body's ability to burn fat by approximately one

third while also increasing the risk of liver and pancreatic cancers.

"Okay," people often say when they read or hear about the top ten foods not to eat, "what can I eat?" Thankfully, God has provided a banquet of wonderful, beneficial things to eat.

A HEALTHY, BALANCED DIET

A great eating program has lots of benefits, including feeling better and looking better. But what does a healthy, balanced diet mean?

Briefly, doctors recommend a diet heavy in fruits and vegetables, protein, complex carbohydrates (such as whole-grain foods, legumes), and healthy fats (including olive oil). There's more about these in chapter 18.

Recent studies by the U.S. Department of Agriculture, the National Cancer Institute, and the U.S. Centers for Disease Control have revealed that a vast majority of Americans—fewer than one-third of adults—are not consuming the daily recommended amounts of fruits and vegetables suggested by the USDA.[5] Specifically the CDC survey showed staggering statistics:

- Only 27 percent of adults ate vegetables three times a day, and only 33 percent ate fruit twice a day. (A serving size is considered to be a half-cup for most fruits and vegetables and one cup for leafy greens.)
- Younger adults, age eighteen to twenty-four, ate

the fewest vegetables of all. Nearly 80 percent of that age group scraped the veggies to the side of their plates if they had vegetables at all.

- Senior citizens were more likely than others to follow mom's advice to eat more veggies, yet only slightly more than a third of that group ate three or more servings each day.

- Seniors also consumed the most fruit, yet only 46 percent ate two or more servings of fruit daily.

- People age thirty-five to forty-four ate fruit the least, with fewer than 28 percent eating the recommended amount of fruit each day.[6]

Previous studies by these U.S. government agencies have clearly linked consumption of fruits and vegetables to a reduced risk of cancer and cardiovascular disease and better weight management through the feeling of fullness and the decrease in the body's energy intake brought on by the foods.

Great Foods

So how can you start to eat a more balanced diet, especially with a greater emphasis on healthy food? My wife, Sharon, has written *The Maximum Energy Cookbook*, and I have written numerous books that focus on a healthy diet, including *Maximum Fat Loss and Maximum Energy* (available by calling 1-800-726-1834 or going online at www.HealthMasters.com).

Briefly, let's list a few of the best principles that Sharon and I have gleaned through decades of nutritional study and practice:

- **Eat a variety of fresh raw fruits and vegetables every day,** focusing on raw and seasonal foods. Avoid overcooking both fruits and vegetables, since too much heat and overcooking can destroy both enzymes and vitamins.

- **Eat a variety of whole grains,** seeking to use foods that are as unprocessed as possible. Most areas of the world have an ample variety of wheat, barley, rice, corn, and buckwheat cereals and whole-grain products. Just remember that grains, not matter how healthy in their original state, have little nutrition when they are overprocessed.

- As much as possible, **avoid foods with chemical additives.** Become an expert label reader.

- **Include a wide variety of seeds and nuts in your diet.** Raw is better. Be careful, since these delightful foods are often high in calories.

- **Use a wide variety of sprouts, herbs, and spices** with both raw and cooked dishes. They are wonderful for seasoning and adding taste, and they are a treasure trove of healthful nutrients.

- **Use extra virgin olive oil often,** especially on vegetable salads and while cooking. Olive oil is an excellent source of monounsaturated oils, the best kind for your heart (more about this in chapter 18).

- Instead of rich, gooey desserts, **use dried fruits** such as raisins, dates, and figs.
- Reduce your intake of red meat. Always seek to use low-fat meats. As mentioned previously (but this is a good time to remind you), avoid pork and pig products.

Isn't it interesting that we often overlook the fact that God placed Adam and Eve in the midst of a garden—a paradise of fruits, vegetables, herbs, grains, and nuts? Today's leading nutrition researchers tell us why: diets rich in these foods help us in so many ways by reducing the risk of many diseases while they provide essential vitamins and minerals, fiber, and other substances that are important for good health.

These are gifts from God. Not only are they good for us, but they are provided in abundance all around the globe. These foods should be a large part of everyone's balanced and healthy eating plan.

Eating natural foods every day can help you in so many ways:

- aiding with weight loss
- bolstering your immune system
- satisfying your body's need for vital vitamins and minerals
- lowering your disease rates

- providing needed nutrition to sustain and restore your organs, tissue, bones, muscles, and skin
- preventing fatty accumulation in blood vessels, which leads to heart disease
- thwarting the risk of cancer and diabetes
- reducing cholesterol levels
- fighting infection
- boosting your energy levels throughout the day
- enriching your life and lifestyle, regardless of your age

These natural foods are readily available, easy to prepare, comparatively economical, and delicious no matter how or when you serve them. There is a wide and interesting array from which to choose, regardless of where you live.

Do you want to safeguard yourself and your loved ones from sickness? With all the other principles of a healthy lifestyle, you can live a longer, healthier life by eating for maximum health.

What could be better?

3

BE WARY OF IMMUNIZATIONS

If you were around for the 1976 swine flu epidemic that swept through the United States, you may have had bouts of déjà vu with recent events. The Bicentennial year outbreak was thought to be closely related to the 1918 flu pandemic that had been especially viral. The government pressured everyone to get vaccinated as swiftly as possible in an unprecedented national effort.

As time passed, the flu threat failed to materialize. What happened, however, was an increasing onslaught of cases with rare side effects apparently linked to the inoculation. In fact, in the 1976 flu scare, more people died of the flu immunizations than from the illness itself![1]

According to one report, "The episode triggered an enduring public backlash against flu vaccination, embarrassed the federal government and cost the director of the U.S. Center for Disease Control, now known as the Centers for Disease Control and Prevention, his job."[2]

EPISODES

The current H1N1 pandemic, as with the 1976 outbreak, quickly provided a wealth of information and
misinformation from a variety of sources: governments,
the health industry, drug manufacturers, media outlets,
and most certainly the Internet. Some voices attempted to
calm the hype. Others ratcheted up the threats.

As information spread like wildfire about both the flu
and the hastily developed H1N1 vaccine, undoubtedly you
asked the same questions that were being asked by people
around the globe:

- What can I do to safeguard my family and myself?
- Will we need to be immunized?
- What are the dangers of the inoculation?
- What if the government requires people to be
  vaccinated? Do I refuse or rush to the front of the
  line?
- Is it safe for pregnant women?
- How about older men and women?

What we do know is that few vaccinations, if any, have
been fast-tracked so swiftly through the U.S. Food and
Drug Administration (FDA). The U.S. Congress quickly
approved a one-billion-dollar grant to the pharmaceutical
companies while simultaneously protecting those manufacturers from product liability claims against the vaccines.
This unsavory combination, laced with an apparent lack of
regulatory safeguards, seemed like a formula for calamity.

I believe that any responsible person should question whether the risk of side effects or injury from any vaccine is a greater risk than the flu itself?

THREE VERY IMPORTANT REASONS TO RETHINK FLU SHOTS

When the flu epidemic hit the world in 1918, over forty million people died. Several thousand people have died, directly or indirectly, due to the current H1N1 flu outbreak. The government feared that the death toll might go much, much higher. Yet rushing out to get a flu immunization, or any influenza inoculation, is not the slam dunk for health that many government and medical officials seem to be saying.

There are three major reasons why government programs to vaccinate 84 percent of the U.S. population with a yearly flu vaccine is so incomprehensible:

1. **An apparent lack of effectiveness.** A recent study published in the October 2009 issue of the *Archives of Pediatric and Adolescent Medicine* found that vaccinating young children against the flu appeared to have zero impact on flu-related hospitalizations or doctor's visits during two recent flu seasons. If you get a flu shot, you can still get the flu (or flu-like symptoms). This is because vaccines only protect against certain flu strains, and it is anyone's guess which flu viruses will be in your area.

The former chief vaccine control officer of the U.S. Food and Drug Administration, Dr. J. Anthony Morris, said, "There is a great deal of evidence to prove that immunization of children does more harm than good." He added, "There is no evidence that any influenza vaccine thus far developed is effective in preventing or mitigating any attack of influenza. The producers of these vaccines know that they are worthless, but they go on selling them anyway."

Unfortunately, flu vaccinations now are also being pushed for virtually all children, not just those under five years of age. I am diametrically opposed to this treatment protocol. Previously, flu vaccines were recommended for five-year-olds and younger. Now the government recommends that children over six months old to eighteen years old be vaccinated, expanding inoculation to thirty million school-age children.

Of course, this ridiculous policy ignores the fact that a systematic review of fifty-one studies involving 260,000 children age six months to twenty-three months found no evidence that the flu vaccine was any more effective than a placebo.

Interestingly, in 2005, the Federal Advisory Committee of Immunization Practices (ACIP) recommended that all children between six months and five years old receive flu shots each year. Now they have expanded their guidelines to include children up to eighteen years old, which means everyone except those between the ages of nineteen and forty-nine years old who are in good health are urged to get a flu shot.

Also interesting is that a majority of the ACIP members who came up with these guidelines have financial ties to the vaccine industry and stand to gain personally for every person who gets a yearly injection. It's actually the only explanation that makes any sense for recommendations as insane as these. It is ridiculous how the pharmaceutical industry is tied to constant payoffs and incentives to promote drug use.

No studies have conclusively proven that flu shots prevent flu-related deaths among the elderly, yet this is one of the key groups in which they are pushed. Additionally a group health study found that flu shots do not protect elderly people against pneumonia, which is the primary cause of death resulting as a complication of the flu. Others have questioned whether there is any mortality benefit with influenza vaccinations. Vaccination coverage among the elderly increased from 15 percent in 1980 to 65 percent now, but there has been no decrease in deaths from influenza or pneumonia. Thus the vaccines neither protect against pneumonia nor decrease death rates.

2. **Mercury and other toxins**: The majority of flu shots contain 25 micrograms of mercury, an amount considered unsafe for anyone weighing less than 550 pounds! And which groups are most sensitive to the neurological damage that has been associated with mercury? The answer is, infants, children, and the elderly. I believe mercury and vaccines are also linked to autism and other learning disabilities.

In 2004, the National Vaccine Information Center described how the Centers for Disease Control officials told everyone to line up for a vaccination that didn't even contain the influenza strain causing most of the flu that year. How stupid is that! Let's inject mercury into the population for no reason! Two-thirds of this year's flu vaccine contains a full dose of mercury! In fact, according to Donald Miller, MD, two-thirds of this year's flu vaccine contains 25 micrograms of thimerosal, which is 49 percent mercury by weight. Each dose of these flu vaccines contains more than 250 times the Environmental Protection Agency's safety limit for mercury.

By now, most people are well aware that children and fetuses are most at risk of damage from this neurotoxin, because their brains are still developing. Yet the CDC still recommends that children over six months old and pregnant women receive the flu vaccine every year. This again is a ridiculous toxic recommendation.

3. **Potential side effects:** In addition to mercury, flu vaccines also contain other toxic or hazardous ingredients, such as formaldehyde (a known cancer-causing agent), aluminum (a neurotoxin that has been linked to Alzheimer's disease), Triton X-100 (a detergent), phenol (carbolic acid), ethylene glycol (antifreeze), and various antibiotics (such as neomycin and gentamicin) that can cause allergic reactions in some people.

   There is also some evidence that flu shots cause Alzheimer's disease. Most likely this is a result of combining mercury with aluminum and formaldehyde.

   Other serious and adverse reactions to the flu vaccine are joint inflammation and arthritis, anaphylactic shock (and other life-threatening allergic reactions), and Guillain-Barré syndrome, a paralytic autoimmune disease, plus an increase in senile dementia.

So why would you take a flu shot every year that has never been proven to be effective, that can give you the very illness you are trying to prevent, and has potentially long-term side effects that are far worse than the flu itself?

Understand that the government and pharmaceutical

corporations have done an excellent job of instilling fear into the population so they believe they must get a flu shot in order to stay healthy. The simple reality is that these influenza inoculations are apparently doing more harm than good.

A large-scale systematic review of fifty-one studies, published in the Cochrane Database of Systematic Reviews in 2006 found no evidence that a flu vaccine is any more effective than a placebo in children. The studies involved 260,000 children, age six months to twenty-three months.

By the way, I have never received a single flu shot, nor have I had the flu in over thirty years.

REASONS TO BE WARY OF IMMUNIZATIONS

Most children in the United States receive thirty-three doses of ten different vaccines before they reach age five, according to a report aired by CBS News in September 2000. The vaccines reportedly provide protection for "everything from childhood diseases like chicken pox to adult diseases like hepatitis B."

Meanwhile, for decades, a growing number of reputable researchers and medical doctors have been suggesting that, in addition to immunities, these vaccines may provide some things that are much less desirable. For some children, they may be causing mental retardation, sudden infant death syndrome (SIDS), paralysis, and death.

As with flu shots, new research appears to implicate childhood immunizations as the suspected cause of a host of autoimmune diseases in genetically susceptible individuals. The list includes cancer, leukemia, rheumatoid arthritis, multiple sclerosis, Lou Gehrig's disease, lups erythematosus, Guillain-Barré syndrome, autistic spectrum disorders, and even attention deficit hyperactivity disorder (ADHD).

One element of mass immunization distresses me. We live in the United States of America, a nation governed by constitutional principles that protect the rights of individuals from governmental oppression. Yet parents who dare to question the wisdom of immunizing their children can face strong-arm tactics from school districts that include the forced removal of their children and even criminal prosecution! The only course left to many is legal action in the courts—courts that appear to demonstrate a strong bias toward the medical establishment and the party line.

Something is seriously wrong with a system that makes conscientious and thoughtful parents feel like criminals because they want to protect their children from what they believe is a very risky and unnecessary medical procedure.

America's Love Affair with Mass Immunizations

The natural tendency for concerned parents is to consult with a trusted family physician for advice and assistance in wading through the conflicting evidence. Unfortunately, even the medical community seems confused. This may be due to the obvious conflict of interest between medical professionals and the high profits generated by mass immunizations and the considerable influence wielded by pharmaceutical giants.

A resolution was presented at the 1982 forum of the American Academy of Pediatrics (AAP) that pediatricians should help inform parents about the risks as well as the supposed benefits of immunizations. This is part of what the proposal said: "The AAP [shall] make available in clear, concise language information which a reasonable parent would want to know about the benefits and risks of routine immunizations, the risks of vaccine preventable diseases and the management of common adverse reactions to immunizations."[3]

The late Dr. Robert S. Mendelsohn was a pediatrician and an instructor at Northwestern University Medical College, associate professor of pediatrics and community health and preventive medicine at the University of Illinois College of Medicine, president of the National Health Federation (NHF), and national director of Project Head Start's Medical Consultation Service. He responded to the AAP proposal and said, "Apparently the doctors assembled did not believe that 'reasonable parents' were entitled to this kind of information because they rejected the resolution!"[4]

Thousands of parents in the United States, Great Britain, Germany, and many other nations refused to accept the party line of the medical and pharmaceutical communities about the total safety of compulsory immunizations. Why? They believe their children were irreparably harmed or killed by complications from childhood immunizations. More and more of them are banding together to establish advocacy organizations and legislative lobby groups. They are also financing lawsuits against officials in school districts, state health departments, and federal agencies when necessary.

They Want to Know Why

These parents want to know why childhood cases of autism have increased 500 percent in just two decades. They also want to know why juvenile cases of asthma jumped 100 percent and juvenile diabetes levels rocketed to the 200 percent mark. For the most part, the persistent questions of these parents are answered by little more than a mountain of excuses and official scorn by the medical establishment. It doesn't matter. These parents and others like them are on a crusade for their children's life.

In the meantime, the World Health Organization is quietly stating what a growing minority of medical experts in the United States believe is the scientifically based truth about disease and immunizations. Research has clearly shown that adequate amounts of vitamin A, zinc, and other essential nutrients significantly reduce the risk and mortality rates of diseases such as measles as well as outbreaks of diarrhea. This is especially true in so-called third-world nations and other areas where malnutrition and poor sanitation conditions exist. Recent research indicates that vitamin A in particular may even lower the risk that HIV/AIDS mothers will pass on the disease to their babies at birth.[5] While the World Health Organization still endorses immunizations in those countries, it continues to cite scientific research that shows proper nutrition is the first line of defense against many viral and bacterial diseases in the third world.

Obscene Seizure and the Custody of Strangers

Who should have the authority to weigh the potential benefits against the potential risks of immunizations for your child? Unfortunately, the decision has already been made for most of us.

In many states, if not most, a government medical official has already made all the decisions for you concerning when, what, how, and how many immunizations your children will receive. If you disagree, your children will be denied access to public education, including colleges and universities.

Don't be surprised if you wake up to the knock of a

lawman with a bench warrant to remove your school-age children from your home just to make sure they receive those immunizations! Does this sound far-fetched? It has already happened.

School officials in Utica, New York, threatened the parents of seventy-seven middle-school students with the forcible removal of their children unless they agreed to submit them to vaccination with the highly controversial hepatitis B vaccine. If the parents refused, the officials were prepared to forcibly remove the children from their homes and turn them over to child protective services on the grounds of parental neglect![6]

This didn't happen in a repressive totalitarian state on another continent. It took place on American soil. And this is not a lone incident.

In response, Jane M. Orient, MD, executive director of American Physicians and Surgeons, spoke out on behalf of the families and said, "It's obscene to seize a child and force him to the custody of strangers just because his parents refuse medical treatment they think is unnecessary or even dangerous. Parents, not...government bureaucrats, should make decisions about their children's medical care."[7]

Government officials often say they are acting in the best interest of children, but the claim is questionable at best in cases where the scientific evidence suggests otherwise. Dr. Orient warned that the latest vaccination rage, the hepatitis B vaccine, "is a potential death sentence for some children. Government studies show that children under the age of fourteen are three times more likely to die or suffer adverse reactions after receiving hepatitis B vaccine than to catch the disease itself."[8]

In spite of the evidence, zealous immunization advocates determined to eradicate disease, even if the effort kills and maims more victims than the disease, have pressed to make the hepatitis B vaccine the latest addition to the compulsory immunization laws of most states.

Ironically, hepatitis B is almost exclusively an adult disease primarily spread through body fluids among those with multiple sex partners, those who use intravenous drugs, or those whose occupations expose them to blood. Children face a very low risk of exposure unless they are infected by their mother at birth.

TOO MANY IMMUNIZATIONS

Most of the children in the United States are required to receive several common immunizations, including, but not limited to:

- DtaP/DPT/DPTH (one of three combined vaccines: diphtheria-tetanus-acellular pertussis, which is a less reactive modification of DPT/diphtheria-pertussis-tetanus/diphtheria tetanus-pertussis hemophilus influenza type B)
- MMR (measles-mumps-rubella)

- conjugated HIB (hemophilus influenza type B)
- hepatitis B
- chicken pox (many states have added or are considering vaccinations for chicken pox and many other lesser diseases)

Perhaps the first question to consider is obvious. Have compulsory immunizations controlled or eliminated childhood diseases? If you believe the continual claims of government and medical spokesmen and state health departments, the nation's childhood immunization programs are humanity's savior from disease.

According to "cause of death" statistics from Metropolitan Life Insurance Company recorded from 1911 to 1935, four diseases topped the list as causes of death for children age one year old to fourteen years old: diphtheria, measles, scarlet fever, and whooping cough.[9]

CHILDHOOD DISEASES DROPPED 95 PERCENT BEFORE IMMUNIZATIONS!

The death rate from these four leading childhood diseases declined from forty-five per one hundred thousand in 1911 to twenty-eight per one hundred thousand in 1935 —or a decrease of 81 percent! By 1945 the combined death rate from these diseases had dropped further, to seven per one hundred thousand. This amounts to a total decline in deaths from the top four childhood diseases of 95 percent—years before mass immunization programs began in the United States.[10]

Perhaps the best way to make sense of the most common immunizations is to examine the diseases they allegedly eliminate or control.

Measles (Rubeola, English Measles)

This common childhood illness is treated with bed rest and plenty of fluids. Most people who attended school in the 1950s and early 1960s remember staying home from class to recover from the measles. They usually aren't remarkable memories, because the symptoms of the disease aren't really remarkable, as long as a child was well nourished and living in sanitary conditions.

Once a child contracts measles, he gains a lifetime immunity. The only dangerous derivative of the measles virus is measles encephalitis, which is said to happen only once in one thousand cases of measles.

Dr. Robert S. Mendelsohn believed that this statistic could only be applied to children living in conditions of poverty or malnutrition. Odds of one in ten thousand or one in one hundred thousand are more likely in the United States and other developed countries![11] Ironically, Mendelsohn and other medical authorities and researchers claim the immunization itself carries a high risk of causing measles encephalitis, encephalopathy (or brain dysfunction), and the nearly always fatal subacute sclerosing panencephalitits (SSPE), which hardens brain matter.[12]

The measles serum has a very checkered history for these reasons:

- **It doesn't seem to work.** According to a Centers for Disease Control report, 40 percent of all cases of measles reported in 1989 were in vaccinated individuals or could be attributed to "primary measles vaccine failure." These same figures showed up in the fourteen measles outbreaks in 1977.[13] One World Health Organization study showed that people who have been vaccinated against measles are fourteen times likely to contract measles than those who have not! One official with the Centers for Disease Control said that in some measles outbreaks, "over 95 percent have a history of vaccination."[14]

- If the vaccination actually offers protection to a portion of the population, those who do get vaccinated evidently have only limited benefit. Blood tests show no evidence of measles antibodies after approximately four years. After measles outbreaks occurred among fully immunized high school and college students, the Immunization Practices Advisory Committee recommended in 1989 that two doses of measles vaccine be required. Since 1990, colleges and universities in twenty-two states established a "prematriculation immunization requirement," forcing students to get two measles shots before they can enroll in college! (Despite scientific evidence that two doses of the vaccine are no more effective than one.)[15]

- Recent research repeatedly points to the measles component of the MMR vaccine as a possible source of the exploding autism epidemic sweeping through the nation. Vijendra K. Singh, PhD, of the department of biology and Biotechnology Center at Utah State University, testified before a congressional committee that, in a study of four hundred people (composed of those diagnosed with autism and a control group exhibiting no symptoms of autistic spectrum disorders), she found a brain protein known as myelin basic protein (MBP) in 65 to 85 percent of autistic children, but only rarely (0–5 percent) in normal children. Further investigation verified that the autoantibodies were created as part of a hyperimmune response to a virus, specifically the measles virus (MV). Singh summarized her testimony with these astounding statements: "This was most probably the first laboratory-based evidence to link measles virus and/or MMR vaccine to autoimmunity in children with autism. Collectively, these observations led me to speculate that autism may be caused by a measles or MMR vaccine-induced autoimmune response."[16]

Mumps

Mumps is a very contagious disease caused by a virus

that focuses on the salivary glands on either side of the neck under the jaw. It causes painful swelling along the jaw line just below the ears, along with fever, headache, muscle aches, and back pain. It may also cause swelling in testicles, ovaries, and breasts.

The disease is uncomfortable but rarely serious. The painful swelling may diminish after the third day, and all symptoms disappear in about ten days. The downside, which is made even more dangerous by the delaying effect of the temporary immunity provided by childhood mumps immunization, is that about one-third of males past the age of puberty who contract mumps develop orchitis, or inflammation of one of the testes (it rarely affects both testicles).

The side effects of the mumps vaccine can be severe, including a risk of contracting viral meningitis, febrile seizures, unilateral nerve deafness, and encephalitis.

RUBELLA (GERMAN MEASLES)

Rubella is a mild disease in children that does not require medical treatment. A child initially runs a fever and exhibits the symptoms of a cold and a sore throat. Then he or she develops a rash on the face and scalp that spreads to the arms and trunk of the body. Unlike measles, the spots in rubella, or German measles, do not run together. With plenty of rest and fluids, the rash and the disease pass after three days, leaving the child with permanent immunity.

The only real danger of rubella is that it may damage the unborn child of a mother who contracts the disease in the first trimester of pregnancy. In Robert S. Mendelsohn's words, "This fear is used to justify the immunization of all children, boys and girls, as part of the MMR inoculation."[17]

Many health providers feel that childhood immunizations deprive young women of the lifelong immunity they would have received from the rubella virus in the harmless childhood stage of life, for the immunizations do not always last. This is one of the really irritating problems plaguing the immunization program: most of the people who come down with this and other childhood diseases consistently show proof of previous vaccinations. As demonstrated elsewhere, this is the problem behind the revaccination of college students.

Recent studies have linked the new rubella vaccine introduced in 1979 with chronic fatigue syndrome (also known as the Epstein-Barr virus). This link was first reported in the United States in 1982.[18]

Although many hospitals require employees (including obstetricians and pediatricians) to take the rubella vaccine, a study in the *Journal of the American Medical Association* noted that nine of every ten obstetricians and more than two-thirds of pediatricians refused to take the vaccine.[19] One can only wonder why they would take such action. We may never know, but it seems to beg the need for some explanation by these physicians who are most familiar with the possible risks involved.

DIPHTHERIA

Diphtheria is a bacterial disease that was widely feared in the previous century when antibiotics were unavailable. The disease was already disappearing before a vaccine became available (probably due to better nutrition, cleaner water sources, and more sanitary living conditions nationwide and particularly in larger cities).

Only five people contracted diphtheria in 1980; only four cases appeared in 1992. The disappearance of this disease before the introduction of vaccines has been explained and documented earlier, using insurance tables. Obviously the disease rarely occurs. When it does, it is effectively treated with antibiotics. Nevertheless, we continue to immunize children against it today.

The diphtheria component of the DPT and DtaP vaccine has not been shown to cause serious short-term side effects. Its long-term effects—as with any injection of foreign bodies into the human body—remain totally unknown. Formaldehyde is used to "stabilize" the diphtheria vaccine, but the dangers of formaldehyde as a carcinogen are well documented. The use of this chemical (and many others, such as mercury and aluminum) in vaccine production will be discussed at greater length later in this book.

In 1975, the Bureau of Biologics and the FDA issued an official report that diphtheria toxoid (which is the "safe" form of the disease used for vaccination) "is not as effective an immunizing agent as might be anticipated."

The report also acknowledged that those who received the vaccination could still contract the disease, noting "the permanence of immunity induced by the toxoid...is open to question." The report noted that about 50 percent of all the people who contract diphtheria appear to have been fully vaccinated![20]

WHOOPING COUGH (PERTUSSIS)

Whooping cough is spread by airborne bacteria from an infected person and is extremely contagious. Common cold symptoms surface approximately seven to ten days after exposure, followed by a severe cough at night. Later the cough occurs in the daytime, characterized by sudden outbursts of convulsive coughing called "paroxysmal coughing." This coughing can frighten parents when their child coughs a dozen times with each breath, especially if the child's face darkens to a bluish or purple hue. The disease gets its name from the whooping noise that a victim makes when he or she breathes in at the end of each coughing bout.

The disease can strike any age group. Currently, between one thousand to three thousand cases of whooping cough occur per year, with between five and twenty deaths annually across the nation. Although the disease is very distressing to young victims and their parents, the incidence of death is virtually negligible. Consistent findings show this vaccine does tend to lower incidences of outbreak cases. Yet it is notorious for wearing out after a few years and often for being totally ineffective.

Consult a doctor if an infant comes down with whooping cough. Hospital care may be required to protect the child from the threat of exhaustion from coughing and pneumonia.

The pertussis or whooping cough component of the DPT vaccine is one of the most controversial of all vaccines. Many consider it to be unpredictable, toxic, and questionable in its ability to actually prevent infection.

Multiple research studies link the pertussis vaccine (whether given alone or as part of a DPT combination) with acute brain injury, anaphylactic shock, shock-collapse, inconsolable crying, febrile seizures, convulsions, sudden infant death syndrome (SIDS), severe and moderate encephalopathy, severe mental retardation, cerebral palsy, blindness, irreversible brain damage, myoclonic twitching, paralysis, infantile spasms, epilepsy, and hyperactivity.[21]

Most parents of vaccinated children probably won't be surprised by these findings. Researchers found that 93 percent of the infants who received the DPT shot experienced moderate to severe reactions within forty-eight hours of inoculation![22] That alone is alarming.

I urge special caution if you or your child has a history of allergies or seizures. The pertussis toxin has another name—histamine sensitizing factor (HSF). That means it dramatically increases the body's sensitivity to the effects of histamine. If your child has severe allergies (especially toward milk or dairy products), he or she may have a hypersensitive immune system that could predispose him or her to a negative (and possibly violent) reaction to the pertussis vaccine.

One physician discovered a history of allergies with twenty of thirty-five children who reacted to the DPT-polio vaccine with persistent screaming, shock-collapse, or convulsions. Another noted that "infants with a family history of fits or allergic conditions are more likely to become ill after vaccination than those without such a history."[23]

Although 95 percent of the children in the United States have been vaccinated against whooping cough, the nation still records about three thousand cases per year, and the vaccine's effect seems to wear off in a few years.

Despite continuous official disclaimers, numerous research studies also point to a probable connection between the pertussis vaccine used in the United States until recently and the rise in autistic spectrum disorders.

Authors Harris L. Coulter and Barbara Loe Fisher, cofounder and president of the National Vaccine Information Center, wrote in their book, *A Shot in the Dark*, "The phenomenon of early-infantile autism was first observed and discussed by physicians in the early 1940s, a few years after the pertussis vaccine became more widely used in the United States." Noting "the brain appears to be isolated from the senses in autistic children," the authors added: "The parallel to certain cases of pertussis vaccine damage is striking.... Both autism and minimal brain damage [ADD or ADHD], as discussed previously, suggest a breakdown in the brain's ability to receive and process information through the senses. The relationship of autism to pertussis-vaccine damage deserves further investigation. Some autistic children share another trait with the minimally brain damaged—a tendency to be hyperactive with all of the associated emotional and behavioral problems."[24]

Very recent research by Dr. Mary Megson pointedly implicates the pertussis vaccine as a possible toxic cause of autism that "inserts a G-alpha protein defect" into genetically at-risk children. This appears to be particularly linked to individuals with a family history of night blindness or irritable bowel syndrome.

Jamie Murphy, author of *What Every Parent Should Know About Childhood Immunization*, noted, "Because whooping cough has become milder in some countries of Europe since about 1970, and because of the ineffectiveness of the triple vaccine, DPT vaccinations were halted in West Germany in 1976 and in Sweden in 1979."[25]

Although reported cases of whooping cough rose after the immunizations were discontinued, the death rate from the disease remained at the same low levels present when the immunizations were being administered. Perhaps the more important observation was that the rates of death or health complications from the DPT shot dropped to zero. Pertussis appears to be a cyclical disease with cases rising in numbers every three or four years, whether its victims are vaccinated or not.[26]

Japanese researchers responded to the DPT crisis by developing a much safer "purified pertussis vaccine" in the late 1970s, but U.S. public health officials waited fifteen years before licensing the acellular pertussis vaccine for American babies. Unfortunately, the DtaP vaccine is more expensive than the DPT vaccine, and the FDA and vaccine manufacturers refused to take the crude and more dangerous whole-cell pertussis vaccine off the market.[27]

This action was even less defensible when clinical trials held in the previous decade demonstrated that the DtaP vaccine was 82–96 percent effective while the crude and toxic DPT vaccine demonstrated a wildly erratic efficiency rate bouncing from 36 to 96 percent. Serious reactions continued to result with the DtaP vaccine, but they occurred significantly less often.[28]

TETANUS

Spores trapped in wounds that have not been properly cleaned spawn this nervous-system disorder. It causes body muscles to tighten and jaw muscles to spasm; it also triggers convulsions, headaches, and depression. Untreated, the condition results in death 50 percent of the time. With proper treatment, victims completely recover in 80 percent of all cases.

Evidently, the disease is virtually 100 percent avoidable when wounds are properly cleaned. Tetanus declined among military personnel from 205 cases per 100,000 wounds in the Civil War to .44 cases per 100,000 wounds during World War II. The disease was rapidly declining long before a vaccine was developed. Throughout World War II, only twelve cases of tetanus were recorded! (Four of the cases involved individuals who were "adequately" vaccinated.) Perhaps this explains why some doctors report that the tetanus toxoid (the "safe" version of the toxin used as a vaccine) does not provide protection.[29]

The tetanus vaccine can have some painful complications, the most serious being demyelinating neuropathy (a degenerative condition of the nervous system), anaphylactic shock, and seriously lowered T-lymphocyte reactions, a crucial component of a healthy immune system. It appears this is yet another example of forcing a little-needed vaccine with potentially harmful side effects into the bodies of young children in the name of immunization without justification.

HEPATITIS B

The newest addition to the list of mandated childhood vaccinations may prove the most difficult to understand. The logic of wanting to protect children from polio or whooping cough is understandable. But in my opinion, there seems to be far less logic for forcing parents in

America to submit their children to the injection of a toxic serum to protect them from a liver disease primarily limited to IV drug users and those with multiple sex partners. Also at risk are health workers who are regularly exposed to human blood products and hemophiliacs who are dependent upon frequent blood transfusions.

In 1991, the Centers for Disease Control and the American Association of Pediatricians launched an aggressive campaign to add the hepatitis B vaccine to the list of recommended and government-funded childhood vaccines. The effort was successful, and most of America's children must receive this toxic serum or be denied access to public education. I personally believe that this effort needlessly placed millions of infants at risk.

POLIO (POLIOMYELITIS)

Polio was the scourge of the 1940s and even confined a U.S. president to a wheelchair. The development of the polio vaccine launched a high-powered national immunization campaign. Ironically, the vaccines developed to protect the American population from polio eventually may have become its most likely cause!

Dr. Jonas Salk, an American physician and microbiologist, introduced a killed-virus vaccine against polio in 1955, but the death rate from the disease had already declined 47 percent in the United States from 1923 to 1953. The disease demonstrated a similar decline in England and other European nations as well.

Ironically, the number of reported polio cases was significantly higher after the mass inoculations than before! In fact, they may have more than doubled in the United States as a whole.[30]

Evidently, the live-virus vaccine introduced four years later by Albert Sabin was little better. The *Washington Post* reported in September 1976 that Salk had testified that the live-virus vaccine was "the principle if not sole cause" of all reported polio cases in the United States since 1961. Even the Centers for Disease Control admitted that the live-virus polio vaccine was the primary cause of polio in the United States!

If the polio vaccine causes polio and the disease was disappearing on its own, then why did the government demand that we mandate the vaccinations?

MONKEY VIRUS CONTAMINATION

It has been known for decades that the simian virus 40 (SV40) grossly contaminated the oral polio vaccine administered to the U.S. school population prior to 1964! One fear is that this virus continues to contaminate polio vaccines used by pediatricians today, because these vaccines are often made by passing serum products through African green monkey kidney cells.

Recent evidence uncovered molecular evidence of SV40 infections in tissue samples from four children born after 1982. What is the significance of this discovery? Since the SV40 virus is a highly carcinogenic (cancer-causing) "latent or persistent monkey virus" known to cross-transmit to humans, it is feared that this virus can cause cancer in human hosts many years after it hides in human body cells. This virus is extremely difficult to discover.

According to Leon Chaitow, author of *Vaccination and Immunisation*: "SV40-contaminated vaccines were used in millions of individuals, and this micro-organism, which is known to be capable of genetically altering other virus (especially let it be noted with Epstein-Barr and cytomegaloviruses) and cellular genetic material, entered the bodies of a generation now in young and middle adult life."[31]

Today, polio has all but disappeared. Should the paralytic form of the disease ever become active in someone's body, doctors have the necessary drugs to deal with it. (Although they have some bad side effects, they appear to be nothing compared to the reported side effects of the polio vaccines!)

DEALING WITH THE FALLOUT

If you are disturbed by some of the information in this chapter, you are not alone. The general public is virtually unaware that mandatory vaccinations have harmed or killed so many children over the last four decades that Congress passed the National Childhood Vaccine Injury Acts of 1986, Public Law 99–660, to officially recognize the reality of vaccine-related injuries and deaths. Its dual purpose was to establish safety provisions (which some claim has essentially degenerated into eager efforts to increase levels of immunization rather than make them safer) and to establish a no-fault federal compensation plan for individuals injured or killed by vaccines.

Barbara Loe Fisher consulted and negotiated with the American Academy of Pediatrics, vaccine manufacturers, and legislative staffs to create the no-fault compensation bill that became the 1986 vaccine injury law. She said:

> The fact that the [U.S. Claims] Court turns down 75 percent of the claims that are made is primarily due to the vigorous, well-financed opposition mounted by federal public health officials and Department of Justice lawyers. Since the National Childhood Vaccine Injury Act was passed in 1986, HHS officials and Justice Department lawyers have systematically gutted the law by passing federal regulations that narrow the criteria that special masters employed by the U.S. Claims Court may use to make awards to vaccine-injured children.... As a result, by 1997 there was a $1 billion surplus in the trust fund that is supposed to be used to provide financial support for individuals injured by mandated vaccines. Federal health officials continue to take actions to further limit the number of awards made for vaccine injuries because they do not want to admit that so many children and adults have been injured and killed by the vaccines they develop, license, regulate, and promote for mandatory use by all citizens.[32]

The fact is that most of the diseases listed above rarely kill under modern health and sanitation conditions.

Although these diseases may cause significant discomfort for victims and their families, there is at least some evidence that those who contract such diseases seem likely to fully regain good health if they have access to adequate nutrition, sanitary living conditions, and competent medical care.

I'll Take My Chances!

It is my personal belief—let me emphasis this—it is my personal belief that individuals can often fare better with the disease rather than the childhood immunizations. However, I do not presume to recommend that you adopt the same opinion solely on the basis of this book or any other single source of information. Conduct your own thorough study of the available medical literature in books, on credible Internet sites, and through consultations with competent health professionals before you make a decision.

As you know, my personal belief in the matter of immunizations is definitely a minority opinion among medical doctors and research scientists (in my mind, the existence of even one competent medical professional who shares my concern about vaccinations is enough to make responsible parents think twice about vaccinating their children). Therefore, it is vital that you reach your own conclusions based on your own study and consultation with your family physician.

One statement in the literature, however, continues to

haunt me. In their chapter on the evolution of mandatory immunizations in this country, authors Harris L. Coulter and Barbara Loe Fisher said: "Curiously, the United States appears to be the only major Western nation with compulsory pertussis immunization.... In fact, the only part of Europe where pertussis vaccination is universally imposed is the [former] Soviet Union and the formerly 'iron curtain' countries of Poland, Hungary, and Czechoslovakia. Mass vaccination in our 'free society' is not voluntary. Since the repeal of the [military] draft in the 1970s, mandatory vaccination remains the only law that requires a citizen to risk his life for his country."[33]

Perhaps the most alarming aspect of increasingly invasive mass immunizations is that the trend seems to be expanding at the same rate as runaway cancer. Coulter and Fisher warn:

> More than 2,000 vaccines are being created in government and drug company labs, vaccines such as live rotavirus (infant diarrhea), salmonella, strep, tuberculosis, gonorrhea, herpes, Epstein-Barr virus, hepatitis A, B, C, D, and E, and cholera. More than 50 different HIV vaccines are being developed to theoretically prevent AIDS, including a live HIV vaccine that will be inhaled and followed by an injection a week later. Scientists are creating a genetically engineered super-vaccine to be squirted into the mouths of babies at the moment of birth that will inject raw DNA from 30 to 40 different viruses and bacteria directly into an infant's cells and be time-released into the bodies throughout childhood. There is little question that federal and state health officials

will try to pass regulations legally requiring that all citizens use many of these vaccines, including the AIDS vaccine.[34]

Perhaps it would be easier for critics to write off such commentary as reactionary and extreme if we didn't already have so many examples of such excessive executive force being exercised by government employees against tax-paying parents who have little say in the formation of such regulations.

CDC Pin Cushions

The "100 percent immunization at any cost" mind-set may well undermine the health, long-term welfare, and constitutional freedoms of an entire nation if left unchecked. I'm convinced Gordon Steward, a leading European physician and respected professor of community medicine at the University of Glasgow, Scotland, was right when he said, "If the Centers for Disease Control has its way, Americans and their children are going to become human pin cushions."[35]

The American public has no place to turn as long as the executive, judicial, and legislative branches of government maintain such a close alliance with the medical and pharmaceutical communities that the value of objective checks and balances seems to be lost. The most prominent group left out of the compulsory immunization profits party may well be the vast majority of trusting American citizens and their children.

The goal of this chapter is not to persuade you to agree with my convictions. It is written simply to provide you with some additional facts so you can make an informed decision. It seems that most doctors, educators, and public health officials often provide information from only one side of the immunization issue.

Only informed parents have the moral, spiritual, and ethical right to make life-and-death decisions concerning their children. For better or for worse, parents have the best shot at truly having their children's best interests in mind when they consider the pros and cons of childhood immunizations. Educate yourself before the last vestige of parental discretion is taken from you.

AUTISM: THE NEW WAVE

As many as one in every three hundred American children fell victim to a mysterious disorder called autism last year that few doctors knew about just fifty years ago. Since then, more than a half million Americans have been diagnosed with autism or some form of pervasive developmental disorder (PDD), making it one of the most common developmental disabilities in the nation. It strikes four times as many boys as it does girls, and it crosses all lines of race, ethnicity, social standing, lifestyle, and educational levels.

Dr. Michael J. Goldberg, a well-known expert in the field of autism and a pediatrician in private practice in

Tarzana, California, put it this way: "While training as a pediatrician, I was told if I saw one autistic child in a lifetime of practice it would be one too many. What I am seeing today is not the autism I learned about in medical school twenty years ago. What was once a relatively rare disorder is now twenty times more likely to occur."[36]

There are differences between classic autism—which occurs in only one or two infants per 10,000 births—and the epidemic of new autistic syndrome cases that occur in one out of every 500 children (rates as high as one to 250 have been suggested), according to Dr. Goldberg.

With classic autism, parents generally notice that something is wrong in infants in the first three to six months of life. Autistic syndrome symptoms, however, generally show up after young children develop normal speech and motor skills, show affection, and demonstrate above-average intelligence.

Autism and autism syndrome conditions are still diagnosed according to American Psychiatric Association guidelines listed in the DMS-IV, but Dr. Goldberg says that autism, particularly autistic syndrome, is now considered a medical condition rather than a psychiatric or mental disorder. He believes that a majority of cases, if not all cases, of autistic syndrome are "immune mediated" (related to dysfunction in the immune or autoimmune system) and are open to medical and nutritional therapy.[37]

Ironically, many medical and governmental sources downplay the apparent surge of new autism cases by attributing them to "expanded" definitions of autism. Dr. Samuel L. Katz, a pediatrician and professor at Duke University, told Ed Bradley on *60 Minutes*: "A child who was called 'autistic' in 1971 is only one of a group who would now be called 'autistic' in 1999 or 2000. The diagnosis has been greatly broadened." When asked if there has been an epidemic of autism, he said, "I would hesitate to describe anything as an epidemic of autism."[38]

When the Government Reform Committee of the U.S. House of Representatives convened a hearing on autism, the session was titled "Autism: Present Challenges, Future Needs—Why the Increased Rates?" At the beginning of the hearing, the committee chairman shared his opinion about the alarming rise in autism cases.

Dan Burton (R-IN), whose grandson developed autism within ten days of receiving several immunizations in five shots, said:

> When asked about the increased rates in autism, many will immediately discount that there even is an increase. Even though the latest statistics from the Department of Education show increased rates in every state. Others will say the increase is due to better diagnostic skills. Others will say it is because the diagnostic category was expanded.
>
> California has reported a 273 percent increase in children with autism since 1998. As for this increase, 21 percent of all autistic children in California live in the 29th district.
>
> Florida has reported a 571 percent increase in autism. Maryland has reported a 513 percent increase between 1993 and 1998. You can't attribute all of that to better diagnostic skills.

In 1999, there were 2,462 children ages 3 to 21 in Indiana diagnosed with autism. That is one-fourth of one percent of all the school children in Indiana, or one in four hundred. Twenty-three percent of these children live in the 6th district. This increase is not just better counting.

If we want to find a cure, we must first look to the cause. We must do this now before our health and education systems are bankrupted, and before more of our nation's children are locked inside themselves with this disease.[39]

I believe that if alarming numbers such as those for ADD, ADHD, and autism epidemics had hit the media for chicken pox or measles, the nation would have risen up in arms and demanded that something be done.

This is even more alarming when you understand that the outcome for children with autism is often very dismal. Once erroneously called juvenile schizophrenia, the condition was considered incurable and untreatable. Victims of autism were routinely institutionalized and virtually forgotten in the nation's mental asylums.

Merriam-Webster's defines autism as "a mental disorder originating in infancy that is characterized by self-absorption, inability to interact socially, repetitive behavior and language dysfunction (as echolalia [strictly repetitive or imitative speech, often without regard to the meaning of the words of sounds])."

The definition of autism was updated in recent years to include a number of similar disorders collectively called autism syndrome or autistic spectrum disorders. According to the Autism-PDD (Pervasive Developmental Disorder) Network, "The diagnosis of autism is made when a specified number of characteristics listed in the DSM-IV are present, in ranges inappropriate for the child's age. Autism diagnosis usually occurs between the ages of three and five."[40]

What Causes Autism?

No one knows for certain what causes autism in infants and young children. A growing body of scientific evidence and cataloged reports of personal experiences lend support to key theories about the condition's primary and secondary sources.

Initially, the medical community rejected its early belief that autism was caused by "refrigerator mothers" who failed to show affection to their children or who were abusive. Later it decided that autism was a psychiatric or mental problem related to mental retardation.

Current research points toward some common risk areas that may potentially cause autism, ADD, and ADHD. Researchers appear to be divided into two camps. The majority considers that autism is related to metabolic or allergic reactions caused by diet, gastrointestinal problems, hormonal imbalances, and yeast infestations. The late Dr. Ben F. Feingold and Dr. William G. Crook have provided some invaluable insights into the interaction of allergies and dietary and nutritional factors with metabolic problems associated with ADD, ADHD, and autistic spectrum disorders.

Other medical specialists, such as Dr. Michael Goldberg, believe autism can be traced to the improper function or regulation of the body's immune system. The condition is complicated by metabolic problems on a secondary level.

In my mind, the most promising cutting-edge research draws from both camps. New findings point to the disruption of G-alpha protein, a protein that is crucial to proper brain function and development.

A study by Dr. Mary N. Megson, a board-certified pediatrician and assistant professor of pediatrics at the Medical College of Virgina, suggested that autism may be linked to the pertussis toxin found in the DPT vaccine. She noted: "A study of sixty autistic children suggests that autism may be caused by inserting a G-alpha protein defect, the pertussis toxin found in the DPT vaccine, into genetically at-risk children.... The far-reaching metabolic consequences [of the blocked neurotransmission it causes] may be enormous, with potential links to not only autism, but dyslexia, attention-deficit hyperactivity disorder (ADHD), bipolar disorder, schizophrenia, chronic fatigue syndrome, fibromyalgia, Type II hyperlipidemia, gluten enteropathy, cancer of the mucous-secreting glands and autoimmune disorders including muscular dystrophy and rheumatoid arthritis."[41]

Megson suspects that unrecognized allergic reactions to childhood immunizations, combined with the introduction of certain foreign cells (called antigens) and toxins, are the culprits behind many childhood distresses.

The G-alpha protein defect depletes the child's body of naturally occurring vitamin A, and it disrupts the immune system. Megson noted a research study conducted by Nevin S. Scrimshaw and others in 1968 that reported a lack of vitamin A is directly linked to infections. The authors of the study said, "No nutritional deficiency in the animal kingdom is more consistently synergistic with infection than that of vitamin A."[42]

SUPPLEMENTATION STRATEGIES

This view is strongly supported by very recent medical research and international health data collected by the United Nations Children's Fund (UNICEF), a relief organization. Three separate clinical trials of children hospitalized with measles—one as early as 1932—showed that children died much less often when given high-dose vitamin A than those not given supplements. The consistent results suggest that boosting vitamin A can rapidly help cells repair and resist infection, thereby saving lives.[43]

Perhaps most interesting of all, Dr. Mary N. Megson's research indicates that a natural form of vitamin A occurring in cod liver oil appears to reconnect the retinoid receptors in cells, which is critical for vision, sensory perception, language processing, and attention. These happen to be key areas that are damaged in autistic children. But remember that vitamin A needs to be balanced with at least 2000 IU of vitamin D3 per day for a child.

A link between intestinal disorders and autism also has been suspected for some time. Previous improvements with some autistic children who received intravenous and sublingual doses of secretin seemed to indicate metabolic problems in the gut. Secretin is a hormone normally present in mammals but conspicuously absent in many autistic children.

Facing a Tide of Negativity

There is hope, but I'm concerned that parents of autistic children may face a tide of negative viewpoints, comments, and predictions that continue to dominate the health arena. The Autism-PDD (Pervasive Development Disorder) Network, a major parent support group, warns parents:

> The autism prognosis is startlingly grim and consistent across a broad range of studies—about 2% will attain normal functioning, with perhaps 40% labeled high functioning autistic.
>
> These high-functioning autistic [children] generally show some oddities of behavior, and have few or no personal friends. Yet, with appropriate intervention, many of the autism behaviors can be positively changed, even to the point that the child or adult may appear, to the untrained person, to no longer have autism. Like any other family faced with this diagnosis, as you explore the options and resources available in your community, you will find on the one hand the unlimited potential your child has, and, on the other, the many limits others try to place on their future. This is where a parent, facing a system with many flaws and pitfalls, must not compromise their vision of their child's future.[44]

Things have changed dramatically since the dark years when the public rarely heard anything about autism. When it did, autism was characterized as a hopeless mental condition from which there was no return to any measure of normalcy.

Dr. Robert S. Mendelsohn made an observation that applies directly to anyone seeking hope and help for an autistic child or a child with autistic-like symptoms:

> When doctors are compared with other people in evaluating retarded or other handicapped persons, those who always give the most dismal predictions and the lowest evaluations are doctors. Nurses are the next lowest, followed by psychologists. The group that always gives the most optimistic evaluation is the parents. When I'm faced with a doctor who tells me a child can't do certain things and parents who tell me that the child can do them, I always listen to the parents. I really don't care which group is right or wrong. It's the attitude that counts. Whatever attitude is reinforced and encouraged will prove true.[45]

In the meantime, there are things you can do to avoid the G-protein problem. Begin by making sure your children have adequate amounts of vitamin A from cod liver oil. Vitamin A palmitate, the form found in most vitamin supplements, is not easily absorbed by youngsters with the preexisting digestive problems so common among those whom Dr. Megson believes are most at risk.

If you plan to have your children immunized, wait as long as possible to allow plenty of time for their nervous system to mature. Space out the injections if possible, and have multiple shots given individually (for example, MMR and DPT).

Heavy Metals and Toxic Injections

It is time to add some additional information to our previous discussions of mandatory immunizations. The information represents some of the latest research on the origins of autoimmune diseases and even of ADHD, ADD, and autistic spectrum disorders. I must warn you that it is extensive and extremely controversial.

We are about to probe a nightmare of heavy metals and the possible contamination of many of the nation's immunization serums. It includes the incredible revelation that, for several decades, our state and federal governments have given our children immunizations using vaccines that may have contained highly toxic chemicals. Some are ranked among the government's top twenty hazardous substances. Under certain circumstances, these substances can maim the body, incapacitate the human brain and nervous system, and even kill.

Some who read this section will say I am absolutely wrong. Others will just as enthusiastically declare that I am right. Frankly, I felt compelled to include this information because I've seen too many children affected under circumstances too suspicious to sweep under the rug of political correctness. Regardless of its origin, we are experiencing an epidemic of biblical proportions, and something has to change. For my part, I feel honor-bound to provide you with the things I've ascertained as a biochemist and health researcher.

The very idea that poisonous substances may be included in childhood vaccines can catch even medical professionals by surprise. Psychologist Bernard Rimland, founder of the Autism Research Institute in San Diego, California, and the parent of an adult autistic child, described his reaction when he first learned about the contents of some of the vaccines being injected into American children.

It happened in the late 1960s when one of Dr. Rimland's graduate students wrote a research paper noting that mercury poisoning mimicked many of the symptoms of autism. The student mentioned that acrodynia, or pink disease, caused a number of symptoms (including those of autism) that baffled the medical community until the cause was finally discovered: mercury in teething lotions and diaper powders!

Dr. Rimland said: "I remember thinking, Interesting... another mystery solved. But only of historical interest. How wrong I was! I had assumed, very naively as it turned out, that the FDA and the drug manufacturers would henceforth scrupulously avoid using mercury. I was aware that minute amounts of mercury, along with other toxins, such as aluminum and formaldehyde, were used as preservatives in vaccines, but, after all, I assumed, since everyone now knew that these substances are extremely toxic, those highly sophisticated vaccine-makers would not possibly use amounts which even approach dangerous levels. Bad guess!"[46]

FORTY-ONE TIMES THE "SAFE" ADULT LEVEL OF MERCURY!

Despite official studies claiming otherwise, many leaders feel convinced that there is a clear cause-and-effect relationship between certain childhood immunizations and the sudden onset of autism and other learning disabilities. Included among them is Congressman Dan Burton from Indiana, who noted during congressional hearings that his grandson developed autistic symptoms after receiving a round of vaccinations. Representative Burton estimated that his grandson had received forty-one times the amount of mercury considered safe for adults—all in one day![47]

According to the position paper of the Consensus Conference on the Mercury Detoxification of Autistic Children released by the Autism Research Institute, "Some infants have been given, in one day, as much as one hundred times the maximum dosage of mercury permitted by the Environmental Protection Agency's standards, [which are] based on the weight of an adult." The paper noted that an infant's system is much less capable of dealing with toxins than an adult's.

The source of mercury in vaccine serums is thimerosal, a preservative that consists of approximately 50 percent mercury. Although the FDA asked drug makers to begin removing thimerosal from vaccines in 1998, fifty vaccines containing the preservative are still in use at this writing![48] (Note: The MMR vaccine is also controversial for its arguably dangerous measles virus, but this multiple vaccine does not contain mercury in the form of thimerosal.)

Dr. Rimland cited two studies confirming the risks associated with vaccines containing mercury. "In one study," he said, "a single injection of hepatitus B vaccine significantly raised blood mercury levels in fifteen premature and fifteen full-term infants, and mercury levels were markedly higher in the preemies. Another study, by the Centers for Disease Control and Prevention, found a slight, but statistically significant, association between mercury from vaccines and neurological disorders."[49]

WEIGHED IN THE BALANCE?

Most parents do not want to do away with the immunization program, but they do want to make sure their children are not exposed to unsafe vaccines. The problem appears to be that almost any negative finding or theory that may lower the national vaccination rate is quickly attacked and silenced for fear it may harm the immunization program. In my mind, the clear short-term and long-term danger to our children's health far outweighs any government concern over the success of a federal program!

It is a fact that mercury is ranked number three in the top 20 hazardous substances ATSDR/EPA priority list, which is published annually by the Agency for Toxic Substances and Disease Registry of the Centers for Disease Control! When you realize the ATSDR lists a total of 275 hazardous substances, it becomes clearer just how dangerous this heavy metal can be—especially to the young.

What is this toxic heavy metal doing in a vaccine serum being injected into the bodies of small children in this country? This isn't 1869 or even 1925. We are supposedly technologically advanced. Shouldn't we know better?

POTENTIALLY DEADLY MERCURY EXPOSURE

The United States currently has a very high mass immunization rate. Most people believe this is very good news. Nevertheless, some fear that America's children have been exposed to potentially damaging levels of mercury and other toxic materials. Those materials include aluminum and formaldehyde. Formaldehyde is a powerful chemical that functions as the primary component of embalming fluid. It is used to make many building materials such as plywood, and it is used in the manufacture of permanent-press clothing, dyes, inks, and explosives.

We have all been exposed to potentially dangerous levels of hazardous chemicals. In 1982, the Consumer Product Safety Commission banned the use of foam insulation made with urea-formaldehyde in homes and school buildings. Vapors from such products were considered poisonous, even at levels as low as .8 parts per million! The National Institute for Occupational Safety and Health (NIOSH) recommends an exposure limit of .016 parts per million for adults in the workplace.[50]

What about liquid formaldehyde in childhood injections? Who wants to believe the most serious exposure of all to our kids would come from an injection of toxins directly into their bloodstream as part of a government disease-prevention program?

PARENTAL DAVID VS. GOVERNMENTAL GOLIATH

The Federal Drug Administration finally did something to stop the use of mercury in vaccines in 1998, but only after informed parents began to make their voices heard in Congress and the national media. It took an incredible amount of effort, courage, and willpower to overcome the medical and governmental Goliath. The shadow of the giant is still there, however, and ADHD, ADD, and autistic spectrum cases continue to flood America's school systems and medical institutions, because a great number of mercury-tainted vaccines continue to be used in this country.

Toxic metals and chemicals are taking a toll apart from the vaccines. Dr. William G. Crook mentioned a few of the environmental hazards playing into the ADHD and hyperactivity problem in the book he cowrote with Laura Stevens, *Solving the Puzzle of Your Hard-to-Raise Child:*

"Before the Clean Water Act was enacted in 1972, oceans, rivers and other bodies of water were commonly used as dumping grounds for some of the most toxic substances imaginable, including arsenic, cadmium, mercury, lead, polychlorinated biphenyls (PCBs) and toxic pesticides."[51]

The late Dr. Ben F. Feingold made this amazing statement about the proliferation of potentially harmful chemicals in 1975 in his landmark book *Why Your Child Is Hyperactive*:

> In 1971, the Stanford Research Institute, under contract to the National Cancer Institute, began work on a system to rank chemicals by their estimated hazard to man. I have been informed by Mr. Arthur McGee, who is in charge of the SRI studies, that since 1839, when organic chemistry began, approximately three million chemicals have been synthesized—compounds which never existed in nature. Of these chemicals, it is estimated that over 30,000 are currently in use for all purposes (industrial, medicinal, agricultural, etc.). Although 5,000 of these compounds have had some tests for carcinogenicity, only 2,000 have been "reliably tested" as to whether they are a cause of cancer. Of the 30,000 chemicals in use today, over 3,800 occur in our foods as additives. Some of the additives have been studied for carcinogenesis, mutagenesis and blastogenesis, but not a single one of the synthetics used in our food has been subjected to the rigid investigations required for licensing drugs.[52]

Apparently, scientists, vaccine makers, and physicians have known about the highly toxic characteristics of mercury and formaldehyde for many decades. Yet they continued to use and dispense relatively high levels of mercury in the form of thimerosal to small children through our nation's compulsory vaccination program. They also use a form of formaldehyde in the production of a number of major vaccines to this day.

Formaldehyde, in the form of formalin, is a 37 percent solution of gaseous formaldehyde with small amounts of methanol. It "is the chemical of choice to inactivate the viruses used in the production of polio, yellow fever, influenza and hepatitis B vaccines," according to Jamie Murphy, author of *What Every Parent Should Know About Childhood Immunization*.[53]

WHY WORRY ABOUT A LITTLE CARCINOGEN?

Jamie Murphy also said that formalin is used to detoxify diphtheria and tetanus toxins, transforming them into toxoids in the process. It has been shown to cause allergic reactions, irritation, and tumors in humans. In addition, it has produced squamous cell carcinomas (cancers) in the nasal cavities of rats.[54]

Although government scientists and medical authorities undoubtedly know about these studies, they don't seem to be worried about "a little carcinogen" being injected into children. Do they know something we don't know?

The only tests I've uncovered for toxicity involved the three usual methods of entry into the body: inhalation, skin contact, and ingestion. No one seems to have any data for the internal effects of injected formalin, but research has shown that an adult will die three hours after ingesting (drinking) just one ounce of the stuff.

Perhaps Jamie Murphy offers the best summary of the risks involved with formaldehyde as a component in most of America's childhood vaccines by asking: "Who would consider using a hazardous waste, carcinogenic in rats, used in the manufacture of inks, dyes, explosives, wrinkle-proof fabrics, home insulation, and as a major constituent of embalming fluid, and inject it into the delicate body of an infant? What could formaldehyde, aluminum, phenol, mercury, or any number of other deadly chemical substances used in vaccines possibly have to do with preventing disease in children?"[55]

WHAT'S A LITTLE FIBROSARCOMA BETWEEN FRIENDS?

Jamie Murphy noted that three researchers conducted a study in 1971 to determine the toxicity levels of seven compounds widely used as preservatives or extracting agents for vaccines: Merthiolate (thimerosal), benzethonium chloride, methylparaben, phenol red, pyridine, ethylene glycol, and ethylene chlorohydrin. He writes, "All seven chemicals produced tumors not only at the injection site, but also in the parts of the body.... Can there be any doubt that at least three chemicals used in vaccines —thimerosal, benzethonium chloride, and aluminum—

are probably causes of induration [hard nodules that appear at the injection site], fibromas [fibrous benign tumors], fibrosarcomas [malignant tumors likely to have a fatal outcome], granulomas, and injection site tumors?"[56]

Some of the other material from which vaccines are made may surprise you. According to Leon Chaitow, author of *Vaccination and Immunisation*, some of the ingredients are quite unsettling to contemplate. For example, diphtheria toxin and antitoxin is derived from putrefying horse blood, the pertussis vaccine is taken from mucus from the throats of infected children, the typhoid vaccine is derived from decomposed fecal material taken from typhoid victims, the Salk polio serum was taken from the kidneys of infected monkeys, and the recently discredited vaccine used ineffectively against swine flu, which had dreadful effects on the recipients, was derived from infected rotten eggs.[57]

ENTER THE OSTRICH AND THE OFFICIAL BOX OF SAND

As a thinking person, university-trained biochemist, and concerned parent, I have to wonder why government officials and key medical leaders continue to ignore these concerns. In my opinion, such clear scientific evidence requires us to rethink our position on the true value of compulsory immunizations in their present state.

An apparent conflict of interest may have a direct

effect on what actually happens in this area. Naturally, most medical and governmental leaders want to preserve their reputations and the status quo. Many in the national educational system want to protect the lucrative subsidies local districts receive from government immunization incentive programs. On the other hand, we want to preserve the lives, health, and future or our children.

Something or someone must give in this situation, and the pressure from informed parents and increasingly bold scientific and medical dissenters continues to grow. While the official denials mount, the runaway epidemic of ADHD, ADD, and autistic spectrum disorders mounts even faster.

This entire debate seems even more risky when you consider just how little it takes to damage or influence the developing nervous systems of growing children. In my mind, it amounts to arguing whether we should give our children just one cup or an entire gallon of unleaded gasoline with their school lunches. This stuff seems unsafe in any amount.

It Only Takes One Molecule

When Nobel Laureate and eminent Stanford University scientist Linus Pauling was asked what amount of a compound is required for sensitization in the human system, he bluntly replied, "A single molecule." As Dr. Ben F. Feingold noted, "Molecules vary in size, but a million small ones can be gathered on a pinhead.... We cannot safely predict that any part per million or billion or trillion will not have an effect on certain individuals or on all individuals."[58]

The good news is that it is possible to remove harmful heavy metals such as mercury or lead from the human body, a procedure that has produced excellent results in children. If you suspect your child experienced an adverse reaction to a vaccination or has been exposed to harmful substances in another way, then the first step is to determine whether or not your child's body contains dangerous levels of heavy metals or chemicals known to accumulate in body tissues.

I strongly recommend that you have your child tested for intestinal dysbiosis, or the abnormal function of the intestinal system. This is a particularly common condition among children with ADHD, ADD, and autistic spectrum disorder, which leads many to believe it may be a contributing or primary cause of these conditions in some cases.

These conditions often occur or are aggravated by a severe yeast overgrowth in the digestive tract that should be treated before any effort is made for mercury detoxification. Even this process may significantly improve or remove many hyperactivity symptoms, according to the research and clinical experience of Dr. William G. Crook and researchers consulting with the Autism Research Institute (ARI), among others.

The Autism Research Institute gathered twenty-five physicians, chemists, toxicologists, and scientists to determine the best way to remove heavy metal contaminants —mercury in particular—from the human body. These medical professionals had treated more than three thousand patients for heavy metal poisoning, including fifteen hundred autistic children. The scientific attendees had a combined total of ninety years of research experience in the toxicology of mercury and other heavy metals.

Choosing the Best Method of Mercury Detoxification

Once the dysfunction caused by heavy metals, harmful chemical deposits, and yeast overgrowth have been treated in a child's digestive system, nutritional therapies will help the child to stay healthy and improve in many areas of behavior and learning ability.

Follow Up with Vitamins

The ARI protocol recommends the supplementation of the following vitamins after the mercury detoxification procedure is complete. This is but a very brief summary of the more detailed recommendations provided in the "Defeat Autism Now! (DAN!) Mercury Detoxification Consensus Group" position paper. These supplements can be obtained by calling us at 1-800-726-1834 or by going to www.HealthMasters.com:

- Ultimate Multiple, which gives foundation nutrition for wellness and disease protection.
- Vaso B6 Plus: Up to 15 milligrams for every 2.2 pounds of body weight of B6 or 3 milligrams for every 2.2 pounds of body weight of pyridoxal-5-phosphate (P5P) to a maximum of 500 milligrams of B6 or 100 milligrams of P5P. (Avoid any preparations that contain supplemental copper. Many autistic spectrum children in particular have an excessive amount of copper in their bodies.)
- Excellent C: Start daily doses at 5–10 milligrams for every 2.2 pounds of body weight (3–6 IU/2.2 pounds) of buffered or vitamin C esters and increase to tolerance. This helps to protect and support healthy connective tissue.
- Super Potent E: This fat-soluble vitamin can accumulate if given in excess. Dosing in the range of 2–4 milligrams for every 2.2 pounds of body weight every day (3–6 IU/2.2 pounds) is within safe limits. Mixed tocopherols are the preferred preparation. This is excellent for heart health, circulation, and cancer prevention.
- Alpha Lipoic Acid: This powerful antioxidant may be particularly helpful in autistic children since many of them show evidence of antioxidant depletion. Start with daily doses of alpha lipoic acid equal to 1–3 milligrams for every 2.2 pounds of body weight and increase to 10 milligrams for

every 2.2 pounds as tolerated. This is a natural product of human cells and so has minimal toxicity. (Note: The authors of the ARI consensus paper recommend that this supplement be used only in conjunction with DMSA, which grabs or binds to excess mercury released by alpha lipoic acid.)

- Melatonin Sublingual: This pineal hormone helps regulate the sleep-wake cycle and is an antioxidant. Doses of up to 0.1 milligrams per every 2.2 pounds of body weight at bedtime should be adequate, although smaller doses may provide the same benefits. (If your child already has a good sleep cycle, I do not recommend supplementation with melatonin.)
- Ultimate D3-5000: This is a superdose of vitamin D and a must for anyone with osteoporosis or osteopenia.
- Cod Liver Oil: Our high-vitamin pure cod liver oil offers more vitamin A and D than any other product on the market.
- Chelation Therapy.

Note: The ARI consensus paper also recommends that you avoid the following substances due to their suspected interaction with mercury or other heavy metals. Consult with your medical provider before using them: cysteine/cystine, n-acetyl-L-cysteine (NAC), chlorella, or other algae.

Call my office at 1-800-726-1834 to order the supplements recommended above. We also carry a great product for children that detoxifies the system and removes mercury and other heavy metals from the body. The reason I promote my supplements so heavily in this book is that most supplements and vitamins don't work. Many are made overseas and are toxic. The supplements my family and I use are the same ones we recommend to you!

4

GET HEART HEALTHY

It is almost ironic when you hear of someone dropping dead from a heart attack or heart disease with no symptoms. One day they seem to be a picture of health, the next day they are dead, and two days later you are at their funeral.

Suddenly a giant void is opened, leaving behind bereaved spouses and children. It is so sad to me to hear of this tragic scenario of events that happens so often. In fact, of the half a million Americans who die of heart attacks each year, almost half of these unsuspecting souls have none of the classic heart attack warning signs.

Let me rephrase that for emphasis. Half of the people who die of a heart attack have normal blood pressure, normal cholesterol, and no previous heart problems!

What all of this means is that you can go to your physician, get great results, drop dead the next day, and be buried three days later.

There has to be a better way!

Tests and More Tests

Obviously, the tests that determine a person's cardiac health are extremely unreliable, yet standard physicians have no choice but to rely on them. They simply check your cholesterol and triglycerides. Then they look at a person's blood pressure and weight and ask you if you smoke or exercise. If they are really thorough, they may check your homocysteine levels (which, by the way, are much more important than just cholesterol) and C-reactive protein levels.

But there is one more thing that I learned about thirty years ago and which the latest research is showing to be one of the most important risk factors of all.

Why is this problem so important to understand? Because all of the other factors—like blood pressure, LDL, and fibrinogen—are merely symptoms of this factor that involves the food that you eat.

So what is this factor and how does food affect it? I am glad you asked.

Blood Viscosity

The risk factor that I learned about thirty years ago is so simple, but it makes a huge difference in your cardiovascular system. It's blood viscosity. Or simply put, how thick is your blood?

I know this sounds incredible, which is why I believe it is so important to emphasize this to you. Frankly, I have had it with people I know dropping dead because their blood is too thick. In many cases their already too thick blood has become much thicker because they have eaten an extremely high-fat meal within twenty-four hours of their death.

To understand blood viscosity, consider the difference between water and room-temperature honey. If you turn over a glass of water, it simply pours out. If you turn over a jar of room-temperature honey, it oozes out. To get the honey to come out faster, some people put it in a plastic container and squeeze it out.

Blood works much the same way. Your heart needs to squeeze your blood by pumping it. But when blood gets too thick, the heart has to pound like crazy just to move it. Some folks call it thick blood, blood sludge, or blood goo. This causes tremendous stress and damage on the arteries, kidneys, and the entire vascular system. It can even run your blood pressure through the roof, causing you to have a stroke.

Most artery damage occurs at the branching of the forks of the blood vessels. If this damage was caused primarily by cholesterol or homocysteine levels, you'd expect it to be throughout the entire cardiovascular system. But it is not. Why you may ask? Because the primary damage is caused by the friction and pressure of this thick blood flowing through these branched areas.

This thick blood produces so much friction that it can erode the inner lining of the artery, then the body has to heal this erosion by patching up the artery. This patch is called plaque. But when the body puts on a patch, it further narrows the artery, which causes more erosion, another patch, and so on. It becomes a viscous cardiovascular constricting cycle.

Other Heart and Blood Risk Factors

In order to paint the whole picture for you, let me cover some of the other factors of heart disease and how those factors relate to blood viscosity:

- **Male or Female**: One of the factors that causes premenopausal women to have lowered heart disease rates is that menstruation thins the entire blood supply. When a women ceases menstruation after menopause, the risk of heart disease for men and women is close to the same. In fact, in some cases it even goes up for women.

- **Body Weight**: High-fat meals and high-sugar carbohydrate meals both increase blood viscosity. In most obese patients, their primary diet consists of high-fat and high-glycemic sugary meals. These high-glycemic meals also increase insulin, which can result in syndrome X. Plus, just eating high-fat meals can cause a weakened cardiovascular system to fail and for you to die in just twenty-four hours.

- **Diabetes**: When diabetics take insulin (which is a salt), it can overionize the blood system, causing additional plaquing. In fact, diabetics run a much higher heart disease rate than the general population. Plus diabetes can make red blood cells stiffer, which also increases blood viscosity.

- **Alcohol consumption**: Alcohol is a diuretic. It makes you urinate. When you urinate, you lose water. When you dehydrate yourself by drinking diuretics, such as alcohol or caffeine, your blood gets thicker, increasing viscosity. This is why, when you fly in an airplane, it has superdry air, and you must drink water continuously. If you don't, you could dehydrate and end up with blood clots.

I remember several years ago when I was speaking with First Lady Barbara Bush about losing some weight. She asked me about former Vice President Dan Quayle, who was suffering from blood clots when he flew, and asked if I could help him. I told her to have him drink twelve to fifteen glasses of no-chlorine, no-fluoride purified water a day when he flew and to follow my cardiovascular procedure. Drinking purified water is the quickest and most reliable way to help your blood. This should be your first step in any cardiovascular healthy heart program.

- **Smoking**: Nicotine constricts blood vessels, increasing blood pressure, and it thickens the blood by increasing fibrinogen and inflammation. Don't smoke. If you do, drink a lot of pure water, avoid diuretics, and follow my cardiovascular program.
- **Cholesterol**: HDL thins the blood. LDL thickens the blood. The best way to elevate HDL is through omega-3 supplements with organic cod liver oil. (More about this later in this chapter.)
- **Blood Pressure**: As I have already said, when you are trying to pump thick blood through your arteries, the pressure goes through the roof. Again, more pressure, more friction, more plaque, and narrower arteries.
- **Age**: As you grow older, everything in your body slows down. This also includes red blood cell replacement. Young red blood cells, fresh out of the bone marrow (God sure did make us amazing!), are soft and flexible. But as with any cells as they age, they incur damage. The damage makes them stiffer, just as aging does to the joints.

  Eventually, the old stiff red blood cells are taken out and recycled in your spleen. But remember, because the blood cells are still somewhat inflexible, they have a difficult time getting through your capillaries. So, again, greater blood pressure is needed to drive them through the capillaries.

BAD NEWS, GOOD NEWS

As important as blood viscosity is to cardiovascular health, there are other vital steps you can take toward a healthy heart. If you want to avoid a stroke, heart attack, or dying from America's number-one killer, you probably need to forget all the mainstream information you have heard.

The truth of the matter is very eye opening. Heart disease was basically unheard of in 1910. By 1930, it caused about three thousand deaths annually in the United States. By 1960, however, five hundred thousand deaths were attributed to heart disease, and despite our spending hundreds of billions if not trillions of dollars since then, the number of heart disease fatalities has never decreased below that level. Several years ago the rates hit one mllion per year—one every thirty-three seconds. Many of us realize that something is wrong, very wrong.

First, let me tell you why there was such a huge spike from 1930 to 1960. That was the era in which junk food (processed) production went crazy in this country. That is also the era that hydrogenated oils were first used. Hydrogenated oils were first used as a substitute for butter. During World War II, there was a scarcity of butter. Then scientists discovered that they could heat corn oil and then bubble hydrogen through it, using nickel as a catalyst. They could take the liquid corn oil and turn it into a solid fat, which was marketed as Crisco.

Yellow food coloring could be added to produce a

butter substitute (margarine). The problem is that this type of fat is not found in nature. It is called a trans fat and is extremely toxic. It causes heart disease, cancer, and infertility. Finally this year, the USDA has required all manufacturers to list the amount of trans fat in their products. But some manufacturers have already found ways to hide this information on their labels.

With all the processed foods we are eating, it is no surprise to see the breathtaking rise in deaths from cardiovascular diseases.

Notice I have not mentioned cholesterol, tryglycerides, or blood pressure. These three can be controlled with dietary changes. Don't forget, half the people who die of heart attacks have normal blood pressure, cholesterol, and triglycerides. Many of them, just prior to dropping dead, have had physicals, EKGs, and stress tests that show their hearts were in great shape. Interestingly, the major drug companies don't want you to have these statistics.

In my book *Maximum Energy*, I wrote about one of my former high-school coaches. His name was Tom. He was a great guy. One day I commented on how good he looked. He said, "I'm sixty-two years old. My doctor told me I have the body of a forty-two-year-old." He was doing some weight training while we talked. He was amazing. Three days later he was dead. He had a massive heart attack. The entire community was devastated.

In the past, as with Coach Tom, the medical community has often been confused. Even with unprecedented heart attack rates over the past years, they have no idea why the rate is so high.

Here is the good news. A new study out of Paris is shedding light on people, primarily men, who are dropping dead from heart attacks for no apparent reason. It seems that one problem, if not the primary problem, is that these victims have high levels of nonesterified fatty acids (NEFA) in their blood. This can cause dangerous ventricular dysrhythmias if you have coronary artery disease and low oxygen delivery to your heart.

Stop! Don't start fussing. I know what you are thinking. *He's doing it again. I don't want this technical stuff. I'm not a biochemist.* Okay, you're right. I'll make it easy. By the way, just for the old university memories, I do enjoy talking and writing like that. But my wife always fusses at me when I do.

So here's the bottom line: high levels of NEFAs are caused by too much omega-6 in the diet. Omega-6 comes from corn, safflower, sunflower, soy, and canola oils.

More Steps to a Healthy Heart

So here's what I recommend for a healthy heart. They aren't casual suggestions, since I take these every day for my heart:

- **Foods high in omega-3:** These include fresh, wild salmon (never use farm-raised salmon). Good plant sources are leaf lettuce, flax seeds, and walnuts.

Plus, remember to use olive oil, grape seed oil, coconut oil, or organic butter in your cooking. It's important to get as much omega-3 as possible.

- **Taking cod liver oil every day**: I am partial to our Cod Liver Oil—Blue Ice Pure (available through www.HealthMasters.com), since it offers more vitamin A and D than any other product on the market. It is fermented cod liver oil, twice as potent with half the dosage!

Our cod liver oil is molecularly distilled, using a patented process, to remove all impurities. Taking one teaspoon a day literally improves vascular integrity and provides anti-inflammatory effects. This is important since cardiovascular disease has been linked to inflammation. One of the biomarkers used to identify the early warning signs of potential cardiovascular disease is called CRP (C-reactive protein). This inflammatory marker indicates potential cardiovascular disease.

Notice that I haven't talked much about cholesterol in this chapter. Here's why. Cholesterol is an anti-inflammatory product. The body produces cholesterol as a defense mechanism to reduce inflammation. So what does mainstream medicine do? It gives us statin drugs to reduce our cholesterol. These statin drugs cause muscle wasting (myopathy), which makes heart disease much worse, plus they cause cancer.

By contrast, fish oil lowers CRP naturally, which then gets the body to reduce cholesterol to a normal level. It really is that simple. Now if you are taking prescription drugs. Don't stop. Go to your doctor and have him help you to reduce or eliminate your dosage. If he won't help, find a medical doctor who will. If you are still worried about cholesterol, there are two products that work great without causing myopathy.

- **Healthy Lipid Profile**: This lowers cholesterol because citrus bioflavanoids antioxidants reduce inflammation. When you provide bioflavanoids antioxidants, your body doesn't have to make cholesterol to reduce inflammation in the arteries. This supplement also helps to balance the LDL and HDL ratio.

- **Cholesterol-X**: This consists of policosanol and a patented magnesium chelate, a combination that acts to reduce cholesterol without causing side effects. It helps to reduce the liver's production of cholesterol.

- **Vitamin E**: I recommend Health Masters Super Potent E, a mixed tocopherol product, which is high in gamma E. This is the most potent E to protect against LDL cholesterol (bad cholesterol) breakdown. When you oxidize or breakdown LDL cholesterol, it's like turning little razor blades loose in your arteries. This oxidized LDL cholesterol creates lesions (little cuts) in the blood vessels. These little cuts then form scars, which can cause blockages in the arteries, heart disease, and heart attacks.

I recommend 1600 IU for men and 800 IU for women daily. By the way, I have been taking 1600 IU for twenty-five years. The study several years ago that concluded vitamin E was bad used chemically produced, cheap, synthetic E. No study has ever shown that natural mixed tocopherol E does anything but good.

- **Magnesium and malate acid**: I am partial to Health Masters Magnesium and Malate Acid. These are natural muscle relaxants that help to lower blood pressure. We also use patented Albion chelate minerals, which are absorbed by the body as food. Magnesium also helps to lower blood pressure and allows more oxygen to be delivered to the heart. If you are taking Health Masters Cholesterol-X, you won't need to add this.

Here are additional supplements that I suggest taking on a daily basis:
- Ossomag, which contains superior calcium, magnesium, and vitamin D3 to reduce and replace bone loss.
- HGH Stimulate, which improves circulatory, immune and nervous system function, memory,

reduces wrinkles, increases bone density, and decreases blood pressure.

- Ultimate Multiple, which gives foundation nutrition for wellness and disease protection.
- Adrenal Support, which helps to restore adrenals and reduces cortisol (the stress hormone that makes you store body fat). This also increases energy levels.
- B Complex, which is important for the support of the adrenal hormone production and the regulation of the body's production of energy through enhancement of coenzyme A production.

Always remember, if you have questions, call us at 1-800-726-1834 or order online at www.HealthMasters.com.

5

Use the Virus Killer

Could influenza and a number of other common illnesses result from little more than a vitamin D and D$_3$ deficiency? If you ask anybody who takes 5000 units of vitamin D a day, they will tell you they just don't get sick anymore. Colds and flu simply happen less and less. How that works is amazing.

Your body makes hundreds of naturally occurring antibiotics called antimicrobial peptides, and people have been looking for a long time to see what can increase the genetic production of these antimicrobial peptides.

Just in the past couple of years, it has been discovered that vitamin D upregulates the production of antimicrobial peptides. It makes sense. Do you get many colds and influenza in the summertime? No, not really. People have always thought that the reason for that is that people are crowded together in the wintertime, but it turns out it's probably simply due to the fact that your vitamin D levels in the winter are a quarter or sometimes one-third what they are in the summertime.

Lots of Theories

Many times when people, even scientists, talk about science, they confuse facts and theories. For example, it is a fact that children with rickets get lots of infections. But scientists will tell you that children with rickets get lots of infections because their rib cages are soft. One part of the statement is fact, and one part is theory.

How about this one. More people get heart attacks in the winter because they are shoveling snow, because they are more often indoors and in crowded situations, or because of influenza. There are so many theories about it. The fact is this: more heart attacks occur during winter. Everything else is theory. It is important to separate fact and theory.

Preventing Disease

The effect vitamin D has on preventing influenza and the common cold should not be overestimated, especially with pandemic influenza. How likely a virus is to kill you depends on not only your innate immunity, that is, how many antimicrobial peptides you have waiting to kill the influenza virus, but it also depends on how many antibodies you have—what is called the adaptive immune system. It also depends on how novel the virus is to the human species and how lethal it is.

In 1918, there are documented cases of people being well in the morning, coughing at noon, turning blue at suppertime, and being dead by nighttime. It was that quick. Even though the majority of deaths occurred in the wintertime in the United States during the 1918 pandemic, there were outbreaks in the summertime. I would caution people not to think that vitamin D is the cure-all for influenza, but I think it's a major weapon in the fight against influenza and even the common cold.

We really just don't know. It wasn't an experiment. We just guessed. And part of that is based on the fact that certain parts of the immune system that might overreact are kept in check. Explain that.

Vitamin D does a couple of things. It not only upregulates production of the cathelicidin and other antimicrobial peptides, but it also dampens the arm of the immune system that is invested and ordered to cause inflammation. Inflammation is what makes the body to respond to it. What is called a cytokine storm, which is what killed many people in 1918, is an explosion of the immune system that strips the epithelial lining of the respiratory tract, and people choke to death because they can't breathe. With this kind of cytokine storm, and there's lots of diseases that deal with excess inflammation, vitamin D makes the immune system smarter.

Immunity and Autoimmunity

In addition to influenza, research shows that vitamin D deficiency and insufficiency are linked to the risk of a long list of illnesses that include the following:

- autoimmune disease
- cancer (including colon and breast cancers)
- chronic pain
- dementia
- depression
- diabetes (both Type 1 and Type 2)
- heart disease
- hypertension
- inflammatory bowel disease
- multiple sclerosis
- obesity
- osteoarthritis
- osteoporosis
- Parkinson's disease
- periodontal disease
- psoriasis
- rheumatoid arthritis
- rickets
- strokes

A recent review presented considerable evidence that influenza epidemics, and perhaps even the common cold, are brought on by seasonal deficiencies in vitamin D.

Results of an RCT support the theory, finding 2000 IU of vitamin D daily for one year virtually eliminated self-reported incidence of colds and influenza. Even the current triple childhood epidemics of autism, asthma, and Type 1 diabetes, all of which blossomed after sun-avoidance advice became widespread, might be the tragic sequel of gestational or early childhood vitamin D deficiencies brought on by medical advice to avoid the sun.

FORMS OF VITAMIN D

Vitamin D comes through both food and sunlight. There are two types of vitamin D found in nature. Vitamin D_2 is formed by the action of UV-B on the plant precursor ergosterol. It is found in plants and was formerly added to irradiated cow's milk. Most milk today contains D_3. Vitamin D_3, or cholecalciferol, is found in animal foods. Both forms of vitamin D have been used successfully to treat rickets and other diseases related to vitamin D insufficiency.

Many consider D_3 the preferred vitamin, because it has more biologic activity. Vitamin D_3 as found in food or in human skin always comes with various metabolites or isomers that may have biological benefit. There are as many as twelve metabolites or isomers in the vitamin D found in animal foods. When vitamin D is taken in the form of fish oil, or eaten in foods such as eggs or fish, these metabolites will be present.

VITAMIN D$_3$

Now let's talk more specifically about vitamin D$_3$. Much current research has been done on this vitamin, which is highly deficient in the normal population.

Vitamin D$_3$ is manufactured in plants, but it is also manufactured by the body from cholesterol as the skin is exposed to the sunlight. Since vitamin D$_3$ is manufactured by the body, many researchers also consider it a hormone. In fact, it is the most active steroid hormone by weight in the body. It is used in hundreds of biochemical reactions throughout the body.

The purity of vitamin D$_3$ is critical. It needs to be from a natural source. Most vitamin D$_3$ on the market are chemical synthetics. Ours from Health Masters is obtained from sheep's wool. I have a pharmaceutical lab manufacture it. This is critical because of its hormone-like properties. It must be pure. Also, it has to be sealed properly by capsulation since it will oxidize very quickly and become useless, if not harmful.

Health Masters Vitamin D$_3$ Liquid is the highest quality product available today. Again, it is the most active steroid hormone by weight in the body.

A PubMed database search yields sixty-three observational studies of vitamin D status in relation to cancer risk, including thirty colon, thirteen breast, twenty-six prostate, and seven ovarian cancer studies. Several assess the association of the vitamin D receptor genotype with cancer risk. The evidence suggests that efforts to improve vitamin D status, for example, by vitamin D supplementation, could reduce cancer incidence and death rates at low cost, with few or no adverse effects.

SUNSHINE

The skin plateau of daily vitamin D production is only twenty to thirty minutes in a light-skinned person. In other words, less than a half-hour of daily exposure of the arms and legs to sunlight will supply us with all the vitamin D that we need, since humans manufacture vitamin D from cholesterol by the action of sunlight on the skin.

Still, this amount of exposure of hands, face, and arms for three times a week provides only 200–400 IU of vitamin D each time, or an average of 100–200 IU per day during the summer months. In order to achieve optimal levels of vitamin D, 85 percent of body surface needs exposure to prime midday sun.[1]

Worse, there are many factors that make it very difficult to obtain even a minimal amount of vitamin D.[2] The ultraviolet effect is limited by:

- Increased melanin pigment increases the exposure time needed for maximum formation, and if you have darker skin, it takes more sunshine to make vitamin D.
- Time of day and time of season.
- Sunscreen, glass, pollution, and lack of exposure.

- Chlorine in swimming pools reduces the skin oils that help in the processing of vitamin D.
- Altitude and latitude.
- Vitamin D levels decline with aging and obesity.

These next statistics are amazing. They show the problem!

- At 34 N (Los Angeles), vitamin D synthesis occurs year-round.
- At 42 N (Boston), vitamin D synthesis ceased from November to February.
- At 52 N (Edmonton), vitamin D synthesis ceased from October to March.

In other words, if you live in the North, vitamin D won't be made by your body due to a lack of sunshine for a large part of the year. No wonder so many people are deficient.

Ultraviolet (UV) light is divided into three bands (sometimes called wavelength ranges). These are commonly called UV-C, UV-B, and UV-A bands, and each has unique characteristics:

- The first, UV-C, is the shortest and most vigorous of the UV bands, burning human skin quickly, even with extremely small doses. Thankfully, UV-C is absorbed by the ozone layer, but it is still present in fluorescent, halogen, and other unique lights, although most approved lights contribute little to skin cancer.[3]

- The second, UV-A, is most responsible for darkening the pigment in our skin. It is sometimes called the tanning ray, and it is less energetic than UV-B. Therefore, exposure to UV-A will generally not result in sunburns unless the skin is especially photosensitive or if excessive doses are used. Because of a longer wavelength, UV-A penetrates more deeply into the skin and is considered to be a major contributor to a growing number of nonmelanoma skin cancers.[4]

- The third band, UV-B is the wavelength that stimulates our bodies to produce vitamin D. While it is sometimes called the burning ray, because it is the primary cause of sunburn, UV-B is also very beneficial by stimulating the production of vitamin D that is so useful and important to maximum health. It does so by causing melanocytes, uniquely effective skin cells, to produce melanin, which is protective and beneficial. This wavelength also stimulates the amazing production of the melanocyte-stimulating hormone (MSH), which is a hormone that is vital to weight loss, energy production, and so many other health-giving processes.[5]

With these three bands in mind, let's revisit the discussion of your location on the globe and the angle of the earth in relation to the sun, since latitude and altitude determine the intensity of UV light.

Specifically, in terms of UV-B (note: a simple meter is available to determine UV-B levels where you live), the wavelength that helps us to produce vitamin D, it is good to remember several key points:

- The reason it is difficult to get adequate vitamin D from sunlight is that, while UV-A is present throughout the day, the amount of UV-B has a direct correlation with the angle of the sun's rays.

- Specifically, many places around the planet have UV-B present only during midday hours.

- Exposure earlier or later, especially at higher latitudes, can cause burning from the UV-A rays long before you can get an adequate supply of vitamin D from UV-B.

- Latitudes higher than 30 degrees (both north and south) have insufficient UV-B sunlight two to six months of the year, even at midday.[6]

- Latitudes higher than 40 degrees have insufficient sunlight to achieve optimum levels of vitamin D during six to eight months of the year.

- In other words, the most beneficial sunning must occur between the hours we have specifically been taught to avoid at all costs—between 10 a.m. and 2 p.m. during summer months (or winter months in southern latitudes). Twenty or more minutes (depending on your skin type and color) provides enough vitamin D before burning occurs.[7]

- Even so, much of the United States has insufficient UV-B sunlight to produce optimal vitamin D levels during at least six months each year.
- In far northern or southern locations, latitudes 45 degrees and higher, even the summer sun is insufficient to provide even minimal levels of vitamin D.[8]

The bottom line is that when you sunbathe with at least 85 percent of your body exposed to the midday sun, your body can produce as much as 20,000 IU of vitamin D, which is one hundred times more vitamin D than a multivitamin and one hundred times more vitamin D than the government says you need!

It seems our body is telling us something. Doesn't it? Sunshine!

VITAMIN D₃: THE MIRACLE VITAMIN

So, theories aside, what are these antimicrobial peptides produced by vitamin D effective against? Are they a broad spectrum?

There are several hundred micropeps, maybe as many as a thousand, in the human body, probably even more than that because they seem to specialize in different things. But the cathelicidin, one of the major groups, has an incredibly broad spectrum of action in both bacteria and viruses. In encapsulated viruses—viruses with a lipoprotein coating around them—it simply destroys the coating or punches a whole in the coating, and the virus or the bacteria dies. It is the same with a number of fungal infections. That's why vitamin D_3 is sometimes called the miracle vitamin. Here are a number of examples:

- **Tuberculosis:** Most infectious diseases common in the wintertime are a target of vitamin D, even some of the more prolonged infections, such as tuberculosis. In fact, it was common knowledge one hundred years ago that sunshine helped tuberculosis. Physicians knew this to be a fact. They published it. But people just forget about it. The reasons sunlight might help fight tuberculosis is because of its relation to vitamin D.

- **Colon cancer:** In an eight-year prospective study of thirty-five thousand subjects, colon cancer was reduced by 80 percent in those with serum 4000 IU a day.

- **Breast cancer:** A recent English study showed breast cancer was five times more common in those with the lowest vitamin D_3 levels.

- **Colorectal cancer:** A Harvard Medical School study showed substantial evidence that higher 24 (OH)D levels through increased sunlight exposure of dietary or supplement intake inhibit colorectal cancer.

- **Prostate cancer:** The biologic evidence for an anti-cancer role of 25(OH)D is also strong for prostate cancer.

- **General Cancers**: Harvard Medical School research adds to the mounting evidence for the influential role of solar UV-B exposure on cancer, particularly for some of the less-well-studied digestive cancers, possibly suggesting that the maintenance of adequate vitamin D levels is more critical for limiting tumor progression than for preventing tumor onset. Our findings are generally consistent with the published literature. Plus, more and more research shows that cancer survival is dependent on a season of diagnosis and sunlight exposure. In fact, a recent study involving over a million cancer patients adds to a growing body of evidence that vitamin D metabolites play an important role in cancer survival. The results show that a high level of vitamin D at the time of diagnosis and during cancer treatment may improve the prognosis of the cancer types studied. The residential and/or occupational sun exposure rate seemed to be positively correlated with a lower risk of overall mortality due to organ cancer. The latter years showed even more dramatic results with the calcium/vitamin D_3 group showing a 77 percent cancer risk reduction, claimed the researchers. There was, however, no statistically significant difference in cancer incidence between participants taking placebos and those taking just calcium supplements. The women—1,179 healthy postmenopausal women who were all fifty-five years or older and free of known cancers for at least ten years prior to entering the study—were randomly assigned to take daily dosages of 1400–1500 mg supplemental calcium plus 1000 IU of vitamin D_3 or placebos. Over the four-year trial, women in the calcium–vitamin D_3 group experienced a 60 percent decrease in their cancer risk compared to the group taking placebos.

- **Heart and blood problems**: Cardiovascular disease is more common in the winter, more common at higher latitudes, and more common at lower altitudes—all apparently related to vitamin D. However, people with 25(OH)D levels above 35 ng/ml were half as likely to have a heart attack than those whose level was less than 35 ng/ml. What most doctors and the public have been told is that high-dose vitamin D can induce calcifications of arteries. But Armin Zittermann, PhD, of the North-Rhine Westphalia Heart Center in Germany, reports that both extremely high and commonly low intake levels of vitamin D induce calcification of arteries. Calcification from overdose of vitamin D requires many hundreds of thousands of IUs and is rare, whereas hundreds of millions of adults are deficient in vitamin D and suffer from calcified arteries as a result of this deficiency. Dr. Zittermann points to a study conducted in Japan where adequate Vitamin D levels achieved via supplementation reduced the death risk from cardiovascular disease by 70 percent compared to those who did not use vitamin D supplements.[9] It is increasingly apparent that excessive calcium, not cholesterol, causes hardening of the arteries and heart attacks. Only about 3 percent of arterial plaque is cholesterol, while 59 percent is calcium, and vitamin D is an anticalcifying agent.

- **Rickets**: The clinical outcome of severe vitamin D deficiency in infants was endemic in Europe and North America during the nineteenth century and the first two decades of the twentieth century. Rickets were everywhere due to lack of sunlight from the Industrial Revolution. However, in the 1820s, Jedrezej Sniadecki noticed that the children of Warsaw had higher percentages of rickets than children in countryside, so he took the city children to the countryside for treatment and achieved excellent results. Similarly, the Floating Hospital in Boston took children with rickets into Boston Harbor for a sunshine cure. Soon, more and more research has shown that vitamin D and sunshine are invaluable in the battle against rickets.

- **Mental health challenges**: There is an increasing amount of research that shows that vitamin D enhances mental health, especially in well-documented studies concerning seasonal affective disorder, premenstrual syndrome, and overall general mood.

- **Multiple Sclerosis:** MS is an autoimmune disease that affects the brain and spinal cord (central nervous system—CNS). The CNS is normally protected from inflammation, but with MS, inflammatory Th1 cells and macrophages mediate CNS pathology. Research shows that MS prevalence increases with latitude and varies with season, peaking in spring and declining in summer. Vitamin D can play an important role.

- **Diabetes:** Type 2 diabetes is associated closely with obesity, and there is a strong inverse correlation between obesity and vitamin D levels. The higher the vitamin D levels, the thinner the patients.[10]

- **Pain:** Vitamin D apparently improves pain. In a study of lower back pain, an initial assessment involved 360 patients (90 percent women and 10 percent men) and found they had an abnormally low level of vitamin D. After treatment with vitamin D, clinical improvement in symptoms was seen in 95 percent of all patients.[11] This is particularly interesting to me since I ruptured a disc in 1988 and went through back surgery. After my wife and I began increasing our vitamin D_3 levels, my back pain has decreased substantially.

- **Sunburn:** Dr. K. M. Dixon of the University of Sydney, working with Professor Rebecca Mason's research group, has presented substantial evidence that vitamin D metabolites protect the skin from sun damage via rapid acting pathways that do not involve genetic transcription.[12] As anyone who has ever taken 5000 IU a day for several months can tell you, your skin is much less likely to burn when you are no longer vitamin D deficient.

- **Osteoporosis and arthritis**: Two randomized vitamin D trials in ambulatory patients on anti-convulsants tested the vitamin's impact on bone. The conclusions were remarkable. In ambulatory adults on antiepileptic drugs, high-dose vitamin D (4000 IU per day) substantially increased bone mineral density at several skeletal sites. Other studies have shown that osteoarthritis of the knee progressed more rapidly in those with 25(OH)D levels lower than 36 ng/ml, and osteoarthritis of the hip progressed more rapidly in those with 25(OH)D levels lower than 30 ng/ml.

- **Kidney disease**: Vitamin D deficiency accompanies the loss of kidney function and is extremely common. Treatment with active vitamin D has improved survival rates in dialysis patients.

- **Influenza and colds**: In terms of the flu, you recover much more quickly from the flu or a cold. More important, vitamin D_3 reduces the risk of ever developing colds or influenza. So how much vitamin D_3 should you take if you get the flu? This is anecdotal and without research, yet some doctors have experimented by taking 70,000 units per day for thirty days. Others suggest 100,000 IU for three days. There are no studies on these levels for the flu. The best treatment is prevention by keeping your vitamin D levels up at 50ng/ml through the winter. If you take more that 10,000 IU a day from all sources, please get your D_3 levels checked twice a year so you can adjust your amount. This is what I do. Getting enough vitamin D is so important that it is worth the test!

In so many more areas—from inflammatory bowel disease, psoriasis, wound healing, and more—vitamin D promotes immunity from a plethora of diseases. This happens because vitamin D is a potent modulator of macrophage functions, promoting differentiation of monocytes into macrophages and then activating phagocytic and antimicrobial activities and enhancing NO production (NO in macrophages promotes mycobacteria killing) macrophages express VDR receptor and can produce vitamin D_3 (1a-hydroxylase). Likewise, vitamin D_3 normally inhibits CD4t-cell proliferation and suppresses Th-1 cytokines (that is, IL-2, IFN-g, TNF-a, and IL-12) and may enhance Th-2 response over Th-1. In layperson's terms, what this all means is D_3 greatly enhances your immune system function.

Peak Athletic Performance

More and more research indicates vitamin D levels of

about 50 ng/ml are associated with peak athletic performance. Of course, recent studies show such levels are ideal for preventing numerous diseases, but it also increases speed, balance, reaction time, muscle mass, muscle strength, squats, reps, and more.

Dr. Heike A. Bischoff-Ferrari, a professor at the University of Zurich, serves as director of the Center on Aging and Mobility at the Department of Rheumatology and the Institute of Physical Medicine at the university. It is significant to note that Royal DSM NV, the global Life Sciences and Materials Sciences company headquartered in the Netherlands, awarded the 2009 DSM Nutrition Award for research on human nutrition to Professor Bischoff-Ferrari in recognition of her seminal contributions to research on vitamin D and its role in human nutrition and health. She has done one of the largest studies of its kind, finding a strong, positive correlation and suggestion of a U-shaped curve with athletic performance on one test that peaked with vitamin D levels of 10,000 IU of 50 ng/ml but deteriorated at higher levels.[13]

It is interesting to speculate that levels around 50 ng/ml of vitamin D may be optimal for athletic performance because such levels are common in humans living in a natural state of sun exposure, such as lifeguards or tropical farmers.

Dr. Yoshihiro Sato, a leading researching on the subject, reported that two years of treatment with 1000

IU of vitamin D significantly increased muscle strength, doubled the mean diameter, and tripled the percentage of fast twitch muscle fibers in the functional limbs of forty-eight severely vitamin D–deficient elderly stroke patients. The placebo control group suffered declines in muscle strength and in the size and percentage of fast-twitch muscle fibers.[14]

To summarize, if you are vitamin D deficient, more and more research indicates that the right amount of vitamin D will make you faster, stronger, improve your balance and timing, and so much more. How much it will improve your athletic ability depends on how deficient you are to begin with. How good an athlete you will be depends on your innate ability, training, and dedication. However, peak athletic performance also depends upon the neuromuscular cells in your body and brain having unfettered access to the steroid hormone, active vitamin D. In addition, how much activated vitamin D is available to your brain, muscle, and nerves depends on having ideal levels of vitamin D in your blood.

Adequate D$_3$ and Good Blood Pressure

A Harvard Medical School study involving 613 men and 1,198 women with measured plasma 25(OH)D levels, prospectively followed for four to eight years, and 38,388 men and 77,531 women with predicted 25(OH)D levels, prospectively followed for sixteen to eighteen years, showed an inverse association between plasma 25(OH)D (25-hydrodyVitamin D) levels and the risk of high blood pressure. Women with a vitamin D deficiency showed more than a twofold increased risk of hypertension compared to women with 25(OH)D levels at or above 3 ng/ml.

Furthermore, in a pooled analysis combining men and women, vitamin D deficiency was associated with more than a threefold increased risk of hypertension. Additionally, in the cohorts with predicted 25(OH)D levels, men in the lowest decile of 25(OH)D levels showed more than a twofold increased risk of hypertension compared to men in the highest decile. Similarly, women in the lowest decile 25(OH)D levels showed a 57 percent increased risk of hypertension compared to women in the highest decile. Thus, the authors of this study concluded, "Plasma 35(OH)D levels are inversely associated with risk of incident hypertension."

When I checked my blood pressure this week, it was 112 over 60. I am fifty-three years old and I feel great. When I had my vitamin D_3 checked this week, it was perfect, around 60. This is one blood test that needs to be done on a semiannual basis.

To ensure that serum 25(OH)D concentrations exceed 100 nmol/L, a total vitamin D supply of 100 microg (4000 IU)/d is required. Except in those with conditions causing hypersensitivity, there is no evidence of adverse effects with serum 25(OH)D concentrations <140 nmol/L, which require a total vitamin D supply of 250 microg (10,000 IU)/d to attain.

Sources of Vitamin D₃

Since this miracle vitamin is so important to people, what should you do to make sure you have enough. Here are a few basic guidelines:

- Spend ten to fifteen minutes in the sun each day, especially from 10 a.m. to 2 p.m.
- Take 2000–5000 IU of vitamin D_3 every day. Even taking 1000 IU of D_3 will raise your level about 10 ng/ml. I take around 5000–10,000 from all sources, although it varies depending on the time of year. I recommend our Ultimate D3-5000 supplement.
- Ask your doctor to check your 25(OH) level. This is really important! Ideal levels are between 40–60 ng/ml. If you take more than 5000–10,000 IU of vitamin D per day, you especially should follow up with lab work at least biannually.
- Add foods rich in vitamin D. These include cod liver oil (two teaspoons add 1000 IU) and such foods as catfish (500 IU from a serving of three and a half ounces), salmon (320 IU from a serving of three and a half ounces). Our High-Vitamin Pure Cod Liver Oil offers more vitamin A and D than any other product on the market.

- If you have hard joint pain, you may be getting too much. Remember: check your vitamin D levels!

In addition, I recommend the following:

- Take at least 800 mg of calcium per day. Our Ossomag is the best source of superior calcium, magnesium, and D$_3$ formula.
- Add our HGH Stimulate, which improves circulatory, immune and nervous system function, memory, reduces wrinkles, increases bone density, and decreases blood pressure.
- Be sure to take our Ultimate Multiple, which gives foundation nutrition for wellness and disease protection.
- Take GHI Cleanse, which is used to treat chronic inflammatory conditions. We use this product daily. It's incredible!

Researchers have calculated that simply increasing levels of vitamin D$_3$ could prevent diseases that claim nearly one million lives throughout the world each year!

It is absolutely tragic that dermatologists and sunscreen manufacturers have done such a thorough job of scaring people out of the sun—your optimal source for natural vitamin D. This is one of the major influences that has contributed to the vitamin D epidemic we are facing, as well as, I believe, the autism increases we are seeing.

The widely dispersed message to avoid the sun as much as possible, combined with an overall cultural trend of spending more time indoors during both work and leisure time, has greatly contributed to the widespread vitamin D deficiency seen today—which in turn is fueling an astonishingly diverse array of common chronic diseases.

Always remember, if you have questions, please call us at 1-800-726-1834 or order online at www.HealthMasters. com.

6

BECOME WATER WISE

All living things must have water to survive. Without water, your body would stop working properly. Water is critical to the way you look, feel, function, and heal. More to the point, nearly two-thirds of your body is water, with the brain (70 percent) and lungs (nearly 90 percent) requiring even more water. More than 80 percent of our blood is water, and plasma, one of the four major components of blood, is 95 percent water. Since blood and plasma help to digest food, transport waste, remove dangerous toxins, and control body temperature, water is crucial to our blood and therefore absolutely vital to life itself.

The average human loses approximately ten cups (about two and a half liters) of water a day through breathing, perspiration, and other bodily functions. That must be replaced by drinking water and other foods containing water, otherwise dehydration occurs.

Dehydration, according to a definition from the Mayo Clinic, means that your body does not have as much water and fluids as it should: "Dehydration can be caused by losing too much fluid, not drinking enough water or fluids, or both. Vomiting and diarrhea are common causes. Infants and children are more susceptible to dehydration than adults because of their smaller body weights and higher turnover of water and electrolytes. The elderly and those with illnesses are also at higher risk."[1]

Mayo adds: "Dehydration is classified as mild, moderate, or severe based on how much of the body's fluid is lost or not replenished. When severe, dehydration is a life-threatening emergency."[2]

Since roughly two-thirds of your body consists of water, wouldn't it seem evident that the connection between health (good or bad) depends largely upon adequate amounts of pure, wellness-giving water? Therefore, wouldn't it be easy enough to conquer the dehydration problem by drinking water?

Symptoms of Dehydration

Mild to moderate dehydration is likely to cause a number of symptoms that may become so common they go unnoticed. These symptoms may include one or more of the following:

- tiredness (even with enough sleep)
- sleepiness (causing even more tiredness), which may range to severe insomnia

- thirst (although this is not always the most reliable measurement of the body's need for water)
- dry, sticky mouth
- dark yellow or amber urine (unless you are taking vitamin supplements, especially vitamin C, good hydration usually produces clear or light-colored urine)
- decreased urine volume (some experts suggest that fewer than a half-dozen wet diapers a day for infants or as much as eight hours a day for older children, teens, or adults may be an indication of dehydration)
- general weakness
- headaches
- lightheadedness
- dizziness

Emergency medical help may be required when these symptoms increase to a point of danger. Indicators may include the following:

- very dry mouth
- dry skin
- dry mucous membranes
- extreme thirst
- extreme fussiness or sleepiness in infants and children
- little or no urination, especially if dark yellow or amber colored

- lack of sweating
- sunken eyes
- low blood pressure
- increased heartbeat
- fever
- mental confusion in older children and adults, and in most serious cases, delirium or unconsciousness

Extreme symptoms of dehydration require emergency care. Thankfully, for most of us who are relatively healthy, mild to moderate dehydration can be solved simply by drinking more fluids, particularly pure water.

Water, Water, Everywhere...

With dehydration in both North America and around the world at epidemic proportions (research shows that at least two-thirds of the U.S. population suffers from some form of dehydration), it would seem to be an elementary, easily fixed problem. The challenges of drinking enough water include these obstacles:

- Water isn't always pure or clean.
- We have access to many alternatives to water, from bottled sodas and caffeine-laced beverages to packaged sugary juices and so-called energy drinks. Many times the beneficial impact of water in these beverages is sorely overwhelmed by the adverse effects of added chemicals and other additives. In fact, when you drink a cup of coffee, a soda, or alcohol, you may be adding to your water deple-

tion, since the substances in the liquid (such as caffeine) act as diuretics.

- Despite the availability of water for most people today, we simply don't take the time or expend the energy to drink enough water every day. In our fast-paced world, it is much easier to grab a snack or a bottle of whatever is handy.

Making things worse, schools, nutritional experts, and even physicians don't always teach the value of drinking enough water, even when dehydration-related illnesses become chronic. There must be a better way!

"LET HIM WHO THIRSTS..."

A simple search through the Bible for water (I found more than seven hundred references, in case you were wondering) shows the significance that God Himself placed on water. From Genesis 1:2 to Revelation 22:17, a literal river of references to water flows throughout Scripture.

It speaks of life coming from water (Genesis 1:20), refers to birth (John 3:5), is compared to the Word of God itself (for example, Psalm 119:9 and Ephesians 5:26), was an important part of the Old Testament Tabernacle and the purification of the priests (Exodus 30:18), points to the purification of the people (Ezekiel 36:25), and was used by Jesus Himself to teach His disciples many lessons, including godliness and humility when He washed their feet (John 13).

God relates the absolute importance of water from

Genesis 2 where the pristine Garden of Eden was watered by a river (verse 10), throughout the wanderings of the children of Israel when life-giving water was produced miraculously at the rock in Horeb (Exodus 17:6), and all the way to the prophetic picture of heaven ("And he showed me a pure river of water of life, clear as crystal, proceeding from the throne of God and of the Lamb"—Revelation 22:1).

We are told: "Behold, God is my salvation, I will trust and not be afraid; 'For YAH, the Lord, is my strength and song; He also has become my salvation.' Therefore with joy will draw water from the wells of salvation" (Isaiah 12:2–3).

In fact, Jesus Christ used water to depict eternal salvation: "But whoever drinks of the water that I shall give him will never thirst. But the water that I shall give him will become in him a fountain of water springing up into everlasting life" (John 4:14).

Is it any wonder we are told, "Ho, every one that thirsts, come to the waters; and you who have no money, come, buy and eat. Yes, come, buy wine and milk without money and without price" (Isaiah 55:1).

All these types and symbols are spiritually important, and it is my prayer that you will study, understand, and accept these eternally valuable principles from God Himself, but I mainly wanted to mention them in reference to the amazing value of water before getting back to the discussion of being water wise in terms of maximum health.

Got Water?

Granted, you can obtain water from any fluid drink or most foods that you eat, but nothing takes the place of fresh, life-giving, sparkling-clear water, nor is anything else so purifying for your system. So how much water should you drink every day? Nutritionists vary on this, but at least eight glasses seems to be a good average. Few Americans, however, even get close.

In its *Statistical Abstract of the United States: 2007* from the U.S. Census Bureau report, the agency notes that Americans drink about a gallon of soda a week, along with a half gallon each of milk, coffee, beer, and water. Water should be the main source of liquid nourishment, but it isn't for most.

It takes a little more time and energy to make sure you have water available, rather than reaching for a soda or other sugary beverage. However, it is a habit you will build if you wish to live longer and healthier. Reach for life-giving water again and again and again.

I suggest that you drink half your body weight in fluid ounces of purified water, per day. If you weigh two hundred pounds, drink one hundred ounces, or ten glasses (ten ounces each) per day.

How About Sodas?

The United States, with less than 5 percent of the world's population, ranks first among nations in consumption of soft drinks, with per capita averages in excess of 150 quarts per year. That translates to 3 quarts per week. The result? Says James A. Howenstine, MD, "The relationship between soft drink consumption and body weight is so strong that researchers calculate that for each additional soda consumed, the risk of obesity increases 1.6 times."

Reporting in *The Lancet*, a British medical journal, a team of Harvard researchers presented the first evidence linking soft drink consumption to childhood obesity. They found that twelve-year-olds who drank soft drinks regularly were more likely to be overweight than those who didn't. For each additional daily serving of sugar-sweetened soft drink consumed during the nearly two-year study, the risk of obesity increased 1.6 times.[3]

Many people have long assumed that soda, which is high in sugar and calories and low in nutrients, can make children fat. But more and more research provides solid, scientific evidence that demonstrates this not only in relation to children but to people of all ages. In addition, sodas also seem to be linked to other problems from tooth decay (sugar and acid in soft drinks easily dissolves tooth enamel) to bone weakening (a highly acidic drink like soda pours phosphoric acid into your body, a chemical that has been shown to leach calcium from bones, and apparently is a major contributor to the rising increase in osteoporosis, and with less calcium available, the bones become more porous and prone to fracture).

There is growing concern that even a few cans of soda per day can be damaging when they are consumed during the critical bone-building years of adolescence and childhood.

Drinking more than one soft drink daily, even if it is the sugar-free kind, may be associated with an increased incidence of metabolic syndrome, which is a cluster of risk factors linked to the development of diabetes and cardiovascular disease, according to a study by the University of Rochester Medical Center.[4]

I have two recommendations for you:

1. Don't drink soft drinks.
2. Don't drink diet soft drinks.

What Should You Drink?

Water! Water is the great healer and wellness builder. Pure water should always be used during any type of detox program, especially since it helps to dilute and eliminate toxins. More important, water should be a major and ongoing part of your dietary intake, especially since there are so many ways through which water brings life and health. Here are just a few ways that water provides maximum health:

- preventing high blood pressure (hypertension is the body's adaptation to dehydration when the blood lacks enough water to freely replenish cells)
- cleansing the body through the skin and kidneys

(without enough water replenishment, the skin and kidneys go into a survival mode as the body locks down to preserve the deleted water supply)

- reducing the frequency and intensity of headaches (headaches are one of the body's most effective ways to signal that something is wrong somewhere, and dehydration almost always causes headaches, even migraines)
- preventing and curing heartburn (this is a major warning signal of water in the upper part of the gastrointestinal tract and a major thirst signal of the human body)
- easing angina (heart pain is the body's way of signaling a water shortage in the heart and lung region)
- alleviating back pain (water shortage in the area that supports the weight of the body, the mostly water cushions in the spinal column and discs, almost always leads to increased pain, a signal of impending danger)
- reducing stomach pain (colitis is often a clear-cut signal of water shortage in the stomach, often associated with equally painful constipation, as the large intestine seeks to squeeze every drop of water from its contents)
- relieving and even curing rheumatoid arthritis (joint pain is another warning signal of water shortage for people of all ages)

- lessening or curing diabetes Type 2 (adult-onset diabetes is another of the body's attempts to deal with severe dehydration as the free flow of insulin is restricted)
- curing asthma and other breathing problems (millions of people of all ages are affected by conditions in which the free passage of air is obstructed as the body attempts to keep from losing water vapor)
- lowering cholesterol (high cholesterol levels are another form of drought management throughout the body, as cell membranes are safeguarded from losing vital water content to the blood)

Pure water is the body's cure-all, literally a fountain of life. So much research is now available that seems to point to water's miraculous curing of a variety of chronic conditions—from a loss of libido to depression, chronic fatigue syndrome, muscular dystrophy, and even multiple sclerosis.

I certainly cannot vouch for all the research, but what I do know from years of experience is that the body's most worrisome conditions always seem to be linked to prolonged dehydration. What I have also seen is that even the worst challenges seem to start clearing up as the body becomes fully hydrated on a regular basis.

Pure Water?

If the answer to most of the questions about health and

wholeness is plenty of clean, pure water, is it a matter of simply going to the faucet and glugging away? Well, drinking plenty of water can be a challenge. Even in modern America, the water that comes out of your faucet is likely treated with the same basic equipment, chemicals, and knowledge that was used one hundred years ago. Mostly, only the organic waste and some heavy metals are removed from water before it is returned to your house. Most treatment plans don't have the technology to take out the chemical contaminants. In fact, municipal plants may actually aggravate the problem by adding fluoride (more on that in chapter 15).

As always, our government has basically ignored the facts that huge amounts of poisons, harmful drugs, toxic chemicals, inorganic calcium, herbicides, pesticides, fertilizers, parasites, fungi, and viruses are being pumped into our home through drinking water. The reality is that more than one hundred million people in this country receive harmful drugs, toxic chemicals, and fluoride in the water from their municipalities and their wells. Even if you live in the country with your own well water, you may be surprised to discover that some of the most toxic water in our country is found in rural wells.

Granted, just drinking more water will make you feel better. As mentioned previously, it is amazing that most people run around in a chronic state of dehydration, even when surrounded with life-giving water. You can change everything by sipping water throughout the day. But drinking the purest possible water is even better!

WHAT ABOUT PITCHER FILTERS?

While writing this chapter, my wife and I were invited to a couple's house for dinner. While we were there, we were offered a glass of water out of a filter pitcher. Our friends said that tap water was really bad because of the contaminants it contained. I don't think they knew how involved I was with water treatment. They were shocked when I told them I didn't trust filter pitchers because they simply did not do a good job. Since my staff and I are constantly being bombarded with questions about water, I figured it was time to give everyone the facts.

I have read that half of all American households now use some kind of filter pitcher. People are becoming more and more health conscious. What saddens me is that these filter pitchers do little more than improve the taste, smell, and color of the still toxic water people are drinking.

Most of the filters use carbon ceramic or alumina. These filters can make the water cleaner and remove some of the smell and taste. They are, however, pretty useless at removing harmful drugs, arsenic, mercury, copper, fertilizers, parasites, inorganic calcium, and bacteria. In fact, the filter can actually breed bacteria and make the filtered water even more unsafe than the original unfiltered water. Always remember that filters catch contaminants like a net. Sooner or later the net fills up, and the filter becomes totally ineffective. This can leave you with a higher risk of contaminants or illness.

What About Bottled Water?

Everywhere I go, people are drinking bottled water. More than half of all Americans drink bottled water, and at least one-third of the public consumes it regularly. Sales have tripled in the past ten years to about $4 billion a year, fueled in part by beautiful pictures of crystal-clear springs surrounded by untouched forests and ice-capped mountains. But does the reality match the digitally edited scenes?

The National Resources Defense Council recently completed a four-year study of the bottled-water industry that included regulatory programs in all fifty states, as well as an in-depth assessment of the Food and Drug Administration (FDA). What they discovered may challenge what you believe about bottled water, including these tidbits:

- **Price**: For starters, people are spending from 240 to over 10,000 times more per gallon for bottled water than what it costs from the faucet.[5]
- **Marketing**: Often the images are misleading, pointing to pristine water sources for the water, which is often not the case. In fact, the NRDC

cited how "one brand of 'spring water' whose label pictured a lake and mountains, actually came from a well in an industrial facility's parking lot, near a hazardous waste dump, and periodically was contaminated with industrial chemicals at levels above FDA standards."[6]

- **Sources**: According to the NRDC, based upon government and industry estimates, between 25 and 40 percent of bottled water is actually bottled tap water, sometimes with purification and treatment, sometimes not.[7]

- **Regulation**: One of the biggest problems with bottled water is that it is an industry that is often unregulated. Out of fifty-two brands surveyed by the FDA, 31 percent contained bacteria, inorganic calcium, and many still contain chlorine and fluoride.

- **Containers**: On top of everything else, have you ever bought bottled water in a plastic jug and gagged because of the taste when you drank it? I know I have. Let me tell you why. The low-grade plastic containers that most manufacturers use can leach poisons, such as methyl chlorides and carcinogens, which damage the reproductive organs.

In spite of these dangers and challenges, millions of people are paying from three to five dollars per gallon for bottled water. They spend more for water in a jug than they pay for automobile fuel!

MY RECOMMENDATION

Over thirty years ago I was told by one of my professors at Florida State University that distilled water was the best and purest water available. Now after nearly three decades of using distilled water, I believe more than ever in its purity.

I use reverse osmosis, that is, distilled water stored in a stainless steel tank or glass (never plastic!). I have become such a believer in this process that my office has carried both distillers and reverse osmosis units, literally changing the lives of my clients.

This is the only type of system that actually removes the water from the contaminants and harmful drugs added to our drinking water, rather than removing the contaminants from the water. Let me explain. The water is boiled and turned into steam. The temperature is 212°F (100°C). This kills cysts, bacteria. and viruses. The steam then rises, leaving all heavy metals (lead, harmful drugs, copper, mercury, and inorganic calcium) behind. The steam is then recondensed using a stainless steel coil. Before it is discharged, it passes through a coconut carbon filter to remove any taste. Then the pure water is collected and stored. If you use a high quality, well-constructed distiller, you will remove literally every kind of bacteria, harmful drugs, viruses, parasites, pesticides, herbicides, heavy metals, chemicals, inorganic calcium, and even radioactive waste.

I know of no other system that always removes all impurities and harmful drugs added to our drinking water without losing its effectiveness over time. Every now and then the boil tank needs to be cleaned. It is supereasy, and I am always amazed at the amount of inorganic calcium and contaminants, literally pounds, that come out of my water. Have you ever heard of hardening of the arteries? The arteries become calcified. The calcium buildup is primarily inorganic calcium—basically dissolved rock—in your water. This rock cannot be used by your body, so it is stored in the soft tissue, joints, and arteries, causing heart problems and arthritis.

The problem with distillers is that they are very expensive. They can cost several thousand dollars. Well, I knew that most of you were not going to be willing to invest that kind of money. So I did some research and found an affordable product that does an excellent job. It is called the Health Masters Water Distiller Model 8800. It is a state-of-the-art countertop distiller.

When I first started looking at a countertop product, I must admit I was a bit skeptical. A system that gives you top-quality water in a compact, good-looking product was more than I expected. I thoroughly inspected and verified its capabilities, and to my delight it passed my standards with flying colors.

Let me detail to you six major criteria for evaluating a distiller:

1. **Ease of use:** If it is complicated, I am not interested. I get aggravated when I use my DVD player. So if it's a hassle, I'm not signing up. Well the Health Masters Water Distiller Model 8800 is simple. Just fill it with tap water and push start. It automatically turns off when the cycle is done. How simple is that?

2. **Investment value:** If you want to spend a hundred dollars on a filter, that is exactly what you will get: a cheap product that is useless. Why waste the money? It's like buying something you know you don't want because it's cheaper than something you want. All that will do is frustrate you. You'll always be thinking, *Why didn't I just buy what I wanted?* Also, when you look at your long-term health investment, a water purifier is a great investment for you and your family. It only costs about twenty-five cents per gallon for pure water using the Health Masters Water Distiller Model 8800. If you're buying bottled water at over a dollar (or more) per gallon and you use thirty gallons a week, that's over two thousand dollars per year, which is over five times the one-time cost of a distiller that will last for many, many years.

3. **Water production:** This incredible unit can make up to six gallons a day of the purest water possible. One of the first things that friends do when they come over to our house is to ask for a glass of

water. Our four children drink water constantly. The reason most kids don't drink water is that it tastes bad. Tap water tastes horrible! My son in college even brings his water jugs home on the weekend so he can have great tasting, healthy water to drink. This unit even comes with a one-gallon Lexan polycarbonate collector bottle that is the highest quality plastic in the industry, avoiding the problem of storing water in cheap plastic whose contaminants leach into the water.

4. **Maintenance and cleaning**: Scale builds up in the boiling tank, making it occasionally necessary to clean the tank. This is a very easy process, and you can use some vinegar to clean very hard water. I use Health Masters Kleanwise Cleaner. Kleanwise is a biodegradable, phosphate-free product that dissolves scale without scrubbing. Also the boil tank is made from high-quality stainless steel to ensure many years of excellent service.

5. **Postfiltration**: Sometimes water quality is so bad that organic chemicals can convert into gas when boiled. However, the Health Masters Water Distiller Model 8800 uses a coconut-shell carbon filter, which removes any gases that may form. After the steam has been converted into water, this is the final treatment. The coconut-shell carbon is the highest grade available. Many other types of carbon filters add silver, which can recontaminate your water.

6. **Guarantee**: I have known the manufacturer of our distillation systems for twenty years. He and his wife actually came to me for nutritional counseling back in the 1980s. This man practices what he preaches. His commitment to you is simple: each unit comes with a one-year warranty and a one-hundred-day money-back guarantee. Missionaries and science labs all over the world use Health Masters distillers. In fact, even the Peace Corps uses these distillers. If all these organizations trust our distillers to purify sewage-ridden, bacteria-filled, disease-laced liquid to get crystal-clear drinking water, I'm sure it can do an incredible job on your tap water, no matter where you live.

That brings me to another point. I live in Polk County, Florida. We sometimes have hurricanes. I have a backup generator, which easily runs my distiller. Had I not had a distiller in recent years, I would not have had purified water to drink. One time we lost electric power for over a week. When it comes to disaster preparedness (no matter where you live or what disasters you may face), you can't go wrong with this distiller and a generator.

I contacted our supplier and told them that I needed special pricing on the Health Masters Water Distiller Model 8800 for the readers of this book. Did they step up! The normal cost is $469.99. Your cost will be $398.99, plus they are including the one-gallon collector bottle. In addition, I have added a copy of my wife's four-hundred-recipe cookbook, *Healthy Country Cooking* ($25 retail), at no extra cost! Please call us at 1-800-726-1834 or order online at www.HealthMasters.com.

Time to Invest in Yourself

It seems that every time I pick up the paper, read a magazine, or watch the news, there are articles about the quality of water getting worse and more drugs being added to our drinking water. That is why I say that there is simply no better time to invest in a high-quality distiller. I have spent three decades drinking distilled water and the past two decades using Health Masters products. During all those years I have continued to research this subject, and I can honestly say that I have not found anything any better (or even close!). That is why I use this product for my family. That is why I highly recommend it for you and your family also!

7

MAKE GREAT CHOICES
ABOUT CHOLESTEROL

It is always a pleasure to sit down on the studio set of the television program *Breakthrough with Rod Parsley*. Pastor Parsley has been a great supporter of my Eat, Drink, and Be Healthy! program, and the results speak for themselves.

When I first met him, his cholesterol was over 600 and his triglycerides were through the roof at over 1000—both dangerously high cholesterol and triglyceride numbers, sometimes even deadly. After following the EDBH program, his cholesterol was reduced to under 200 and his triglycerides normalized.

He was living proof of one of the most common problems among humans who live into our modern society. When the blood fats get that high, the blood viscosity increases because the blood gets too thick. This makes it very difficult for the heart to pump. Consider, for example, how it is easier to pump water than axle grease.

Once Pastor Parsley increased his water consumption (which helps to thin the blood—I recommend one half of your body weight in fluid ounces per day, so a person weighing two hundred pounds should consume one hundred ounces of water per day) and reduced certain animal protein, his blood thinned, and his cholesterol and triglycerides were normalized.

Six medical doctors had told him that it would be impossible to reduce his cholesterol without a lifetime dependence on statin drugs.

The Biggest Medical Mistake

Let's talk about cholesterol. Rod's was ridiculously high and it had to come down. But always remember that you cannot live without cholesterol. The liver produces large amounts of it. Total cholesterol of around 250 used to be considered normal. Overnight, Big Pharma (the huge pharmaceutical companies) decided that 200 was the proper number. Now, it is 160.

There is sparse research to substantiate these numbers. I personally believe it is simply pulled out of thin air so that another one hundred million people can be told they are ill and need to be on drugs for the rest of their life to control their cholesterol.

Let me share with you some interesting facts. Cholesterol has never been proven to cause heart disease! I personally believe cholesterol under 250 should be considered a normal range. The food that you eat only has a moderate effect upon cholesterol. Statistics prove that your body needs it, and your liver continues to make it. Statistics prove that people with cholesterol above 200 actually live longer. Low cholesterol under 200 actually increases death rates.

As for men, not much testosterone can be produced with low cholesterol. You lose muscle mass and increase body fat when the numbers get too low. Plus many men can't think clearly, and many men feel terrible taking statin drugs. Worse, cholesterol (statin) drugs put you at greater risk of cancer, depression, memory loss, nerve damage, skeletal muscle damage (necrosis), and kidney damage. According to the *Journal of the American Medical Association* in its May 2003 issue, if you take statin drugs for thirty years, you only live six months longer. That's probably because other death rates are increased from the drugs themselves.

What I'm going to reveal to you in this chapter, in my opinion, is the biggest medical mistake of the past fifty years. Cholesterol of 250 or lower is not the culprit in heart disease. The problem is that standard medical procedure won't admit to being wrong. After all, the use of cholesterol drugs is a $16-billion-a-year enterprise. In 1983, the National Institutes of Health (NIH), a completely pro–big pharmaceutical agency that believes everyone is sick and needs to be on drugs, decided that high cholesterol was the culprit in heart disease.

The biggest problem the NIH had in the 1980s was that medical doctors were not convinced that cholesterol was bad. Remember, doctors know that the liver manufactures huge amounts of cholesterol, unless it is drugged by statins not to do so. It's amazing that in 1900 we had no statin drugs and had one of the healthiest populations on earth with almost no heart disease and no statin drugs.

Consumers, on the other hand, had already been brainwashed in the 1970s by bogus studies and media and research misinformation. Back in the 1950s, studies showed that powdered egg yolks caused heart disease. The truth is that powdered eggs do cause heart disease because they are oxidized, and thus they cause inflammation. That's why I tell you to never to use powdered eggs, Egg Beaters, or anything artificial. Use organic eggs. They don't cause heart disease. And always prepare eggs either soft scrambled or over easy in real organic butter, and don't throw the yolks away. They are healthy and they're good for you. They are loaded with sulfur, and the sulfur helps to maintain good, healthy skin, hair, and nails.

Cholesterol is so important that every cell in your body contains it. The human body would die without it. And guess what organ has the highest concentration of cholesterol? Your brain! You can't think clearly or remember without it. That's why, when you artificially lower it, in many cases, you don't think clearly and your memory goes to pot, then your liver makes extra cholesterol to make up for what you don't get in your diet. That's why it is difficult to lower cholesterol using diet alone. The drugs stop the liver from producing this essential nutrient, because your liver fights back on a low cholesterol diet to keep you healthy. Remember, cholesterol is used as a blood lubricant by the body to keep the blood flowing properly.

The reality is that people with high cholesterol (160–250) statistically live the longest. Remember, the government's own Framingham study shows that older people with the lowest cholesterol had some of the highest death rates. Yale University's Dr. Harlan Krumholz found that elderly people with low cholesterol die more often from heart attacks than those with high cholesterol. His findings were published in the *Journal of the American Medical Association*. Here are the facts:

- People of all ages with low cholesterol have higher death rates from gastrointestinal and respiratory diseases (nineteen studies using sixteen thousand people).
- Low cholesterol increases rates of infection.
- People whose cholesterol is below 160 are twice as likely to die than people whose cholesterol is between 160 and 250.
- Low or high cholesterol deaths from heart disease are about the same, but low cholesterol has a much higher cancer rate. That's probably because cholesterol of less than 160 is normally obtained by using statin drugs. Statin drugs all have one

common side effect: they all cause cancer. A French study revealed that cancer rates climb steadily as cholesterol levels fall below 200.

The reality is that the heart researchers know the truth, but they are too arrogant to give us the facts. After all, fifty years of entrenched dogma is hard to change or at least admit to. Plus, much of the cholesterol research is paid for by the drug companies, and their data is kept secret.

Always remember that this cholesterol lie was started by a bunch of no-eggs, tree-hugger doctors, drug companies, and researchers who refused to admit the truth about the major cause of heart disease.

A Look Backward

In 1973, I was a senior in high school, and Richard Nixon was president of the United States. He decided to declare war on cancer. What a joke that has been. The big shots of mainstream medicine decided that they could, if given enough money (around a trillion dollars to date), cure cancer. In the process, they decided to do a seven-year study using thirteen thousand men. More than half had high blood pressure and were smokers. The other half had maximum medical supervision and a lot of don't eat this, don't eat that, no eggs, no red meat dietary restrictions. Guess what happened after seven years of deprivation? The boys who ate normal lived longer. Wow, imagine that. How many times have you heard me say that organic beef, organic eggs, and organic butter are not on my top ten list of foods *not* to eat (see pages 17–19).

Researchers even found that the blood pressure medication of the control group may have caused the deaths of the healthy participants (remember, according to the May 2003 *Journal of the American Medical Association*, thirty years of high blood pressure medicine only increases life expectancy by nine days, and the medicine has so many bad side effects). These findings, by the way, were revealed in 1982. However, the medical researchers and pharmaceutical companies hushed it up. Way too much money was and is being made by selling drugs.

Even the British medical journal *Lancet* wrote that two hundred men without any prior heart disease have to swallow 357,700 statin tablets over five years to save one of them from dying of coronary heart disease. This is due to the fact that no exact knowledge exists as to which of these two hundred will benefit from the treatment.

At one point, television ads even said that Lipitor has not been shown to prevent heart disease, cardiac disease, or heart attacks. It's amazing to me that we are spending $16 billion on these drugs that are, in my opinion, unnecessary and are probably causing a lot more health problems because of their consumption.

By the way, don't blame your doctor for prescribing cholesterol-lowering drugs for you. He's only following today's standard medical procedures; he has to if he wants to keep his license. Also remember, almost all of the continuing education provided to doctors after medical school is provided free of charge by guess who? The drug companies. Imagine that. Anyone think that's a conflict of interest? What a horrible, unfunny joke.

Cholesterol Recommendations

So I know your next question: Should I be concerned about my cholesterol? The answer is a very loud YES! I like to keep mine around 200. Your body needs it, but it needs to be watched. Also, the lipid profile is important. It's important to keep the HDL cholesterol high and the LDL low.

Here are my recommended supplements for my healthy cholesterol and heart program. All of these products help to maintain healthy blood chemistry. I take them every day:

- Ultimate Multiple, which gives foundation nutrition for wellness and disease protection.
- HGH Stimulate, which improves circulatory, immune and nervous system function, memory, reduces wrinkles, increases bone density, and decreases blood pressure.
- CoQ10Max, which is a critical healthy heart supplement.
- Ultimate D3-5000, which research suggests helps to prevent high blood pressure and boosts immunity.

- Super dose vitamin D, a must for anyone with osteoporosis or osteopenia.
- Vascular Relaxant SR, which lowers blood pressure and cholesterol—a superior product produced from sustained-released Niaspan (niacin extended-release tablets).
- Healthy Lipid Profile, an all-natural formula for lowering cholesterol, provides anti-inflammatory benefits, maintains healthy lipid levels, and promotes cardiovascular health.
- High-Vitamin Pure Cod Liver Oil, which offers more vitamin A and D than any other product on the market.
- Cortico B5-B6, which offers water-soluble B vitamins to ensure strong bones, balance, and mobility.
- Excellent C, which helps protect and support healthy connective tissue.
- Super Potent E, which is excellent for heart, circulation, and cancer prevention.
- B Complex, which is important for the support of the adrenal hormone production, regulation of the body's production of energy through enhancement of coenzyme A production.

If you have questions, call us at 1-800-726-1834 or order online at www.HealthMasters.com.

Just remember that high cholesterol levels can increase

your risk for heart attacks and strokes. Lowering cholesterol will reduce this risk while keeping the heart and blood
vessels healthy. Not all cholesterol is harmful, however.
There are both good and bad forms of cholesterol, and the
balance between the two is vital to your health.

What we are learning is that diet, weight loss, and
exercise will help you in your quest to achieve ideal
cholesterol levels and maximum health!

8

Exercise Your Way to Health

No matter what age you are, once you cross the line from teenager to twenty-something, you begin losing up to 7 percent of your total muscle mass every decade for the rest of your life—unless you begin a regular program of exercising. Worse, your overall body weight tends to increase. It doesn't take a rocket scientist to figure out what replaces your muscle mass: fat!

However, there is good news. Many, many studies increasingly show that the loss of muscle mass can be greatly reduced or actually prevented if you follow a consistent program of exercise that includes a balance of cardiovascular, flexibility, and strength training. That program, along with eating wisely, getting plenty of sleep, and drinking lots of pure water—along with all the principles you learn in *Maximum Health*—will keep your energy levels high, help keep weight gain under control, and reduce or prevent muscle mass loss. This is true regardless of your age!

AGE-RELATED RESEARCH

Two recent studies should be especially encouraging, regardless of your current age. The *Journal of Gerontology* reported the results of tests by two leading universities on men and women ages sixty to seventy-five. One study used men only. Scientists found that leg muscle strength increased up to 84 percent over sixteen weeks among those who did aerobics and weight-training exercises at an intensity that matches gym rats in their twenties. Increases in muscle fiber size among the older exercisers was reported to be proportionate to the gains showed by younger exercisers. "Elderly men cannot only tolerate these very high workloads," the *Journal* reported, "but will exhibit muscular changes similar to their younger counterparts."

The studies used healthy men who kept active but did no regular weight training. Nine were put on a training program that had them doing leg extensions. The men first did ten repetitions at 50 percent of the maximum they could lift at one time. They then did three sets of six to eight repetitions at 80–85 percent of their one-time maximums. The men did this twice a week. The other nine did no weight training and served as a comparison group.

Although both groups were similar at the start, the exercisers had pulled well ahead at the end of the sixteen weeks. They averaged 50 percent better on the extension, 72 percent better on the press, and 84 percent better on the half squat, the study said.

The scientists also found the exercisers gained endurance. As a result, the men's hearts had to work less at a given intensity in a treadmill test. There was no such improvement in the nonexercising comparison group.

The exercise paid off in lifestyle improvements. All of the men indicated they felt better. They were doing more things. They felt much more comfortable and much stronger in their daily activities.

The companion report in the *Journal of Gerontology* took a closer look at changes in the size of the cells among both women and men who trained. The cells in the exercisers grew by 30 percent, the study said. That's similar to what's found in men in their twenties who weight train. The research is in line with other studies on resistance exercise, and the gains can be especially dramatic among people who have done no previous exercise.

Get Moving!

Therefore, the idea that older people must resign themselves to inactivity and frailty is clearly old-fashioned and outdated. Although age does mandate limits on how much strength an exerciser can gain, researchers increasingly are unsure what the limit might be. If you are younger than the men and women in the research study, you have even more reason to get moving!

The only limit, apparently, is in the minds of the exercisers. Even in veteran athletes, gains through more intensive training are very possible. The best part, as mentioned previously, is that for previously sedentary seniors, the gains can be dramatic!

Exercise Stimulates, Satisfies Appetites

One of the most exciting benefits of exercise is related to appetite. A recent study of fifty-eight overweight and obese adults who started an exercise regimen showed that exercise tended to cause hunger to grow before a meal, especially when compared with formerly sedentary days in which hunger was not as pronounced. Yet those exercisers also reported being much more satisfied by healthy meals than they had been before becoming more active. The lead researcher in this study was Dr. Neil King, an associate professor at Queensland University of Technology in Brisbane, Australia.[1]

The results of the study, published in the *American Journal of Clinical Nutrition*, included fifty-eight overweight men and women who went through a twelve-week supervised fitness program that was specifically designed to burn five hundred calories each exercise session. A wonderful result of the study, as almost anyone who exercises regularly can tell you, was that the participants were generally more successful in losing weight than previous attempts at weight loss simply through dietary changes.

Other research from this study shows that exercise has health benefits such as improved cardiovascular fitness, lower blood pressure, and reduced cholesterol—even when total weight loss is not dramatic.

After twelve weeks, a majority of the participants (thirty-two) had lost the expected amount of weight based on the calories they burned during exercise. Some had not lost as much. Regardless, according to Dr. King, "The key messages are exercise is good for you, don't expect unrealistic weight loss, and don't give up exercising just because of lower-than-expected weight loss."[2]

MORE REASONS TO EXERCISE

As with Dr. King's Queensland University of Technology research, numerous studies with people of all ages show conclusive proof that an active program of fitness that involves a balanced program of cardiovascular, flexibility, and strength training increases overall physical performance and muscle tone, while decreasing disability and pain. There are so many benefits to fitness activities that focus on strength training, especially as you add more and more candles to your birthday cake. Let me list a few of my personal favorites:

- **Better weight management:** When you follow a regular fitness training regimen, especially when you include strength or resistance training, you gain muscle mass. More muscle mass means a higher metabolic rate, as much as 15 percent in some studies. A higher metabolism means increased weight control, since the active tissue in muscle consumes calories, as opposed to stored fat that uses extremely little energy.

- **Increased bone density:** Fitness is great for all ages, but some of the most dramatic studies now include research on postmenopausal women. Studies, including several that have been published in the *Journal of the American Medical Association*, reveal that strength and fitness training not only increases bone density, but even grandmas and grandpas who pump iron can also reduce the risk of bone fractures.

- **More effective control of glucose:** The statistics of people being diagnosed with Type 2 diabetes is mind-boggling, over 300 percent during the past half-century! Today, in the United States alone, more than fourteen million men and women have this diabolical disease that is often linked to heart disease, blindness, amputations, and more. Thankfully, statistics also show that positive lifestyle changes—including diet, physical activity, and strength training—can produce a dramatic impact on diabetes for people of all ages and races, including older adults.

- **Improved sleep**: Study after study shows that people, regardless of age, enjoy deeper and more beneficial sleep when they exercise regularly. The reasons are many, from falling asleep faster to sleeping more deeply, awaking less often during the night, and sleeping longer. Get moving and dump the sleeping aids.

- **A healthier cardiovascular system**: Exercise, especially as your body gets leaner and meaner, can reduce the risk of heart disease, which is why the American Heart Association recommends exercise and strength training as a significant way to reduce risks while building better cardiac health. In fact, both exercise and strength training are becoming more and more of a standard therapy for cardiac rehabilitation patients.

- **Better balance**: It wasn't that long ago that falls and fractures meant an end to mobility, even among younger people. Thanks to numerous medical, product, and lifestyle improvements, even older people are not only coming back stronger than ever from broken bones as a result of falling, but they are becoming proactive about increasing flexibility and balance through strength training. A research project in New Zealand signals a new wave of thought, since the study of octogenarian women pointed toward a whopping 40 percent reduction in falls through the most basic fitness, balance, and strength training!

- An enriched life: It has been proven that strength training, as part of an overall fitness program, works powerfully in the area of self-image. Researchers are not conclusive whether people feel better about themselves when they get stronger and more buff, or whether the fitness and strength training itself produces beneficial biochemical changes in the body. My studies have shown that it is a balance of the two. Regardless, people of all ages who work out regularly almost universally see a dramatic improvement in self-confidence and self-image.

Exercise is often directly linked to reducing obesity, diabetes, back pain, arthritis, osteoporosis, and depression while controlling weight, increasing bone density, improving glucose control, enhancing sleep, building cardiac health, building better balance, and enriching life. Think about the possibilities for you!

THREE KINDS OF EXERCISE YOU NEED DAILY

Your fitness program should include a regular regimen that includes a balance of three major kinds of exercise:

1. **Cardiovascular Training**: This is often called aerobics. No matter what you call it, you should be involved with some type of activity that requires

physical exertion to the point that your heart rate is accelerated for a sustained period of time. There are many types of beneficial cardiovascular exercise, including outside activities (which can include walking, jogging, running, bicycling, jump roping, swimming, and skiing), indoor activities (including treadmills, stationary bicycles, stair climbers, rowing machines, elliptical trainers, and ladder climbers). Cardiovascular exercise involves using the larger muscles, like those in your legs.

2. **Flexibility Training**: Often referred to as stretching, this often-neglected area of fitness is always important, regardless of your age, as it can help prevent joint, ligament, and muscle problems that can occur when vital areas of the body are not properly warmed up and stretched. Flexibility is especially important because having flexible muscles allows your joints to move through a full range of motion. You need a certain amount of flexibility to move smoothly, avoid muscle tension, and to protect your body from injury—all of which is possible through stretching. In fact, you will undoubtedly discover that proper stretching both before, during, and after other forms of exercise will help you to reduce the risk of injury, reduce muscle soreness, improve your posture, lessen lower back pain, increase blood and nutrients to the body's tissues, improve your coordination and

balance, reduce stress, and enjoy all of your exercise program more fully. Don't go overboard or force your body to do too much, especially at first. Hold a comfortable position until you feel a gentle pull on your muscle. It shouldn't hurt, or you are doing too much. Try to hold each stretch for fifteen to thirty seconds or more to maximize flexibility benefits. And don't bounce! Again, stretch before, during, and after your other exercise programs. After your overall workout, try to work and stretch all of the muscles you have used, especially those that seem chronically tight.

3. **Strength Training**: I recommend that people work toward devoting thirty to forty-five minutes to strength or resistance training at least three times a week, regardless of your age. There are a few basics to include, whether you are working out by yourself in the den or hanging out in a gym filled with glistening equipment. Squats, push-ups, lunges, pull-ups, and sit-ups are all good compound strength movements, meaning that each exercise uses a number of the major muscles in your body. You can vary each exercise, depending upon your fitness level, preferences, and comfort zones. Add weights and other forms of resistance training as desired to work out your legs, chest, shoulders, stomach, biceps, triceps, and back.

What really matters is starting with multijoint exercises that simultaneously use different muscle groups, which is the fastest way to increase both lean muscle and strength. You will have plenty of time to graduate to isolation exercises later. Right now your emphasis should be on working out regularly, not being the next Ms. or Mr. Universe.

Get started with a range of simple cardiovascular, flexibility, and strength exercises at least two to three times a week, building up to five or six days each week. You will be amazed at what you can do and what it does for you!

It is always advisable to check with your physician before making major lifestyle changes. However, it is vitally important to know that a balanced program of cardiovascular, flexibility, and strength training can make your life better in so many ways. It is never too early or too late to make the decision to become more active!

For more information on my men's and women's exercise videos or my Forever Fit at Twenty, Thirty, Forty, and Beyond series, call us at 1-800-726-1834 or order online at www.HealthMasters.com.

GETTING STARTED

You don't have to fill your closet with the latest togs, join an expensive gym, or replace your den furniture with a roomful of weightlifting equipment. Do what you can. Start with a small set of dumbbells from Walmart or a sporting goods store. If you feel adventuresome, get a weight bench and a fifty-dollar set of barbells. Or you can go hog-wild with a personal trainer and glistening weight machines. Better yet, order my exercise DVDs and work out with me properly in the convenience of your home!

One thing I do recommend, regardless of your level of exercise, is to make sure you get good-quality, well-fitting, comfortable shoes. There are few things that bring your exercise program to a halt quicker than turned ankles, bruised heels, or tender toes that are often caused by ill-fitting fitness shoes. There are a number of different well-known brand names and styles, but it is especially important to get shoes that maximize support and balance.

Eight Questions to Help You Stick with Your Exercise Program

One of the biggest downfalls to any fitness program is sticking with the regimen. No matter how good your intentions are, if you quit, there will be no positive results and no maximum health. I have spent most of my adult life working with people who are great at sticking with their goals and those who are lousy at it. Here are eight of the best questions you should ask yourself during the coming days, weeks, and months:

1. **What motivates you?** More important, what de-motivates you. Success depends upon figuring out what works, doing more of it, and eliminating what keeps you from achieving your goals. As you

begin your fitness regimen, take time to evaluate yourself. Jot down your thoughts. When you understand what lights your inner fire, you will discover the first gigantic step in sticking with a program that can change your life forever.

2. **What are your goals?** Unless you think them through and write them down, you probably won't achieve what you want to accomplish. As you go through self-evaluation (as described in the first step), you will begin to see more clearly what motivates (and demotivates) you, then you can determine what you want to shoot for. Write it down. Edit yourself. Set long-term goals (one to two years), midrange goals (three months to a year), and short-term goals (the next three months). Refer to them often. It's always easier to get over the rocky roads when you have a clear picture of the mountaintop, and you won't accomplish anything unless you have a map of where you want to go.

3. **What is the best fitness program for you?** Some people enjoy biking, while others hate it. Some people like walking in the park, while others are terrified of being outdoors. Yes, we need to be open to new things, but you won't be successful over the long haul unless you tailor your training program to achieve your goals. Make sure both your goals and your program are realistic and spent doing

things that you enjoy, since not being realistic is almost always a surefire way to get discouraged and quit. Whatever you design for yourself, your training program should always include a balance of cardiovascular, flexibility, and strength training, along with a fitness-maximizing diet.

4. **Have you shared your goals with someone you trust?** Better yet, have you found a training buddy who will start the program with you? Encouragement means so much when you feel like quitting. Companionship can be very important to the entire process. Whether you work out together or just share what you are doing with the other person, by linking with another person, you build your chances of sticking with your program and reaching your goals.

5. **Are you spending time imagining what it will be like to achieve your goals?** The power of visualization is incredible. It is important to see it before you can believe it, and until you believe you can do something worthwhile, you won't stick with the program successfully. Use your God-given ability to merge images with your thoughts and feelings. See yourself finishing the distance you have set for yourself. Visualize yourself lifting your desired weight or crossing the 5K finish line. Imagine yourself standing on the scale the moment your reach your desired weight. How will it feel? What

will it mean to you? A vivid imagination can fuel the fires of your dreams and can help get you past the challenging times when you feel like quitting.

6. **Are you finding ways to learn more about fitness?** Knowledge is power, and the utilization of that knowledge is effective power. I believe that with all my heart, or I wouldn't have spent most of my adult life developing the finest products from the best material I could find. Read books. Watch DVDs. Go to fitness seminars. The more you learn about a cardiovascular, flexibility, and strength training, along with a fitness-maximizing eating program, the more you will be motivated to do more. As you do more, you will find yourself motivated to learn more. It is a life-changing cycle that will propel you toward all your goals.

7. **Are you rewarding yourself?** As you reach short-term, medium-range, and long-term goals, determine ahead of time what you will do to reward yourself. Maybe it will be a new pair of running shoes. How about a special meal? Perhaps it could be a weekend at a favorite resort. The point is that you don't have to spend a lot of money to create a meaningful celebration. Mainly, looking forward to predetermined perks makes your strength training program more rewarding and motivates you to make your program into a vital, ongoing part of your lifestyle.

8. **Are you setting your own pace and reaching your own goals?** Exercising your way to maximum health can be dramatic at times, but it usually involves lots of slow and steady progress as well. People who are only motivated by incredible bursts of success won't last long. True success requires a commitment to sound principles. Just because you don't look like airbrushed models or chiseled magazine athletes doesn't mean that you should become disillusioned. Just because you haven't finished a marathon or bench-pressed four hundred pounds like someone you know doesn't mean that you should quit out of frustration. Keep your own goals at the forefront. Don't build your success on what someone else does or wants for you to do. Building a strong, fit body means developing a long-term healthy lifestyle that you choose!

Let me tell you candidly that there are many times I don't want to exercise. The weather is lousy. I have something else I need to do. I am in a hotel waiting to do a television interview, and I'm pressed for time. I do it anyway, because I have kept at it so long that it is an ingrained habit that I don't want to break. The results are much too important to me. Plus, I know that exercising every day, regardless of the circumstances, is the right thing to do so I can be all that God created me to be.

Stick with these eight basic keys and you will begin to see significant changes in your body and outlook on life. Keep a journal or logbook that includes details about your workouts, your body measurements, and other important details. Soon, you won't have to worry as much about sticking with your exercise program, for you will see the results right in front of you—both in your notes and in the mirror!

9

SAFEGUARD YOUR HEALTH
WITH SLEEP

A recent Harvard University survey has revealed that more and more people—up to three-fourths of all Americans—have sleep problems at least several nights a week.[1] This is echoed by many researchers who point to seventy million or more Americans who suffer chronic insomnia from one cause or another.[2] Worse, according to the National Sleep Foundation (NSF), there are now more than seventy different sleep disorders, many of which are severe enough to interfere with daily activities several times a month.[3] On the far end of the spectrum, according to psychologist Charles M. Morin, PhD, a professor in the psychology department and director of the Sleep Disorders Center at University Laval in Quebec, Canada, as many as 10 percent suffer from chronic sleeplessness.[4] Although insomnia is considered by many to be an adult-onset problem, nearly 70 percent of children experience one or more sleep problems several nights a week.[5]

While sleep is absolutely essential for health and well-being, most sleep-related problems go unreported, undiagnosed, and untreated—as though the problem will go away on its own. Nothing could be farther from the truth.

An Increasing Challenge

Certainly almost everyone reports an occasional bout with sleeplessness with resulting drowsiness or reduced effectiveness at school or on the job. However, chronic sleep loss can contribute significantly to health problems such as high blood pressure, immune system weakness, weight gain, and so much more. More to the point, the Harvard Women's Health Watch offers six important reasons for why sleep is so vital:[6]

1. **The body's immune system**: "Sleep deprivation alters immune function, including the activity of the body's killer cells." Better sleep patterns can even reduce the risk of major diseases such as cancer.

2. **Cardiovascular health**: "Serious sleep disorders have been linked to hypertension, increased stress hormone levels, and irregular heartbeat." Elevated cardiovascular risks can also lead to strokes. Unfortunately, these heart-related problems then build up with time, rather than showing up immediately.

3. **Memory and learning ability**: "Sleep helps the

brain commit new information to memory through a process called memory consolidation." As any college student can tell you, when you sleep after learning material, you tend to do better on tests. However, research shows that sleep loss especially interferes with the learning of young people in our nation's schools, with 60 percent of grade-school and high-school children reporting that they are tired during the daytime and 15 percent of them admitting to falling asleep in class.

4. **Weight control and metabolism:** "Chronic sleep deprivation may cause weight gain." Sleeplessness often affects hormones, the appetite, and the way your body processes food and stores carbohydrates. This can lead to obesity and the onset of problems caused by overweight, including diabetes Type 2.

5. **Emotional disorders:** "Sleep loss may result in irritability, impatience, inability to concentrate, and moodiness." Worse, you may be too tired to care about moodiness and the problems it causes in work performance and relationships, especially as emotional disorders sometimes lead to depression, bipolar disorders, as well as alcohol and drug abuse.

6. **Heightened danger and risks:** "Sleep debt contributes to a greater tendency to fall asleep during the daytime." One can only imagine how many job-related errors, traffic mishaps, and home accidents

are caused by chronic and pathological sleeplessness. In fact, according to research by the National Commission on Sleep Disorders (1998) and reports from the National Highway Safety Administration (2002), accidents are often attributed to a severe lack of sleep. According to the NHSA, falling asleep while driving is responsible for at least 100,000 crashes, 71,000 injuries, and 1,550 deaths each year in the United States. Young people in their teens and twenties, who are particularly susceptible to chronic sleep loss, are involved in more than half of the fall-asleep crashes on the nation's highways each year.

7. According to the Department of Transportation (DOT), 1–4 percent of all highway crashes are due to sleepiness, especially in rural areas, and 4 percent of these crashes are fatal.

By any definition, enough sleep is absolutely necessary for survival. Even animal studies have shown this. Lab rats, usually with a normal life span of two to three years, only live an average of three weeks when deprived of regular sleep, almost always developing outward signs of immune impairment, such as sores and abnormally low body temperatures.

What about human studies?

Again and again, research has shown that sustained sleeplessness, even after one day, begins to show measured decreases in the metabolic activity of the brain, reduced concentration, impairment of thinking and motor skills, decreases in body temperature, reduced immune function, lessened release of the human growth hormone (especially important for children and young adults), and increased heart rate problems.

Equally significant is the fact that sleeplessness is a significant factor in causing people of all ages to get along successfully and to be socially well adjusted. Conversely, deep rest replenishes the areas of the brain that control both emotions and social interactions.

How Much Sleep Is Enough?

Everyone's sleep needs vary. In general, most healthy adults need an average of eight hours of sleep a night. Some people can function without sleepiness or drowsiness after as little as six hours of sleep, while others need ten or twelve hours for peak performance. Although infants have the greatest overall sleep time than any other age group (as much as a total of fourteen to fifteen hours), that time decreases during the first year into an overnight period with a nap or two during the day.

Sleep needs vary throughout life, but contrary to common myth, the need for sleep doesn't decline with age, although some elderly adults may desire an extra hour or so of sleep. However, sleeplessness may be exacerbated as you grow older by the increasing number of medical conditions related to aging, from sleep apnea (interrupted breathing during sleep) to musculoskeletal pain and other diseases that add to nightly restlessness.

What Causes Sleeplessness?

According to sleep researchers, stress is usually listed as the number-one difficulty with sleeping. Stressors may include job-, family-, school-, illness-, or death-related problems. The good news is that when the stressor diminishes, the sleeping challenge lessens as well. The bad news is that stress that begets insomnia often begets more stress, which becomes an ever-worsening cycle, sometimes long after the original stressor is gone or reduced.

There are many more causes of sleep problems:

- Following an erratic sleep schedule (which includes irregular work times that necessitate varying bed-times, as with the 20 percent of Americans who work shifts)
- Overweight or obesity, which is often accompanied by sleep discomfort, apnea, and a myriad of other health-related problems
- Exercising too close to bedtime
- Nightmares, especially common among children, but also occurring occasionally among people of all ages
- Doing mentally challenging activities prior to bedtime

- Drinking alcohol in the afternoon or evening
- Drinking beverages or eating foods containing caffeine in the afternoon or evening
- Jet lag and traveling across time zones
- Interruptions from children, family members, or friends
- An uncomfortable mattress or pillow
- A bedroom that is not conducive to sleep (too light, too noisy, too hot, or too cold)
- A sleep partner who is detrimental to deep sleep (snoring, tossing and turning, irregular sleep patterns)
- Body pain (such as backaches, twitching muscles, restless leg syndrome, neuropathy of the feet or hands, or a thousand other things that make it uncomfortable to lie still)
- Pregnancy
- Premenstrual syndrome (PMS)
- Menopause (especially when accompanied by hot flashes)
- Medications (especially decongestants, antidepresants, asthma, high blood pressure, and steroids)
- Over-the-counter diet pills, especially those containing stimulants
- Energy drinks containing caffeine or stimulants
- Psychiatric disorders such as postpartum blues,

depression, and bipolar disorder that sometimes lead to a disruptive cycle of both fatigue and restlessness

- Tobacco use, since smokers tend to have increased breathing problems, and heavy smokers tend to wake up after a few hours when the body signals nicotine withdrawal

A Special Problem with Young People

According to a long-term study published in the April 2004 issue of *Alcoholism: Clinical and Experimental Research*, young teenagers whose preschool sleep habits were poor were more than twice as likely to use drugs, tobacco, or alcohol. This finding was made by the University of Michigan Health System as part of a family health study that followed 257 boys and their parents for ten years.

The study found a significant connection between sleep problems in children and later drug use, even when other issues such as depression, aggression, attention problems, and parental alcoholism were taken into account. The results were so compelling that researchers now suggest that early sleep problems may be a marker for predicting later risk of early adolescent substance abuse—there may be a common biological factor underlying both traits.

There is a long-known connection between sleep problems and alcohol abuse among adults, but this Michigan study was among the first to delve into the correlation between drug use and sleep disorders among young people.

How Do I Get a Good Night's Sleep?

According to sleep researchers, taking a sleeping pill or other medication should not be considered as a long-term solution. Natural is always better, and here are several proven techniques to combat the most common sleep problems:

- Avoid long naps during the daytime (although many find a fifteen- to thirty-minute power nap to be advantageous, especially in the middle of the day)
- Seek a regular bedtime, preferably at 10 p.m. (many studies promote going to bed even earlier, especially during the wintertime)
- Set aside at least eight hours for sleep
- Develop a regular presleep ritual, including personal hygiene and family routines (such as bedtime stories with your children)
- If possible, try to wake up without an alarm clock (whatever you do, don't keep hitting the snooze button)
- Avoid eating meals (especially spicy, sweet, or caffeine-laden foods) within four to five hours of bedtime

- Avoid drinking alcohol or caffeinated beverages at least four to five hours before bedtime
- If you smoke, avoid tobacco use for two to four hours before bedtime, and never light up if you awake at night
- Exercise regularly, but not within two to three hours of bedtime
- Consider a warm bath or shower thirty minutes or more before bedtime
- Minimize light (including LED lights), noise (some use white-noise machines or earplugs), and excessive temperatures in your bedroom
- Invest in a comfortable mattress and foundation, along with bed linens and pillows
- Keep pets out of the room, especially if they snore or cause allergic reactions
- Turn off the television
- Clean the clutter out of your bedroom and remove everything from the room (such as computers and files) that remind you of work
- If you simply can't sleep, go into another room and read a book (remember how that always seemed to work when you were in college and didn't want to sleep), then return to your bedroom when you get drowsy
- Be aware of the supplements that help with sleeplessness (more about that later)
- Consider brewing a cup of prebedtime tea that

contains chamomile, a natural muscle relaxant and sleep promoter

- Meditate on scriptures such as Psalm 4:8, 91, 127:1–2; Proverbs 3:21–24, the Lord's Prayer (Matthew 6:9–13)

If you continue to have sleeping problems on a regular basis, seek medical and psychological help, especially if you are also battling symptoms of depression, such as feelings of helplessness and hopelessness, loss of interest in daily activities, appetite or weight changes, sleep changes (either insomnia or hypersomnia-oversleeping), irritability or restlessness, loss of energy, self-loathing, concentration problems, unexplained aches and pains, and thoughts of suicide.

In addition to medical and psychological help, it is important to know that nearly every city of any size has sleep clinics staffed with professionals who specialize in sleeping disorders.

SLEEP RECOMMENDATIONS

Here are my recommended Health Masters supplements:

- **Enhanced Sleep Support:** Our blend of patented extract of magnolia officianalis and a proprietary extract of ziziphus spinosa helps to normalize night-time stress hormones while enhancing sleep. It is an all-natural herbal blend that reduces stress and anxiety, is nonaddictive, and can be taken nightly for an indefinite period of time. It is especially excellent for those with stress-related sleeplessness, cortisol-related weight gain, low daytime energy, or anxiety and nervous disturbances.

- **Melatonin Sublingual**: A natural product of the pineal gland, this helps you sleep like a baby. Research continues to show that the use of melatonin can synchronize the circadian clock to environmental cycles and can have beneficial effects for treatment of sleeplessness.[7]

- **Magnesium and Malate Acid**: These are natural muscle relaxants, which help to lower blood pressure. It also uses patented Albion chelate minerals, which are absorbed by the body as food. Remember metallic minerals are rock and are absorbed very poorly by the body. I go into detail on the different types of minerals in my home study series, *Forever Fit at 20–30–40–50 and Beyond*. Magnesium also helps to lower blood pressure and allows more oxygen to be delivered to the brain and heart.

- **Ossomag**: Our excellent calcium, magnesium, vitamin D, and microcrystalline hydroxapatite concentrate supplement helps promote sleep as well as reverses bone loss, which is great for fractures and teeth.

If you have questions, call us at 1-800-726-1834 or order online at www.HealthMasters.com.

FOR MORE INFORMATION

Let me offer a number of excellent resources that may be helpful on this subject:

- American Academy of Sleep Medicine, www.aasmnet.org
- American Insomnia Association, www.americaninsomniaassociation.org
- Mayo Clinic Sleep Center, www.mayoclinic.com/health/insomnia/
- National Institutes of Health National Center for Sleep Disorders Research, www.nhlbi.nih.gov/sleep
- National Sleep Foundation, www.sleepfoundation.org
- Sleep Research Society, www.sleepresearchsociety.org

10

Discover Natural Solutions for Stress and Anxiety

Mike Smith (I have changed his last name, but he is famous for a chain of restaurants) came to my home with William Wise, a friend. William brought Mike to see me because Mike was terribly depressed and having anxiety attacks and suicidal thoughts. His medication only made matters worse. Mike told me how he had lost a fortune through bad business partners and that recently his oldest son had been killed on a motorcycle. The depression brought on by these incidents completely debilitated him. He would spend days in bed and never leave the house.

Mike was in bad shape. When I examined his diet and saw what he was eating, I placed Mike on my Healthy Brain Program.

Several months later, Mike was a new man and felt great. His anxiety was gone. He was a new person. I'll explain to you the protocol I shared with him and why, but first let's allow him to tell us what happened.

In December 2008, I met with Dr. Broer through the referral of a friend, William Wise. At that time, I couldn't walk a hundred feet without being out of breath. After my son died, I wouldn't leave the house. I was depressed, dizzy, and drowsy. My heart was racing, and I had panic attacks. The antidepressants I was on had horrible side effects. They actually made me suicidal. I even enrolled in an online psychiatric support group for help.

In January 2009, I started on Dr. Broer's Healthy Brain Program. The results have been nothing short of miraculous! All of the symptoms I listed above are gone. I feel absolutely great! My business has prospered. It's amazing what happens when you give your brain what it needs.

I really believe that this program could be beneficial to everyone. I recommend Dr. Broer's Healthy Brain Program for everyone. It has truly changed my life. I feel great!

You can order the program I developed for Mike at either www.HealthMasters.com or by calling 1-800-776-1834.

Nutrition Is the Brain's Fuel

First, let's start with nutrition and how it affects behavior and brain function. When proper nutrition is not given to the body, many of the genes responsible for keeping us healthy are not activated. This is particularly true in prenatal nutrition.

If certain nutrients are not available to the fetus, lifelong health problems can occur, including breast cancer and other types of degenerative disease. Please read my wife's book, *Train Up Your Children in the Way They Should Eat*, especially if you are pregnant or you have young children. It will really help you to have healthy children. Plus do your research on immunizations!

Recently the best friend of my niece, Julie Rogers, lost a three-month-old due to sudden infant death syndrome several days after receiving a DPT shot. One study has shown that over half the deaths attributed to SIDS occurred within a week of the child's receiving A DPT shot. Those are horrible odds!

Proper prenatal nutrition has been shown to reduce breast cancer and many other diseases later on in life, especially in the developing fetus. Always remember, the brain never rests. The brain burns a huge amount of fuel. The burning of all of this fuel, especially low-nutrient fuel, produces a lot of free radicals. If your diet does not contain sufficient quantities of the antioxidants A, C, E, selenium, and omega-3 oil, your brain is being slowly poisoned, causing Alzheimer's, Parkinson's, and Lou Gehrig's disease. These free radicals actually destroy the structure of the brain, including the all-important mitochondria and your DNA.

It is a fact that the brain uses 20 percent of all oxygen in the blood, and it is also a fact that the brain uses 25 percent of all glucose in the blood, even though the brain is only 2 percent of the total body weight.

Your brain components are constantly being replaced. The primary need of the brain is omega-3 fat DHA, and the brain uses it in only two weeks. A deficient brain will begin to deteriorate and change in structure in just two weeks without a constant supply of omega-3 DHA in our blood. Health Masters Cod Liver Oil contains the finest quality DHA and omega-3 supplements available on the planet, as far as I'm concerned. I take cod liver oil and omega-3 capsules every day.

Several weeks ago, Mike was feeling so good, he neglected to take the cod liver oil for ten days. He immediately started relapsing and having anxiety symptoms again. He came by my house, and I fussed at him and immediately gave him four tablespoons of cod liver oil. I sent him to the office to replenish his supply. He's doing great again.

Nutrition and Behavior

Significant brain research has been going on for over a century. Back in 1935 it was shown that hypoglycemia, or low blood sugar, can cause or initiate anxiety, neurosis, hysteria, and psychosis. When Mike was tested for hypoglycemia, he tested positive. That's why I started him on our Fit Food Protein, which is a 100 percent New Zealand organic whey protein powder. It has never been heated over 85 degrees, and it stabilizes blood sugar. I told Mike to drink two scoops two to three times a day, either in water or raw certified cow's milk. He noticed an immediate difference in his mood swings and energy levels.

By 1973, additional studies showed a 74 percent increase in schizophrenia and hyperactivity with hypoglycemia. Plus 60 percent of hypoglycemic patients had alcoholism in their family. High blood sugar causes a rise in insulin. The problem is that the insulin reduces the blood sugar so much you get hypo, or low blood sugar. This presents a major problem for the brain. It doesn't get enough glucose, which severely impairs cognitive function. Bad diets and hypoglycemia also increase criminal behavior, probation violation, drug abuse, suicide, childhood felonies, and abnormal EEGs (electroencephalograms), which measure brain wave activity.

Another component of Mike's program was Health Masters E-400 with Selenium. Vitamin E helps to thin the blood to increase the blood flow to the brain. Selenium deficiency radically affects brain function, causing confusion and depression.

Sugar Consumption and Behavior

With Mike, as with most Americans, sugar was one of the biggest culprits. In the 1900s, the average American ate about 4 pounds of sugar per year. That has increased to an average of 129–160 pounds of sugar per year, depending on whom you read—a whopping 2,500 percent increase!

Sugar affects all kinds of violent, antisocial, and criminal behavior. Multiple studies in prisons have shown that when inmates were given extra sugar, their violence increased. When they weren't given sugar, the violence decreased.

Sugar is hidden in foods. Matter of fact, the majority of our sugar (43 percent) comes from fruit juices and sodas. What folks don't realize is that there are thirty-five grams of sugar in just a few ounces of apple juice. You should never give children or infants juice to drink. It is way too much sugar for their body to process properly.

Also, you should never drink soda. One soda has up to twelve teaspoons of sugar. Since 1974, soda consumption has doubled. Today, the average teenager consumes fifty-four teaspoons of sugar a day. From 1972 to 2001, adults from forty-nine to fifty-nine years of age have had a 250 percent increase in soda intake. Adults over the age of sixty had a 300 percent increase.

Sugar dramatically increases preradical activity in the brain. In other words, it causes the brain to deteriorate. As mentioned earlier, if you have bad quality glucose or bad quality food, you massively increase the products in the brain that cause free radical damage.

Sugar makes every cell, particularly in the brain, age very, very quickly. It causes cross-linkage in cells, makes the skin sag, and ages the whole body. People who eat a lot of sugar have six times the incidences of Alzheimer's. By the way, 50 percent of the American population has functional hypoglycemia. Basically what that means is, if you eat the wrong foods, your blood sugar spikes then drops because of insulin, and you feel horrible. When you have hypoglycemia, your sugar goes up so high and the insulin reduces the sugar to such a low level, you feel like you will pass out. You can actually end up with permanent brain damage and or seizures. You can actually die from hypoglycemia if your blood sugar gets too low. You can have a seizure and die.

Nutrition and Crime

Almost all violent felons in prison are alcoholics, and they have hypoglycemia. In fact, the most violent offenders in prison are alcoholics: 97 percent of alcoholics are hypoglycemic compared to 18 percent in a controlled study. Alcohol is a tremendous source of energy because it releases sugar so quickly into the blood, but it also causes tremendous toxicity of the brain. When you treat hypoglycemia and you stabilize the blood sugar, like I did with Mike with the Health Masters Fit Food Protein, 71 percent of the alcoholics become sober. Think about that!

The most violent crimes, auto accidents, and road rage are all connected to alcohol consumption. By the way, Alcoholics Anonymous (AA) only has a 25 percent sober rate. So I suggest to AA, they need to check people's blood sugar to find if they have a problem with hypoglycemia.

Now, this is interesting, if you take the temporal lobe of the brain, which is the part of the brain that contains memory, and you electrically stimulate it, you create instant violent behavior. The behavior is so violent that the subjects actually attacked the researchers.

What is also interesting is that hypoglycemia attacks the temporal lobe of the brain, causing anger. In many cases, these people lose all control. They will become very violent. They will stab people. They will kill people. In fact, most alcoholics are very, very violent. When they are admitted into emergency rooms, in many cases, it takes many people to subdue them.

I remember when I was young, we used to talk about someone being a mean drunk or a passive drunk. Most drunks that I knew were mean. The sad part of it is that in many cases the alcoholism was brought on by hypoglycemia. The problem is we didn't know about this back in the 1960s. Today, we know that if an alcoholic can simply stabilize the blood sugar, alcoholism simply goes away. The lowering of blood sugar of an alcoholic can actually drive him or her wild, like an animal. High hypoglycemia can cause extreme anger.

HYPOGLYCEMIA AND AGGRESSIVE BEHAVIOR

Back in the 1980s, I worked with a lady named Bonnie. She was hypoglycemic. When she would show up at the office, you never knew if you were getting Bonnie 1 or Bonnie 2. Bonnie 1 was extremely nice. Bonnie 2 was a total nightmare that you wanted nothing to do with. We found that Bonnie had hypoglycemia. When we stabilized her blood sugar, we were able to completely control the hypoglycemic symptoms.

Sugar plays a strong role in human behavior. Cecilia Rosenfelt, a medical doctor, wrote that blood sugar imbalances or hypoglycemia is one of the primary causes of marital discord. If a spouse had a blood sugar condition, in many cases, he or she was impossible to live with and given to fits of rage. When that person's blood sugar was stabilized, often the rage completely went away.

Again, back to Mike, this is why I recommended that he start taking our Fit Food Protein. I wanted to stabilize his blood sugar.

Everyday Substances That Cause Health and Personality Problems

While we are on the subject, let's talk about aspartame and MSG (monosodium glutamate). Both release insulin, which causes hypoglycemia. Diet sodas and MSG both cause weight gain because they release insulin and actually force the body, in many cases, to become hypoglycemic.

How often have you seen people drink diet sodas while thinking they are losing weight, yet in reality, they are gaining weight because the aspartame releases the insulin to cause hypoglycemia? The insulin is a hormone that stores these extra calories from sugar as fat, plus you have constant sugar cravings because of the hypoglycemia.

Likewise, MSG can induce intense rage. Studies have shown that if you inject MSG into the brain of a mouse, the mouse can attack a cat and actually kill a cat. MSG is in almost every corn chip and potato chip you are going to eat. Then, when you combine a diet soda with the aspartame and the chips with MSG, people rage severely.

Think about how many children eat this way on a daily basis. It is no wonder we have out-of-control children in school classrooms. These children are drugged into a stupor with Schedule II drugs. How sad is that! The MSG goes into the blood sugar, and the person goes into a severe rage. MSG actually kills brain cells because of too much calcium influx into the neuro cells, causing them to die. This is one of the reasons for extreme headaches when you eat MSG. Another reason for MSG extreme headaches is because of the type of hypoglycemia that is induced. When you have low blood sugar headaches, in most cases, they are in the back of the head. High blood sugar headaches are usually in the front of the head or around the temporal lobes.

The problem is clear: 40 percent of the calories in children's diets are from sugar. A study of children showed that the top 25 percent were hyperactive. High sugar intake seriously reduces their mental performance to the point that children simply can't think.

Several years ago, I wrote *The Maximum Solutions to ADD, Autism and the Learning Disabilities of Children.* The book is out of print, but we are able to reprint multiple chapters of that book and make those available to you from my office.

The point is that there is a strong relationship between serotonin and sugar levels. Serotonin is that feel-good chemical in your brain. This is why, in many cases, women who are menstruating crave sugar, because they are trying to elevate their serotonin because they are having mood swings. Also, children taking SSR (selective serotonin reuptake inhibitors) in many cases actually lower their own serotonin levels. This is why there is a black-box warning on Prozac and Zoloft regarding children and warning you explicitly that it induces suicidal behavior in children. Anytime you lower serotonin levels, you have a problem with suicidal behavior in adults or your children. If you can avoid serotonin reuptake inhibitors, DON'T USE THEM. There are all kinds of natural ways to increase serotonin without the use of these suicide drugs.

Mike and many other clients have proven this again and again. I am not saying SSRI prevents suicide, but I am saying it can lead to suicidal tendencies, as the labels clearly state. I personally do not ever recommend their use.

High sugar intake seriously reduces mental performance. Remember that. You simply can't think. Therefore a person with hypoglycemia wants to stay away from high glycemic foods such as sugar, white potatoes, pastas, white rice, and anything that will elevate sugar and cause a rise in insulin, which drops the sugar too quickly. Juices, white potatoes, and sugar need to be avoided completely, along with sodas, including diet sodas. Never use them!

Interestingly, one of the most reactive foods for hyperactivity in children is soybeans (more about that in chapter 13). Yellow dyes are bad, and soybeans are bad for kids with ADD and ADHD. Some of the red dyes also are bad.

Nutrients and Behavior

In 1985, J. Egger and C. M. Carter did a study in which they placed seventy-six hyperactive kids on a low-carbohydrate diet and also eliminated food dyes. Over 80 percent of these children improved on the diet, and 28 percent of these children returned completely to normal. They had the highest reaction from Yellow Dye #5, sodium benzoate, and soy products. The reactive food was soybeans. Nearly three-fourths of children who were ADD and ADHD reacted to soy products as well as pasteurized cow's milk (64 percent) and chocolate (59).

Let me stop here for a second. I don't put raw certified cow's milk into that category. I've never seen a child react against raw certified cow's milk. But you need to be very careful. Make sure to use state-certified cow's milk if you are going to drink raw milk, and make sure you know the dairy. We lived off of raw cow's milk for thousands of years, but the pasteurization process has only been around for the past few decades, and we have seen a tremendous amount of health problems in our families and children because of all of the processing in the food that we eat, including cow's milk.

Serotonin also helps the brain resist violent acts, including suicide. Corn is low in tryptophan, and it also lowers serotonin levels. Almost all cereal products are made from corn. You have to have tryptophan in your diet to maintain serotonin levels. It's very, very important.

We have 5HTP Tryptophan product we use now in our office. It is phenomenal. It's one of the best things I've ever seen to elevate serotonin naturally, and it helps to stabilize and elevate moods and keep people from being depressed. Low niacin B_3 can also increase the risk for mental illness. We have a very good product called Vascular Relaxant SR that also helps to reduce cholesterol levels.

I put Mike on all of these products because I knew they would work. Niacin also helps to reduce the incidences of mental illness. Deficiencies of niacin can cause diarrhea, dementia, and schizophrenia.

Vitamins A, B, C, D, E, and K are all associated with brain function. Again we put Mike on the vitamin C and vitamin D_3 from HealthMasters. I put him on 20,000 IUs of vitamin D initially for the first thirty days. We talked about the importance of vitamin D supplementation in the flu vaccine chapter (chapter 3) and what it did as far as increasing brain function, decreasing the risk of mood problems, increasing mood, and increasing serotonin. All these vitamins are critical.

Deficiencies in any of these specific nutrients can cause behavioral and brain problems. Just B_1 thiamine deficiency can cause mental depression, memory failure, chronic fatigue, and personality changes. The problem, most of the time, with B_1 is that it is a supplemental deficiency and can't be detected, but the problems are still there. It's kind of like coming down with scurvy because you don't have enough vitamin C. Scurvy has been shown to have been a clinical definition of vitamin C deficiency, so they treat it by giving you vitamin C. Eating sugar and carbohydrates depletes B_1. A recent survey of adolescents shows that 60 percent were deficient in iron, 57 percent were deficient in vitamin A, 43 percent were deficient in vitamin C, 39 percent were deficient in B_1, 30 percent were deficient in protein, and 16 percent were deficient in riboflavin.

Studies have shown that using a very good multivitamin like our Health Masters Ultimate Multiple can reduce almost all of these symptoms and can increase CAT scores in children. Also you can increase CAT scores by removing dyes from your children's diet. Dyes and additives can cause brain problems. By changing the diet of children, you can have a profound influence in their behavioral and cognitive functions. Even marginal deficiencies can cause brain problems.

BRAIN ALLERGIES

Food allergies directly affect brain function. Foods that cause allergies can actually be absorbed as macromolecules by the intestinal tract through a condition called leaky gut syndrome. When this happens, you have a situation where the immune system causes an immune reaction. The immune reaction is not localized to the torso; it also goes to the brain. When the brain has an immune reaction, it releases glutamate, which causes neurological dysfunction. In other words, food allergies cause neurological dysfunction.

Guess what one of the primary causes of food allergies is? Soy products!

Primary allergy reactants are soy (88 percent), pasteurized milk (60 percent), corn (50 percent), gluten, pasta, and pastries (100 percent). When you have these common allergens in your food supply, the side effects from the chemicals released into the brain include lethargy, stupor, disorientation, paranoia, delusions, hallucinations, agitations, rage, panic attacks, criminal behavior, seizures, and even schizophrenia.

Consider a study done with schizophrenics. They were taken off of gluten completely—bread, pasta, rice, and pastries—everything with gluten in it. Within a short time, 100 percent of the schizophrenics returned to normal. When given just a little bit of gluten, they became schizophrenic again and had to be rehospitalized. It is amazing to me how food affects everything.

Vaccinations and Brain Function

In chapter 3 we discussed immunizations. It is certainly worth revisiting, especially in a chapter on stress, anxiety, and personality disturbances. Some people ask about overvaccinating. I believe that most immunizations are overvaccinations. They cause neurological affects. When you inject a vaccine into the body, it causes an immune response, both in the body and in the brain. This immune response in the brain goes on for years. The neurological toxins used in many vaccines can cause an ongoing immune response in the body and the brain. This inflammation of the brain simply will not calm down. It goes on for years and years and years.

To prevent overvaccinating, you may be able to get a religious exemption to immunizations so that your children can still attend public or private school.

Some may say, "Well, you should immunize your kids." Why? We have seen that children who have been diagnosed with autism in many cases have been diagnosed after their second measles booster. Do your own research! Look at the dangers of immunizations. Google it on the Internet. You're going to find that everything I'm telling you about immunizations is true.

MORE PROBLEMS FROM DIET

In chapter 2 we discussed high animal fat, such as lard. This can also cause a problem with the brain. On my top-ten list of foods to never eat is high-fat luncheon meats. I include bacon, sausage, ham, pepperoni, and hot dogs. Pork is one of the worst foods you could eat. It can cause all kinds of problems with the brain, including brain parasites!

It's so important and so easy to have proper brain health and good brain chemistry, but there are certain things you need to eliminate from your diet. Avoid the Top Ten Foods Not to Eat (see pages 17–19). Avoid the chemicals we talked about throughout this chapter. And make sure you take the supplements we talked about.

Thirteen Critical Supplements for the Healthy Brain Program

Here are my recommended Health Masters supplements:

1. HGH Stimulate
2. Fit Food Protein
3. Ultimate Multiple
4. Cod Liver Oil—Blue Ice Pure
5. B Complex
6. Norwegian Omega-3
7. Excellent C
8. Cortico B5-B6
9. Zinc Glycinate
10. Super Potent E
11. Memory Support
12. Ultimate D3-5000
13. 5-HTP

If you take all of these products every day it will greatly influence and affect your brain chemistry. If you start this program, you will feel so good and have so much energy.

You will have the same results that Mike and so many others have achieved!

If you have questions, please call us at 1-800-726-1834 or order online at www.HealthMasters.com.

11

CLEAN OUT YOUR ARTERIES

A frequent topic of my newsletters is the continual deterioration of the cardiovascular system, which occurs with the aging process. The deterioration I am speaking about is the slow closing of veins, arteries, and capillaries—all seventy-five thousand miles of them—through calcium and fat plaquing. Let me share an amazing product that can actually reverse this process.

In 1938, German scientists discovered a new compound called ethylenediaminetetraacetic acid (EDTA). The elements that made up this amino acid are similar to common household vinegar. However, EDTA has an amazing ability to grab hold of metals and chemical toxins in the bloodstream. Once EDTA grabs these metals and poisons, it dissolves them, allowing them to be flushed out of the body through stool and urine.

Now let us fast-forward ten years to 1948, in which a group of 240 factory workers manufacturing lead batteries were diagnosed with lead poisoning. After years of being exposed to lead, many received bad news. They had only months or maybe a year to live. Others would slowly lose their hearing, vision, and ability to control their bodily functions. In addition, their heart and kidneys would be damaged and eventually stop working.

The good news is a group of American scientists had learned about the breakthrough technology discovered by the Germans in 1938. These workers were administered EDTA and recovered. It was an incredible story, and EDTA worked so well for these factory workers that it soon became the approved treatment for all heavy metal poisoning. In fact, years later, when navy sailors were exposed to lead paint, the U.S. Navy administered EDTA to them.

CHELATION THERAPY

In the 1950s, Dr. Norman E. Clarke, chairman of the research department at Providence Hospital in Detroit, Michigan, began researching the effects of EDTA chelation therapy on cardiovascular disease. When Dr. Clarke used EDTA to treat patients with lead poisoning, he noticed an incredible effect. While the lead and toxic metals were being flushed out of the patient's blood, so was the dangerous substance known as calcium plaque. This is the same plaque that can easily clog all of your veins, arteries, and capillaries. (This plaque can become so hard, that doctors performing bypass surgery have actually cut their gloves on it.)

After EDTA was found to be effective in chelating and removing toxic metals from the blood, it wasn't such a large jump in reasoning to wonder if hardened arteries could be softened if the calcium in their walls was removed. The first indication that EDTA treatment might benefit patients with atherosclerosis came from Clarke. In 1956, he reported that patients with occlusive peripheral vascular disease said they felt better following treatment with EDTA.

Chelation, as it has been called since then, refers to the ability of certain chemicals to bind with calcium, iron, and other metals and remove them from the body. Presumably, as calcium is "clawed out" of constricted vessels (*chelation* comes from the Greek word *chele*, meaning "claw"), plaque also could be slowly dissolved away. Just as this chelation therapy not only saved the lives of these factory workers and sailors, this amazing discovery for cleaning out arteries became what I believe is the biggest breakthrough in the history of cardiovascular health. In fact, the more we learn about chelation, the more mysterious and wonderful it seems to get.

PLAQUE DANGERS

What causes arterial plaque? Plaque that accumulates on the inner walls of your arteries is made from various substances that circulate in your blood. These include calcium, fat, cholesterol, cellular waste, and fibrin, a material involved in blood clotting. In response to plaque buildup, cells in your artery walls multiply and secrete additional substances that can worsen the state of clogged arteries. As plaque deposits grow, a condition called atherosclerosis results. This condition causes the arteries to narrow and harden, and the process seems to stem from damage to the arterial wall. This damage, which enables the plaque deposits to build up, may result from several causes:

- **High "bad" cholesterol and low "good" cholesterol**: High levels of "bad" cholesterol, or low-density lipoprotein (LDL), are major contributors to arterial plaque formation. But everyone also has "good" cholesterol, or high-density lipoprotein (HDL), circulating in their blood. HDL is believed to remove some of the bad cholesterol from plaque in clogged arteries and to transport it back to the liver, where it is eliminated.

- **High blood pressure**: Having high blood pressure increases the rate at which arterial plaque builds up. It also hastens the hardening of clogged arteries.

- **Tobacco**: Smoking seems to increase the rate of atherosclerosis in the arteries of the heart, legs, and the aorta, the largest artery in the body.

- **Drinking water that contains inorganic calcium**: Plaque can also be caused by drinking water that is not distilled. Remember most water contains large amounts of inorganic minerals, particularly metallic calcium. The body cannot use this calcium, unlike the calcium from good food and supplements. So when you ingest it, it is stored in your soft tissue, helping to contribute to the calcium plaque that stores in your arteries. It is important to avoid drinking water that contains inorganic calcium. It can literally turn your cardiovascular system into stone.

Plaque often starts to develop during the childhood or teenage years. Then clogged arteries develop in middle age or later. Depending upon where the arterial plaque accumulates, clogged arteries in different parts of the body can lead to multiple medical conditions, which include the following:

- **Coronary artery disease**: As plaque accumulates in the arteries carrying blood to the heart, it results in coronary artery disease, or heart disease. This condition leads to heart attacks and is one of the leading causes of death in the United States.
- **Carotid artery disease**: Carotid arteries run up either side of your neck, supplying oxygen to your brain. The accumulation of arterial plaque in the carotid can lead to a stroke.
- **Peripheral artery disease**: As plaque builds up in the blood vessels that carry blood to your legs, it

can reduce the amount of oxygen delivered. The reduced blood flow can cause you to experience pain, numbness, or serious infection in your legs and feet.

Chelation Benefits

When you reduce the calcium plaque and toxic minerals, there have been multiple side effects recorded in medical research and literature. These include:

- patients who had angina were pain free
- improved circulatory health
- cleaner, sharper thinking
- improved vision
- restored hearing
- improved sense of smell
- increased energy level
- increased libido

In fact, over 1,823 clinical and scientific studies have shown that using a chelating agent such as EDTA is 82 percent effective in eliminating plaque from your arteries. Interestingly, the standard medical procedure for individuals with blocked heart arteries is bypass surgery. I have a simple question: If those few inches of arteries are blocked and then replaced, how are you going to clean and replace the other seventy-five thousand miles of arteries, veins, and capillaries?

The point here is that plugged arteries are an indication of an overall problem. Remember, the same blood vessels that feed your heart also nourish your skin, strengthen your bones, and keep your vision and hearing working at peak capacity. Without proper blood, even sexual function stops.

When you flush this calcium plaque from your entire circulatory system, life-giving blood can once again surge through your entire body, as it did when you were younger, helping to improve every aspect of your health.

BENEFITS AND DRAWBACKS

There are two types of chelation therapy: intravenous chelation therapy and oral chelation therapy. With intravenous chelation therapy, a needle is inserted into a vein. Through this, EDTA is administered into the bloodstream. A series of treatments will need to be administered. Oral chelation therapy usually comes in tablet form, but it is also available as oral sprays, powders, and suppositories.

While the effects of intravenous chelation therapy have been well documented, there are several drawbacks:

- It is extremely time consuming, taking from three to five hours at least one or two times each week.
- It requires medical supervision, which is often difficult to find.
- IV needles are needed.
- It costs up to three hundred dollars per treatment,

often costing thousands of dollars for a correct protocol, then up to ten more treatments every year thereafter.

- Insurance usually never pays for the treatment.

Needless to say, many of us simply can't afford the investment, time, and energy required to go through intravenous chelation, nor is it that easy to find a great facility. However, chelation experts now believe that oral chelation is quite effective in reducing calcium plaque in the arteries and joints. It has also been shown to increase the concentration of calcium in your bones, where it is needed.

MORE PROOF NEEDED

Frankly, all that we have read and experienced with oral chelation wasn't enough for my colleague Brian Blackburn, a pioneer in natural health and supplement development, or me. Our years of research led us to develop a product that is the best oral chelation product I have ever found. We didn't stop with EDTA. We went much further.

Our chelation therapy product contains the following ingredients:

- **EDTA** has the ability to bind with virtually every metal in the periodic table. EDTA is FDA-approved for lead, mercury, aluminum, and cadmium toxicity. There is a benefit in combining EDTA with other chelators, because alone it acts slowly and could potentially lead to a redeposit of metals. It is important to replace beneficial minerals, such as zinc, copper, iron, cobalt, and manganese that are bound by EDTA.[1]

- **DMSA** is a nontoxic, water-soluble dimercapto-succinic acid employed as a metal chelator since the 1950s.[2] Containing two sulfhydryl groups, this relatively stable compound with a high affinity for toxic metal penetrates tissue deposits of the metal and rapidly eliminates the chelated toxic metal through urine and stool. It is the best oral chelation known. It is approved by the FDA and actually works in the cell membrane to eliminate aluminum and mercury. It also does a great job on calcium plaque.

- **Cilantro** (coriandrum sativum; Chinese parsley, coriander) suppresses the deposition of lead by chelating the metal.[3] A sorbent prepared from cilantro was found to have good efficiency in removing organic and methyl mercury.

- **Chlorella** (green algae) has the ability to take up toxic metals in its environment, preventing heavy metals excreted through the liver from being reabsorbed back into the gut. Chlorella's influence is synergistic with that of garlic and cilantro. Researchers observed a dramatic reduction of 66.03 percent in blood lead levels in a group of mice receiving chlorella extract concurrent with lead exposure.[4]

- **Garlic** in a variety of forms has been shown by researchers to be beneficial in the management of heavy metal toxicity, especially lead, cadmium, and mercury.[5]
- **N-Acetyl-L-Cysteine** (NAC) has the ability to interact with reactive oxygen species (ROS) and stimulate the body to produce glutathione enhancing cell survival after exposure to heavy metals or toxins.[6]
- **Alpha Lipoic Acid** is mostly known for its attribute as a powerful antioxidant. However, it may also directly chelate heavy metals especially copper, arsenic, cadmium, and mercury.[7]

Our product, Chelation Therapy, is an extraordinary all-natural combination of unique and therapeutic ingredients formulated to support the safe and effective removal of heavy metals. It is designed to protect against heavy metal–induced free radical damage.

Before we decided to release this product, we wanted a clinical trial to prove it works. So we did just that. The results were spectacular! Check out these numbers related to the approximate average increase in urinary excretion of these toxins:

- aluminum—5000 percent
- arsenic—8 percent
- cadmium—20 percent
- lead—40 percent
- mercury—90 percent

Needless to say, we were excited. These numbers are huge! They show the incredible effectiveness of our oral chelation therapy. Simply put, this product works, and it works extremely well. By the way, to our knowledge, this is the only oral chelation product that has been clinically tested.

CHELATION THERAPY

Our product is your personal in-home chelation program, administered without painful needles or a high price tag. In fact, our Chelation Therapy will cost you around $1.06 daily. You just take four capsules at bedtime. You will to need to be on our Ultimate Multiple along with the Chelation Therapy to be sure you are you getting the necessary daily supply of your patented chelated minerals. Take four of the Ultimate Multiples with breakfast. This will help to gently and effectively flush out the hardened plaque, lead, mercury, aluminum, and other toxins, as well as increase your blood flow. That means you can once again experience more energy and sharper, clearer thinking, not to mention all of the other benefits I have already mentioned.

We have had a massive demand for this product, and I believe you may benefit from it on your journey to maximum health. If you have questions, please call us at 1-800-726-1834 or order online at www.HealthMasters. com.

12

Build Health with Supplements

I *get all the nutrition I need from food.*

I wish I had a dollar for every time I heard that from people. Nevertheless, and at times in spite of what they adamantly say, most of my clients agree to take the supplements I recommend. Invariably, several months later they admit they are feeling better than they've ever felt in their lives! (Some won't admit that the supplements have helped, but most do.) Most then become such advocates for nutritional supplementation that you couldn't talk them out of taking their supplements!

Many people simply grow up believing that if a person eats three balanced meals a day, he or she will live a long and healthy life. The balance back in the 1940s, 1950s, and 1960s was one that called for protein, grains, fruits, vegetables, and dairy products at every meal—a program called the four food groups.

Today, we would likely say that a person needs to be eating considerably more fruits and vegetables than grains or protein, and that virtually all dairy products should be nonfat.

Either way, what home economists of that earlier time did not say was that much of the food that was available on the market had been stripped of its nutritional content or had been subjected to a wide variety of additives and pesticides that have since been shown to be harmful to the human body.

Let me sum up what we know in one simple phrase: Food today is not what it was a hundred years ago! Here are three quick reasons why so much has changed:

1. Many of the vitamins and minerals that were readily available in the foods consumed a century ago simply aren't in the foods we buy in must supermarkets today. Many of the soil's nutrients are now missing, and so many additives are being infused into our foods.

2. Today's cooking methods can destroy many of the vitamins in our foods. Not only are fewer foods eaten raw today, but many are being boiled and microwaved to the point that less and less nutrients reach your plate and body.

3. Advances in medications and medical treatments can also destroy or diminish the value of vitamins in your body. We live in a day when we are quick to take drugs to cure whatever ails us—from analgesics to antidepressants, cardiovascular drugs,

and sleeping aids—yet we are reluctant to take the supplements that can help keep us from so many of the most common ailments in the first place! In fact, every year in our nation, several hundred deaths are directly attributed by poison control centers to the use and abuse of drugs, yet there is a large body of research to indicate that vitamin deficiencies are linked to the diseases that these drugs and medicines are supposed to treat.

These widespread trends have important health implications for those seeking maximum health. Not only do we need to avoid negative forces that diminish the value of nutrients in the body, but we also need to find a way to ingest more and more vitamins and minerals.

OUR NEED FOR VITAMINS

I want to focus first on what is missing. We have known for decades, even centuries in some cases, that vitamin deficiencies can lead to disease. For example, each of the diseases listed below is the result of an important molecule or substance:

- **Anemia**: a deficiency of iron, and in some cases an insufficient amount or insufficient absorption of vitamin B_{12} (cobalamin)
- **Beri-beri**: an insufficient supply of vitamin B_1 (thiamin)
- **Goiter**: a deficiency in iodine

- **Osteoporosis**: an insufficient supply of calcium and vitamin D
- **Pellagra**: an insufficient supply of vitamin B$_3$ (niacin)
- **Scurvy**: a deficiency of vitamin C
- **Spina Bifida**: an inadequate amount of folic acid (a B vitamin)

Many other diseases may be linked to vitamin deficiencies or perhaps a combination of insufficient vitamins and other nutrients. The research is growing in this area.

What we do know is that every human being is unique. We each need a distinctive nutritional profile. Perhaps someday in the not-too-distant future we will be able to determine the exact amounts of which nutrients are missing from our bodies for individual maximum health. Today, what we do know is that most people need more of certain vitamins on a fairly routine basis. The exact amount may vary, but the general guidelines are known.

WHAT ARE VITAMINS?

Vitamins are organic compounds that contribute to normal growth, development, and metabolism in the human body. With few exceptions, vitamins cannot be made in the body but must be supplied through food or drink. Vitamins are produced by living materials—plants and some animals. By contrast, minerals come from soil.

Vitamins have no calories and are not the fuel that runs the body. Rather, they are like the ignition switch that sparks the fuel and keeps the engine running smoothly. Vitamins work in combination with other nutrients and have many diverse roles. They play a vital part in the formation and maintenance of blood cells, hormones, creation of genetic material, and the functioning of all cells and tissues of the body. Vitamins are necessary to convert the calories in carbohydrates, protein, and fat into usable energy. Vitamins help form the enzymes that trigger and become catalysts for important metabolic and physiological processes in the body.

When vitamins are not present in sufficient quantity—either because we have not eaten sufficient vitamins or have not been able to fully absorb the vitamins we have eaten—our metabolism is impaired.

There are two general types of the vitamins that are required for health:

1. **Water-Soluble:** These vitamins dissolve in water and are not stored by the body to any great degree. As a result these vitamins need to be supplied regularly to the body:

   - B_1 (thiamin)
   - B_2 (riboflavin)
   - B_3 (niacin)
   - B_5 (panothenic acid)

- B_6 (pyridoxine)
- B_{12} (cobalamin)
- folic acid
- biotin
- choline (part of the B complex)
- inositol (part of the B complex)
- PABA (para-aminobenzoic acid)
- C

2. **Fat-Soluble**: These vitamins dissolve in fat and in substances that dissolve fat. They are stored in the liver and other tissues. Fat-soluble vitamins include:

- A
- D (sometimes called the sun vitamin because a form of cholesterol in the body is converted into vitamin D when ultraviolet rays from the sun hit the skin)
- E
- K

FACTORS THAT CAUSE A VITAMIN INSUFFICIENCY

There are a wide variety of causes behind the depletion of vitamins in the body. Shortly I will discuss environmental stressors. General reasons for vitamin insufficiency can include the following:

- tobacco use
- overuse of processed salt

- mineral oil
- perspiration
- antacids
- surgery
- fluoride
- polluted air or water
- lactation (nursing mothers)
- extreme cold or heat
- chlorinated water
- aspirin
- diuretic drugs (often part of high blood pressure medication)
- sleeping pills
- pregnancy
- sickness or accidents
- rancid fats
- estrogen
- cortisone
- food additives
- oral contraceptives
- prescription drugs
- laxatives
- tranquilizers
- emotional strain
- diarrhea (losing abnormal amounts of water from the body)

Any one of these factors can cause the body to need more of one or more vitamins or minerals.

ENVIRONMENTAL STRESSORS

Let's get more specific. Throughout this book I have pointed to a number of harmful substances that we need to avoid. All of the things that I have noted—tobacco, alcohol, aspartame, drugs, heavy metals, and home- and medicine-related chemicals—act as stressors on the body. Other things that cause the body to experience stress at the cellular level include:

- unnecessary x-rays and other forms of radioactivity
- radiant energy, including the energy emitted by computer screens, microwave ovens, fluorescent lights, cell phones, high-voltage electric power lines, and even energy from electric blankets
- ozone and other harmful chemicals in smog
- chemical fumes
- pesticides and fungicides
- harmful toxic substances often found in homes, such as asbestos, vinyl chloride, and formaldehyde (often found in plywood, particle board, paints, plastics, and detergents)

Arguments have been made about the degree of toxicity and health hazard posed by each of the above categories, and we can be sure of this: Taken as a whole, the stressors that permeate our world weaken our immunity and make us more susceptible to disease. Without a doubt, our world is much more toxic in terms of chemicals and radiation than any prior time in history!

ANTIOXIDANTS TO COMBAT
ENVIRONMENTAL STRESSORS

Environmental stressors are a major cause of free radical production. A free radical is a molecule that has lost an electron and seeks to steal an electron from another molecule or get rid of its unpaired excess electron. Free radicals essentially wreak molecular havoc in the body. They tend to disfigure and corrode the protein, fat, and DNA of cells they encounter, setting off destructive chain reactions that break down cell membranes and cause cells to disintegrate.

Granted, none of us can ever totally avoid free radicals. Our bodies produce a certain number of them. But most of the free radicals produced in our environment are the by-product of smog, high altitude, exposure to x-rays, toxins in water and food, ozone, pollens, molds and dust, sunlight, and so forth.

The bad news is this: free radicals impair the immune system and simultaneously cause cell damage. Cell damage has been associated with many degenerative diseases, such as arthritis, Lou Gehrig's disease, some types of cancer, Alzheimer's disease, heart attacks, atherosclerosis (hardening of the arteries), Parkinson's disease, cataracts, cerebral vascular changes (that lead to dementia or senility), and degenerative diseases linked to cell damage.

Here is the good news: free radicals are rendered harmless by antioxidants. An antioxidant is a a substance that can donate a sought-after electron to a free radical without becoming dangerous itself. When an antioxidant comes into contact with a free radical, it puts an end to the havoc that the free radical can cause!

The top five antioxidants are these vitamins and minerals:

1. vitamin A (retinal or retinyl)
2. vitamin C
3. vitamin E
4. selenium
5. beta carotene

Many other minerals, herbs, and other substances are also excellent antioxidants:

- bioflavonoids
- CoQ_{10} (coenzyme Q_{10})
- zinc
- garlic
- ginseng
- manganese
- molybdenum
- echinacea
- milk thistle
- L-Cysteine
- grape seed extract (and also red wine extract)
- ginkgo biloba
- glutathione
- pine bark extract

- pycnogenol
- copper
- DHEA
- melatonin
- alpha lipoic acid
- wheat and barley grass
- B vitamins (folic acid, riboflavin, B$_{12}$)
- carotenoids (lycopene, alpha-carotene, cryptoxanthin, leutin/zeaxanthin)

RESEARCH HIGHLIGHTS RELATED TO ANTIOXIDANT VITAMINS

There are a number of studies that have specifically linked antioxidants to building good health. Let me summarize just a few of the key findings:

- **Vitamin C:** It is very difficult to overestimate the value of this vitamin in combating degenerative diseases associated with advancing age. Gladys Block, an epidemiologist at the University of California, summarized more than 10 large-scale population studies on the relationship between vitamin C–rich foods and vitamin C supplementation and cancer. With only a handful of exceptions, every study pointed toward a positive benefit from vitamin C. More than 110 of these studies found statistically significant reductions in the risk of virtually all kinds of cancer with a high intake of vitamin C.[1] Cancer patients and others with degenerative diseases seem to have a much greater requirement for vitamin C than normal, healthy individuals, perhaps because all available vitamin C is mobilized toward resisting and repelling malignant cells.

- **Vitamin E:** Natural, mixed tocopherol vitamin E is another superantixodant with amazing properties. One study conducted by the New York Academy of Science shows that even though immune response declined with age, it reverted almost to the level of young people after an administration of 400–800 IU of vitamin E. Study after study has shown that vitamin E seems to enhance or recharge the immune system, with white blood cells increased by 10–50 percent within thirty days, and other immune-related systems improved as much as 80–90 percent! Vitamin E has been shown to lower the risk of breast-, epithelial-, and carcinogen-related cancers. A study involving women with low levels of vitamin E in their bloodstreams were found to have four to five times the risk of developing pancreatic, stomach, and urinary tract cancers.[2] Similar studies have correlated low vitamin E with lung and colorectal cancers.

- **Selenium:** This is a tremendous immune-boosting substance that greatly stimulates the antibody response against germ infections. It works with vitamin E synergistically—that is, the two substances work especially well when taken together. More than four hundred research articles have documented the role of selenium in cancer prevention. In fact, some studies have shown that supplemental selenium could reduce cancer deaths by as much as 50 percent.[3]

- **Lipoic Acid**: Often referred to as alpha lipoic acid, this substance especially protects the liver and detoxifies tissues of heavy metals, such as excessive iron and copper. It also helps detoxify metals such as cadmium, lead, and mercury. It enhances the power of vitamins C and E, as well as glutathione (an amino acid). It has the unique property of being both fat-soluble and water-soluble, therefore it is used throughout the body as a potent antioxidant.[4] A number of studies have shown alpha lipoic acid to be a potent substance in protecting against heart disease, cancer, cataracts, diabetes, and other diseases. It seems especially good in protecting against nerve tissue damage.[5] In its use by diabetics, it appears to have a great ability to normalize blood sugar levels, and it has been used for more than thirty years in Germany to help protect diabetics against retina damage, cataract formation, and nerve and heart damage.

- **CoQ$_{10}$**: Coenzyme Q$_{10}$ is a vital catalyst for the production of energy in human cells. Studies have shown a great effect on stimulating immunity by boosting production of immunoglobulin (antibody G or lgG) with only 60 mg a day. This rise of antibodies usually occurs between one and three months after supplementation begins.[6] Several very encouraging studies have shown that CoQ_{10} may be very helpful for breast cancer patients. In one study, patients were given high doses of antioxidants, essential fatty acids, and CoQ_{10}, with a highly significant number of the patients experiencing tumor remission.[7] CoQ_{10} has been linked to protection of the brain, especially in protecting the cell's mitochondria, which may be helpful in combating Alzheimer's disease, Lou Gehrig's disease, and some forms of dementia.[8] One of the best features of CoQ_{10} is that it appears to have virtually no side effects. It is one of the safest substances ever tested, even at very high doses, with no significant toxicity in long-term studies recorded to date.

- **Glutathione**: Many call glutathione the master antioxidant because it protects every cell in the body, which means it also protects every tissue and organ. It is especially powerful against natural and man-made oxidants. It helps detoxify the liver and protects the integrity of red blood cells. It has been shown to deactivate at least thirty cancer-causing substances![9] It works synergistically in the body with vitamin C and selenium. Glutamine is an amino acid, available as a supplement, that helps boost blood levels of glutathione.

POWERFUL ANTIOXIDANTS

Thousands of research articles have been published in medical and nutritional literature on the value of these antioxidants. Below is a brief summary of potential benefits and sources.

- **Vitamin A**: Infection fighting; helps repair damage to the linings of respiratory, digestive, and urogenital tracts; helps protect against cancer (especially in an elderly person).
  Source: Fish liver oil (cod liver oil).
  Normal Dosage: 7,500 IU daily in the form of fish oil. Toxicity is uncommon at doses less than 100,000 IU daily (any symptoms of toxicity declined within a short time after discontinuing use). The human liver stores up to one million IUs of vitamin A.[10]

- **Beta-Carotene (a form of vitamin A)**: Limits oxidation-type reactions; neutralizes free radicals inside the cell; protects lipoproteins from oxidation.
  Sources: Carrots, spinach, kale, tomatoes, papaya, apricots, melons, sweet potatoes.
  Normal Dosage for Vitamin A and Beta-Carotene: 20,000–50,000 IUs daily. I recommend a formula

that has a balanced mixture of vitamin A (retinal) and beta-carotene.

Carotenoids

- **Lycopene:** Reduces risk of some cancers and cardio-vascular disease.
  Sources: Tomatoes, apricots, pink grapefruit, guava, watermelon.
- **Lutein (zeaxanthin):** Prevents age-related macular degeneration.
  Sources: Spinach, broccoli, kale, collard and mustard greens, hot chilies.
- **Alpha-Carotene:** Inhibits production of cancerous skin, liver, and lung cells.
  Sources: Pumpkin, cantaloupe, carrots, corn, yellow and red peppers.
- **Cryptoxanthin:** High levels seem to reduce cervical cancer risk.
  Sources: Peaches, tangerines, papaya, nectarines, oranges.
- **Bioflavonoids:** Decreases risk of some cancers; decreases risk of cardiovascular disease.
  Sources: Most fruit (grapes, plums, apples, cherries, white rind of citrus fruit), onions, buckwheat.
  Normal Dosage for Lycopene, Lutein, Alpha-Carotene, Crypotaxanthin and Bioflavonoids: 7,500 IU in form of fish oil.[11]
- **Vitamin C:** Fights viruses; helps in synthesis,

formation, and maintenance of collagen (skin and muscle tone); fights infections and inflammation; preventive and life-extending effects in some cancers.

Sources: Citrus fruits

Normal Dosage: The older we grow, the less able we are to store and use vitamin C. Thus, we need even more vitamin C. Up to 10,000 mg/day for those with disease; 3000 to 6000 mg/day for those who are healthy. Take in divided dosages. Suggestion: start with 1000 mg/day and increase dosage by 500 mg until you experience soft stools and mild diarrhea. Then cut back to previous level. That is likely your optimal need level.[12]

- **Pycnogenols (grape seed extract and red wine extract)**: Helps lower cholesterol; helps with vascular disorders; helps prevent hardening of arteries; protective effects against heart disease, cancer, arthritis, non-germ diseases associated with free radicals.

  Sources: Dark grape juice and red wine; maritime (Landes) pine bark

  Normal Dosage: Available in a number of products, most nutritionists recommend 1 mg per pound of body weight (150-pound person would take three 50-mg capsules).[13]

- **Vitamin E**: Both immuno-protective and immuno-stimulating; blocks negative prostaglandins that slow immune system; protects cell membranes against viruses; anticancer properties.

Sources: Wheat germ oil, soybean oil, safflower oil, whole grains (wheat, oats, rice), peanuts, leafy green vegetables, eggs, cabbage, asparagus, spinach, broccoli.

Normal Dosage: 400 IU daily for women; 800 IU daily for men. Make sure vitamin E is from natural d-alpha tocopherols. If you have high blood pressure, are using anticoagulation drugs, or take medications for blood pressure control, consult a physician before taking more than 800 IUs due to vitamin E's blood-thinning properties.

- **Selenium**: Reduces risk of some cancers; enhances effects of vitamin E; protects against coronary artery disease, strokes, and heart attacks.

  Sources: Fish, liver, garlic, asparagus, mushrooms, Brazil nuts, brewer's yeast, fresh garlic.

  Normal Dosage: 200–400 mcg (micrograms, not milligrams) daily.[14]

- **Zinc**: Promotes T-cell immunity; antibacterial activity; helps in production of DNA and RNA; promotes wound healing; helps infertility and prostate problems; helps prevent hair loss; helps with macular degeneration.

  Sources: Herring, wheat germ, pumpkin seeds, milk, chicken, turkey, lean ground beef, liver, eggs.

  Normal Dosage: 30–50 mg daily. Be sure to use a

formula balanced with copper (zinc:copper ratio of 10:1)

- **Lipoic Acid** *(alpha-lipoic acid)*: Helps improve blood flow to nerve tissues; improves glucose use in the brain; helps normalize blood sugar levels; helps boost energy; protects liver; detoxifies tissues.
  Sources: Red meat, potatoes.
  Normal Dosage: 20–50 mg daily. Diabetics have been treated with dosages up to 300–600 mg daily for neuropathy. Not recommended for pregnant women.

- **CoQ$_{10}$ (Coenzyme Q$_{10}$)**: Cancer-protective and cancer treatment properties; boosts immunity antibodies; protects brain tissue.
  Sources: Supplement form only.
  Normal Dosage: 30–60 mg daily for healthy people. Some recommend 90–120 mg for those who have heart problems.

- **Glutathione**: Protects against cancer; helps sustain rejuvenated immunity; helps cholesterol from becoming toxic; helps with Type 2 diabetes; helps prevent macular degeneration.
  Sources: Whole fruits and vegetables; walnuts, orange juice, raw avocado, acorn squash, asparagus, grapefruit, watermelon
  Normal Dosage: 2000–8000 mg daily. Doses up to 40,000 mg have been used in studies with no noticeable adverse effects. Glutamine works

synergistically in the body with vitamin C and selenium.[15]

REMEMBER: The processing of vitamin supplements greatly affects their potency and effectiveness. There is no such thing as a "cheap, good vitamin." I do not recommend products such as One-a-Day, Flintstones, etc. In my opinion, 90 percent of the vitamins sold today are an ineffective waste of money. If you would like information on top-quality supplements by brand name, which are the ones I use, call my office at 1-800-726-1834.

HERBS ALSO HAVE ANTIOXIDANT PROPERTIES

A number of herbs also have excellent antioxidant properties and have been shown to help build immunity. These include the following:

- Astragalus (*Astragalus membranaceus*): Commonly used in traditional Chinese medicine as an immunity stimulant, this herb is called an adaptogen because it helps cells in need, especially cells that have been subjected to chemotherapy and radiation.[16]

- Echinacea (*Echinacea angustifolia and purpurea*): This powerful herb appears to kill bacteria, viruses, and other infectious agents, as well as some cancer cells. It has interferon-like properties. It also has anti-inflammatory properties with no reported cases of toxicity. It is best to not use echinacea all the time; however, since it seems to work best if you alternate one or two weeks of echinacea with one or two week without it. I generally don't take echinacea unless I am feeling run down or have been exposed to someone who is sick.

- Golden Seal (*Hydrastis Canadensis*): This herb soothes mucous membranes of the respiratory, digestive, and genitor-urinary tracts. It helps promote against bacteria, protozoa, and some fungi. It helps inflammation of the gallbladder and stimulates secretion of bile. It is nontoxic, but it should not be taken by pregnant women or for long periods of time. Golden Seal seems especially potent when combined with echinacea.

- Cat's Claw (*Uncaria tomentosa*): Preliminary research has shown this herb to be beneficial in the treatment of cancer, arthritis, bursitis, rheumatism, genital herpes, allergies, ulcers, systemic candidasis, PMS, toxic poisoning, and numerous bowel and intestinal disorders. Found high in the Peruvian rain forest, Cat's Claw has been used for hundreds, perhaps thousands of years. Many are beginning to see it as a major cleansing agent. Very often, the intestinal tract needs to be cleansed before genuine healing can occur, and Cat's Claw can be very helpful with this cleansing.[17]

- Garlic: Germs don't seem to be able to live in the presence of garlic.

- Milk Thistle (*Silybum Marianum*): This herb is

particularly helpful against liver toxins, especially those that seem to be alcohol induced, as well as chronic hepatitis, chemically induced fatty liver disorders, cirrhosis or hardening of the liver, hepatic organ damage, and psoriasis.[18]

OUR NEED FOR MINERALS

Many people think of minerals as being related only to the health of bones and teeth. In fact, minerals are important to the proper function of the brain and heart, as well as to the muscles and the nervous system. Minerals are found in all soft tissues and in blood.

Minerals are vital to the production of enzymes and hormones, the creation of antibodies, and in keeping the blood and tissue fluids at the right pH (not too alkaline and not too acidic).

Some minerals have electrical charges that act as something of a magnet to attract other electrically charged substances to form complex molecules, conduct impulses along nerve pathways, regulate the fluid pressure between cells and blood, or to transport substances in and out of cells. These minerals include sodium, potassium, and calcium.

Even though minerals are found in soil and water, they cannot be assimilated in that form. In fact, high concentrations of some minerals dissolved in drinking water are sometimes harmful to the body. Plants convert inorganic minerals into organic substances often called second-stage organic materials. We human beings then eat and are able to assimilate the minerals that have been absorbed and converted by the plants. Soil that has been depleted of many of its minerals does not produce nutritionally rich foods, so it helps to know where your vegetables and fruits were grown.

Minerals not only help the structural components of the body, but they also serve as catalysts that help regulate other bodily processes. In this regard, they are similar to enzymes.

Throughout history, minerals have been used to treat anemia, dermatitis and other skin diseases, epilepsy and other convulsive disorders, tooth problems, premature gray hair, rickets, parasitic infections, stomach problems, diphtheria, rheumatism, muscle pains, burns, pleurisy, insanity, yellow fever, tuberculosis, and varicose veins. Some minerals have even been administered through the years to help those who are suicidal, as well as those who have engaged in criminal behavior, including homicide!

The big seven among minerals include the following:

- calcium
- chloride
- magnesium
- phosphorus
- potassium
- sodium
- sulfur

There are also essential minor minerals, called trace elements or micronutrients, that are found in the body in smaller amounts. These include boron, cobalt, copper, chromium, iodine, iron, manganese, molybdenum, selenium, and vanadium.

In some cases, too much of a trace element or mineral that exists naturally in the body can also be toxic, as with gold, silver, nickel, tin, arsenic, barium, bromine, and cadmium.

Mineral Deficiencies

The majority of Americans have a great deficiency when it comes to ingesting minerals that are vital for health. The percentages of those who do not take even the barest of minimum recommended amounts is staggering:

- calcium—68 percent of us do not get enough
- magnesium—75 percent
- manganese—50 percent
- copper—81 percent
- iron—58 percent
- zinc—68 percent

In general, mineral deficiencies occur more often than vitamin deficiences. Those who seem especially at risk for mineral deficiencies include the following:

- those who eat low-calorie diets
- pregnant women

- elderly men and women
- vegetarians
- those who take certain drugs (including diuretics)
- those who live in areas where the soil has been especially depleted of certain minerals

Minerals work in balance with other minerals. A large intake of one mineral can actually produce a deficiency of other minerals. This is especially true for trace minerals such as iron, zinc, and copper, and these need to be taken in balanced formulas. The same is true for calcium, magnesium, and phosphorus, which work well as a team.

Colloidal mineral supplements are best. Colloidal minerals are those provided by plant sources. They are 98 percent absorbable by the human body. These minerals and trace elements from plants are at least ten times more absorbable than metallic minerals because they are seven thousand times smaller than our red blood cells. And they are negatively charged, so they have a natural attraction to the intestinal lining, which is positively charged.

MINERAL RESEARCH CONTINUES

One thing we know with certainty in the nutritional and scientific world is that we are just beginning to understand our need for trace minerals. Much remains to be learned. It is also very likely that we haven't discovered all of the trace minerals yet!

Let me give one example of our need for continued

research. Indium (element 49 on the periodic table) was relatively recently discovered. It was patented for nutritional use in 1980, with a patent update in 1999. It appears to work primarily by helping the body to absorb and use more of the other health-beneficial trace minerals that would be absorbed and used otherwise.

A homeopathic remedy called indium metallicum has been used for nearly seventy years for a variety of problems, from migraines to headaches, acne, mouth sores, sore throats, neck and shoulder stiffness, muscle pain, and backache.[19]

Back in the 1970s, Dr. Henry Schroeder found that indium supplementation caused a lower incidence of tumors.[20] In fact, indium caused a lower incidence of cancerous tumors 40 percent of the time! Other studies noted that indium seemed to inhibit the growth of human cervical malignant carcinoma, neuroendocrine tumors, pancreatic tumors, and even bone cancer tumors.

One researcher sorted through volumes of data and found that subjects taking indium had 22 percent less cancer and 46 percent fewer malignant tumors than non-indium users.[21] This researcher discovered more than forty reported benefits from indium.

Note carefully that indium did not cure these cancers, but rather it was useful in inhibiting the growth of cancerous tumors. It also significantly helped many of the cancer patients with the pain they experienced as a result of their cancers.

Indium also seems to be useful in lowering body weight. Even back in the 1970s, researchers noticed that at the lowest levels of supplementation, weight loss and/ or lack of weight gain was noticed.[22] This was especially true for women. In his 1971 study, Dr. Schroeder found that women who gained weight did not add any fat as part of that weight, but women who did not use indium added 20 percent of their weight as fat. Men who used indium maintained more muscle mass that is normally lost to age-related declines in growth hormone.[23] The weight-related effects of indium appear to be the result of indium's beneficial effect on the thyroid gland.

Is it safe? The Food and Drug Administration has since indicated that it would take twenty thousand times more than that used for nutritional purposes to cause indium to be toxic in the body. In other words, it would take twenty full bottles of indium preparations to achieve an overdose level.

When combined with chromium, indium supplementation seems very effective in helping to lower blood pressure. Indium has also been shown to be helpful in controlling eyeball pressure as well as inflammatory opthalmopathy (which is related to Grave's disease and thyroid eye disease). It has also been helping in controlling Type 2 diabetes.

The only people who have not shown significant general health and psychological improvement are Type 1 diabetics, those over age fifty who have serious mineral deficiencies and a variety of health problems, young people who do not yet have any decrease in hormone output, and people with a highly weakened immune system.

Those who take indium need to have a source of iodine in their diet. Iodized sea salt can supply this.

EIGHT CRITICAL SUPPLEMENT RECOMMENDATIONS

This chapter has given you the basics for what will hopefully be a lifelong search for the perfect combination of vitamins, minerals, and herbs for your body. To get started, let me recommend the following:

1. **Take a multiple vitamin every day.** I am partial to Health Masters Ultimate Multiple. This is an easily absorbed, biologically assimilated multiple vitamin that everyone can use. I believe this is the best multiple vitamin on the planet, period! If you want a product that will make you feel better and feed your cells, this is it. From personal experience, I know that you will feel better in thirty days.

   I always try to provide people with the best products possible. They are the same products that my family and I use every day.

   Remember these facts: never use tablet vitamins if at all possible. There is so much glue and heat used in producing these products it is literally impossible for your body to break them down. They go right through your body unused. Also, don't use gelatin capsules. Use only cellulose fiber capsules. Gelatin capsules are probably a pork by-product. Less than 1 percent of all products use cellulose fiber capsules because of the cost. They are much more expensive than tablets or gelatin capsules. All of my Health Masters products use only cellulose capsules.

Plus, my multiple vitamin uses only activated B vitamins. Most cheap vitamins use cyancobal amine. This is a cyanide B_{12} vitamin and is very toxic. The body cannot use it. It is poison. Our B_{12} is methyl cobal amine, which is highly absorbable. A lot of times cheap products will list their B_{12} as cobal amine. They won't tell you whether it's methyl cobal amine or cyancobal amine. Guess why? It's because they use the cheap cyancobal amine, and they don't want you to know this.

2. **Take at least a teaspoon of cod liver oil.** Our Cod Liver Oil—Blue Ice Pure is produced in Norway to our exact specifications. The cod is seasonally fished and exclusively harvested from the icy blue waters of the Arctic Ocean to ensure a premium quality, natural high vitamin cod liver oil.

3. **Take a vitamin formulated specifically for your memory and brain.** Ours is Health Masters Memory Support. It is a nutrient and botanical blend for optimum cognitive function and memory enhancement.

4. **Take vitamin E.** I am partial to Health Masters

Super Potent E. This is a mixed tocopherol product, which is high in gamma E. This is the most potent E to protect against LDL cholesterol (the bad one) breakdown.

When you oxidize or breakdown LDL cholesterol, it is like turning little razor blades loose in your arteries. This oxidized LDL cholesterol actually creates lesions (little cuts) in the blood vessels. These little cuts then form scars, which can cause blockages in the arteries, heart disease, and heart attacks.

I recommend 1600 IU for men and 800 IU for women daily. I have been taking 1600 IU for twenty-five years.

In case you are worried about the study from several years ago that concluded vitamin E was bad for you, you should know that the study used chemically produced, cheap, synthetic vitamin E. By contrast, no study has ever shown that natural-mixed tocopherol E (such as we use in Health Masters Super Potent E) does anything but good. Best of all, it helps to boost brain power.

5. **Take magnesium and malate acid**. Our brand features Health Masters Magnesium and Malate Acid. These are natural muscle relaxants, which help to lower blood pressure. We use patented Albion chelate minerals, which are absorbed by the body as food.

Remember that metallic minerals are rock and are absorbed very poorly by the body. Magnesium also helps to lower blood pressure and allows more oxygen to be delivered to the brain and heart.

6. **Use a supplement that boosts your immune system.** Our product is Health Masters Ultimate Immune Booster. This one is important since xeno-estrogens cause cancer. They come from chemicals and pesticides in our environment. They get into our liver and become carcinogens.

   Our immunity booster has been clinically proven to reverse and neutralize environmental carcinogens. It has also been shown to kill lung cancer cells in vitro. This is one of the only substances known to man that is not toxic and will kill lung cancer cells (our product is made from broccoli). It has five U.S. patents from Johns Hopkins University. Always remember, cancer is a continuum, the cells are always forming. This product is incredible for your lungs, colon, breast tissue, and ultimately your brain!

7. **Take vitamin C.** Ours is Health Masters Excellent C, a functional vitamin C formula. It has an added 7.5 mg of BioPerine per capsule. BioPerine is a proprietary, patented piperine extract that has been shown in clinical studies to increase the bioavailability of vitamin C by up to 40 percent.

Vitamin C provides valuable antioxidant protection and supports the production of collagen and healthy connective tissue. Excellent C is buffered to help prevent potential stomach upset often found with high dietary ascorbic acid intake.

8. **Add a vitamin B complex supplement.** Ours is called Health Masters B Complex. This supplement supplies significant amounts of water-soluble B vitamins.

A vitamin B complex is important for the support of the adrenal hormone production, regulation, and the body's own production of energy through its enhancement of coenzyme A production. Activated B vitamins are utilized in the finest formulas like ours for optimal effectiveness.

All of these high quality supplements can also be purchased by calling my office at 1-800-726-1834 or ordering online at www.HealthMasters.com.

Safeguard yourself and your loved ones by building your health with supplements!

13

Don't Use Soy!

Does soy turn little boys into little girls? Here is the shocking truth. This information may totally change your health and your family's health. Be prepared for an awakening unlike any you have ever experienced concerning your food and this ingredient. A further warning: this chapter will not be politically correct.

I have done over five thousand radio and television talk shows. I have spoken to over a million people at seminars and over the air. I can tell you that I rarely get this emotional about any particular topic, but this one has really disturbs me. The truth about soy needs to be told.

Basic Ingredients

Genistein is the plant estrogen found in soybeans. It is not identical to estrogen in the human body, but it is close enough to fool the body into thinking it is human estrogen. When soy formula is fed to infants, their genistein (phytoestrogen or soyestrogen) levels are twenty times higher than breast milk. However, the estrogen equivalent is much worse than that. This is because the phytoestrogens are only part of the soy problem. If all soy factors are taken into account, the result is worse than a horror show. There are actually fifteen thousand times more of these estrogen-mimicking compounds in soy formula than is in mother's milk or goat's milk formula.

So what does this mean? Well, for starters, a baby who only gets soy formula is getting the equivalent of five birth control pills a day! This is why I will not sell soy protein in my office.

Soy Popularity

It has only been over the last forty years, and particularly the last twenty years, that soy has ended up in approximately 60 percent of our food. Many vegetarians and some religious groups who eat large amounts of soy protein products get very upset with the facts I am now telling you.

We have become a nation obsessed with soy: soy drinks, tofu, soy milk, soy protein, soy burgers, and even soy pet food. Only in the past few years have we begun discovering that soy can sometimes damage the thyroid gland, causing a decrease in energy. Soy can damage the pancreas and cause an increase in diabetes. Soy interferes with calcium absorption. Plus soy formulas use toxic oxidizing omega-6 oils, which interfere with infant brain development.

DIFFERENCES

Here are some more interesting facts concerning babies. Infants need omega-3 fat in high concentration for proper brain development. That is why I recommend the use of goat's milk formula with cod liver oil. (This is explained in my wife Sharon's book, *Train Up a Child in the Way They Should Eat*, which is available online and through at my office at 1-800-726-1834.)

An infant girl and an infant boy have different types of brains. Obviously a little boy has different DNA than that of a little girl. In the first few months of life, little boys undergo a testosterone surge. This is the hormone surge that allows proper secondary sexual characteristics in men.

When you pump this little boy up with the equivalent estrogen of five birth control pills, the testosterone surge may not take place properly. This can cause his brain development to become feminized, and he can develop the brain of a little baby girl. Second, his reproductive organs, including his testicles, may not develop properly and in many cases are undersized. He therefore may not produce sufficient testosterone to obtain proper secondary male sexual characteristics, size, strength, deep voice, facial hair. Plus this hormonal imbalance can lead to gender confusion. This has been widely known in scientific circles for many years.

Soy estrogen can also cause hyperfeminization in girls.

They can develop breasts earlier, perhaps as young as five or six. They can go into puberty as early as nine years of age. This also leads to obesity and increased risks of breast cancer.

These statistics are even worse in the black community, where children in many cases have shown an adverse reaction to cow's milk. A large percentage of black children are put on soy formulas. Possibly this is one reason why black girls have noticeably higher rates (as high as 50 percent) of premature puberty. Even the American Academy of Pediatrics says, "Healthy full-term infants should only be put on soy formulas when medically necessary." However, to date soy formulas are 25 percent of the U.S. infant formula market. That doesn't make sense. Why not use goat milk formula instead!

In addition to other challenges, soy can cause a huge increase in allergies. Plus, the processing of soy products in many cases produces the by-product MSG (monosodium glutamate), which is a neurotoxin that can cause brain damage.

Here are even more specific conditions that can be caused by soy:

- infertility
- delayed puberty in boys
- lowered sperm count
- gynecomastia in men (feminine-looking chest)
- heart disease
- asthma

- digestive problems
- uterine cancer
- allergies
- hypothyroidism
- immune disorders
- diabetes
- childhood leukemia
- calcium deficiencies
- depression
- insomnia
- rheumatoid arthritis
- anemia
- chronic fatigue
- eczema
- cognitive and mental decline
- hair loss
- psychosexual problems
- low blood pressure

BENEFITS?

So why do we keep hearing so many great things about soy and all of the many benefits that are touted. Here is a multipronged reality check:

- Soy does not reduce heart disease.
- Soy does not help with menopause-related symptoms.
- Soy does not lower breast cancer rates.

- Soy does not lower cholesterol.
- Soy does not reduce hot flashes.

We have been told so many half-truths, distorted statistics, and outright lies over the years by manufacturers and marketing experts:

- NutraSweet is safe. (It is not! It is poison.)
- Splenda is safe. (It is not! It is poison.)
- Fluoride toothpaste is safe. (It is not! It is poison. Read the label.)
- Chlorine is safe. (It is not! It is poison.)
- Fluoride water is safe. (It is not! It is poison.)
- Hydrogenated oils are safe. (They are not! They are poison.)
- Shellfish are safe. (They are not! They can be toxic.)
- MSG is safe. (It is not! It is a poison that can destroy brain cells.)
- Pasteurized homogenized milk is good for you. (No, it is actually bad for you.)
- Red wine is safe. (It is not! It can be addictive, plus it increases the risk of pancreatic cancer, breast cancer, cirrhosis of the liver, alcoholism, and osteoporosis.)
- High fructose corn syrup is safe. (It is not! It contributes to obesity.)

Add soy to that list. In fact, countries such as New Zealand, England, France, and Israel are in the process of banning infant soy formula or placing other regulations on its use with babies.

If you were told to use soy formula for your children, don't blame yourself for what has already happened. This is a tragedy of international proportions brought on us by greedy international food corporations. They, however, knew what they were doing.

But now you know. And you should also know that the industries (and the high-powered, well-paid marketing firms they hire to promote their products) are interested in one thing: profit!

Do you remember when a panel of top scientists were called before the U.S. Senate on behalf of the tobacco industry in the 1990s, and how they swore under oath that tobacco and nicotine were not addictive? They were experts and they were persuasive, but they definitely were not telling the truth.

What I have told you is the truth!

HEALTHY ALTERNATIVES

Now, perhaps you are wondering, "If I don't use soy, what is a safe replacement for cow's milk and other sources of protein?"

I like raw, certified, grass-fed, organic, no-hormone cow's milk for children (and even adults) over the age of two. Infants and children younger than two can be given goat's milk. (Again, get a copy of Sharon's book and use the formula in her book.) Also, organic eggs are a great source of protein.

At Health Masters, we offer cold-temperature processed 100 percent New Zealand whey protein that is excellent (Health Masters Fit Food Protein)! It tastes great and is great for you.

These high-quality products can be purchased by calling my office at 1-800-726-1834 or ordering online at www.HealthMasters.com.

Here's to your maximum health!

14

Indulge Without Sinning

When I was a kid and had no knowledge of nutrition, I used to eat Carnation Instant Breakfast. I liked it because it was so convenient and easy to use. I had no idea how horrible it was for me, but the idea, especially the ease of use, has always intrigued me. I guess it was perfectly natural, after dedicating my life to helping people live healthier and longer, to also make it my mission to develop a product that was as easy to use as the instant breakfast product, tasted great, and was actually healthy to use as a breakfast replacement.

So I called my buddy Brian Blackburn, with whom I had worked on several different projects. We both researched like crazy and jointly developed the finest, highest-quality instant breakfast protein supplement on the market today. I call the product Health Masters Fit Food Protein. It's a great food supplement. It comes in both delicious natural chocolate and natural vanilla and fructose-free vanilla. I have learned that if you regularly skip breakfast or chose to eat junk food when you are in a hurry or on the go, then you owe it to yourself and to those you love to have this healthy option that can keep your diet and health on a healthy track.

Treat Yourself to a Great Morning Jump-Start!

Many health experts agree that breakfast is the most important meal of the day, yet millions of people skip breakfast altogether. Or they consider a cup of java and a pastry their breakfast, which is not quite the way to optimize your health. After the fast of eight to ten hours, it is important to supply your body with high-quality food choices to start your day.

One of the most popular ways to use our Fit Food Protein supplement is as a snappy breakfast supplement. You will want to make this part of your no-nonsense breakfast, and here are several quick reasons:

- You can whip up a smart, nutritious drink quickly, and it's portable for those mornings when you're really in a rush.
- This convenience helps to ensure that you and your family don't miss out by skipping the most important meal of the day.
- It gets you out the door quickly each day, fueled

with a high-quality, low-carbohydrate, protein-rich supplement to help meet your protein needs.

- Fit Food Protein supplement supports healthy blood sugar levels with a glycemic index of 23.
- It contains a good balance of vitamins and a great morning jump-start.
- It sustains you for hours, unlike many carb-based cereals, providing you with prolonged energy throughout the morning.
- It makes a convenient and delicious morning smoothie—finally a breakfast supplement beverage without guilt.
- It prevents grabbing unhealthy but convenient fast food and can become your go-to meal supplement when you're rushed, haven't been to the store, or you're feeling less than creative in the kitchen.
- Best of all, Fit Food Protein supplement tastes great!

For the sake of refueling your body with real nutrients in the morning, you can't beat the simplicity and speed of whipping up this protein supplement. You can also add this to state-certified raw milk, kefir, or your favorite yogurt. Or you can mix in some nuts or a tiny bit of fruit for flavor. (Some parents even hide powdered or liquid vitamins, cod liver oil, or other nutrients their kids wouldn't otherwise take in their protein drink, but remember, don't tell the kids!)

From now on, get your day off to a jackrabbit start!

Super Nourishment

Besides the "we've got to get out the door quick" benefit of this product, Fit Food Protein supplement packs a powerful punch on a cell-nourishment level. This is a world-class protein supplement, and here are ten remarkable reasons:

1. It is bioactive. The whey protein concentrate in the Fit Food Whey Protein Supplement comes from New Zealand, known for its highly strict world standards for dairy processing. Guaranteed to be 100 percent pure, this high-biological value, 100 percent New Zealand whey concentrate contains a rich array of essential and nonessential amino acids (including more than five grams of branched-chain amino acids) and high levels of immunoglobulins to support your immune system and intestinal function. The immunoglobulins resist peptic digestion. The immuno stimulatory function of immuno-globulins increases your defenses against bacteria, viruses, and parasites, reduces inflammation, and may reduce the likelihood of allergic reactions. Whey protein is the gold standard of protein for serious athletes. It supports healthy blood pressure, LDL cholesterol, and C-reactive protein levels. By the way, many protein supplements claim to use New Zealand protein, but we have found these products to be only 9 percent New Zealand protein; the rest is junk protein. Sadly, as long as others

include a trace amount of New Zealand protein, they can call it New Zealand protein. We go to the extreme, but we won't settle for less than 100 percent pure New Zealand whey concentrate in our product.

2. Oat fiber and chicory inulin supply six grams of fiber per serving of Health Masters Fit Food Protein supplement. This controls cholesterol and stabilizes blood sugars. Plus it greatly helps with body-cleansing bowel movements. The secret is the oat beta-glucan.

3. Glutamine and glycine, in combination with the cysteine-rich whey protein, promote glutathione synthesis, which helps to combat free radicals. Glutamine, which is crucial in nitrogen metabolism, is important for replenishing amino acid stores especially after exercise or stress. This amino acid aids in intestinal cell proliferation, thereby preserving gut barrier function and intestinal health. Glycine is an inhibitory (calming) neurotransmitter, an important constituent of collagen and a building block for other substances.

4. Taurine, a derivative of sulfur-containing cysteine, helps to grow strong hair and nails and to slow the aging process.

5. Medium-chain triglycerides are a rapidly absorbed, easy metabolized, and quick form of energy.

6. Defeat free radicals with potent antioxidants.

7. Support balanced blood sugar levels.
8. Enhance muscle endurance (great for weight training). It increases lean muscle mass, and it thereby speeds up your metabolism.
9. Aid liver detoxification
10. Support immune function

And Health Masters Fit Food Protein supplement is also 100 percent natural and free of any artificial flavors or sweeteners. That means no chemical hazards and no chemical aftertaste. Chocolate and vanilla flavors contain natural xylitol and fructose sweeteners, which do not impact blood sugar levels.

Accept no substitutes. This is the protein superstar!

WHY WHEY?

The foundational ingredient in our Fit Food Protein supplement is whey protein, considered by many to be protein's superstar and nature's richest source of biologically active protein.

Whey is one of the worlds oldest health foods. In 420 BC, Hippocrates, known as the father of medicine, recommended the health-boosting benefits of whey. Whey is beneficial because the very first protein source you were designed to ingest as a newborn is mother's milk, and the single most important nutritional protein in breast milk is whey protein. In fact, mothers' milk is 70 percent whey.

Whey protein contains all the essential amino acids, plus it boasts the highest protein quality rating among all proteins. It is a complete protein, giving newborns a healthy start in life. From that start, you are designed to build a strong immune system and attain a normal growth pattern.

A 1987 *Immunology Journal* article reports that whey protein supports optimal immune system response by replenishing glutathione (GSH) levels in the blood through its critical precursor, cysteine. Intercellular levels of glutathione and its precursors increase when you eat protein. Then glutathione is stored in your cells for later use.

YOUR BODY'S BEST-KEPT SECRET TO HEALTH AND WELL-BEING

As you have learned by now, antioxidants are very important for a healthy immune function because they neutralize free radical activity. Surprise! Glutathoine (GSH) happens to be your body's best-kept secret in the war against free radicals and aging, and it is a part of our product Fit Food Protein. Glutathione acts as your body's master antioxidant and detoxifier. It is a tri-peptide made up of the amino acids cysteine, glutamine, and glycine. There are higher levels of GSH in non-denatured whey protein like Fit Food Protein than any other protein you could eat. So how does glutathione promote your good health?

- It supports your immune system. Healthier people have higher GSH levels than immune-depressed people. Lymphocytes, cells vital for your immune response, depend on GSH for proper function and replication.

- Glutathione decreases signs of aging. GSH levels drop as you age. Research shows that a tendency toward degenerative diseases and aging are related to the cells' ability to robustly recover from oxidative insult. This ability can be determined by measuring intracellular stores of glutathione.

- It helps to detoxify your liver. Your liver is your body's major detoxifier. High concentrations of GSH locate there to carry on biochemical detoxification. GSH detoxifies pollutants, carcinogens, and poisons, like those found in fuel exhaust and cigarette smoke.

- Glutathione supports good athletic performance. Strong muscular activity generates oxy-radicals, leading to muscle fatigue and reduced athletic performance. GSH neutralizes those radicals and promotes muscular development.

GSH relies on naturally occurring cysteine for its production. Cysteine is scarce in the standard American diet, leading to glutathione deficiencies. Heat and processing denature (destroy) cysteine, so it's important to use a whey powder that uses raw milk with minimal heat processing, like Fit Food Protein.

Keeping the Best Tasting, Healthiest Protein Healthy

As you are likely aware, I am a huge advocate of consuming certified raw milk products and avoiding all pasteurized milk dairy products. Certified raw milk is one of the most profoundly healthy foods you can consume.

Once milk is heated, nutritional breakdown and chemical modification begin. Both of these denature the milk and, by extension, the whey proteins inside. Pasteurizing destroys enzymes, weakens vitamins, denatures or damages fragile milk proteins, destroys vitamin B_{12} and B_6, kills beneficial bacteria, and promotes pathogens. I firmly believe that pasteurized milk is the number-one cause of food allergies in this country and is associated with a broad range of other symptoms.

What's more, once the protein is denatured, the vital protein-bound fats are cut loose. Even today's most expensive whey products—isolates, ion exchange concentrates, and hydrolyzed form—are denatured by-products of cheese manufacturing that fall short of preserving the biological activity of the whey proteins. These damaged proteins leave just a slim range of proteins to contribute to your health.

Fit Food Protein never uses cross-flow filtration, microfiltration, hydrolyzation, ion exchange, or any process that could denature the original proteins as found in pure raw milk.

Fit Food Protein is a customized, non-denatured, whey protein powder. It undergoes a unique pasteurization process to keep the full range of the fragile immune balancing and restoring components of fresh raw milk. It's never heated above 85°F.

Fit Food Protein is an exceptional-quality, natural whey protein. It took years of work to perfect the proprietary filtration and drying methods to lessen processing and retain critical nutrients. Some vendors of whey powders will tell you that processing methods don't matter. That is simply not true, due to the negative impact of heat and filtering. I want you to have access to every bit of protein available in the same natural, life-supporting form that exists in nature.

How Could You Possibly Go Wrong with All These Benefits from Whey Protein?

My commitment to providing you with the finest quality whey protein—without stripping it down via heat and processing—means you get all the powerful and important benefits from natural whey. How about these ways to help your well-being?

- Lactoferrin enhances iron absorption when needed and also supports immune health and optimal inflammation levels.
- Immunoglobulins provide numerous immune system benefits.

- Bovine serum albumin—along with lactoferrin and immunoglobulins—contains generous amount of cysteine and glutamine (necessary for glutathione production).
- Covalent-bonded cysteine is the critical precursor of the intracellular production of glutathione (GSH), your master antioxidant and detoxifier.
- Active peptide gives specialized, paired amino acids that display a helpful information transfer factor effect on the immune system. These also boost glutathione.
- Growth factors (growth-promoting protein fractions) help regenerate aged or injured cells, build and retain muscle, process energy efficiently, and support healthy blood sugar and brain chemicals.

WHY DOES IT MATTER WHAT THE COWS EAT?

You may be trying to use as much natural, pesticide-free food as possible. And I would encourage you to do so. That's why I'm especially pleased to be able to offer you Fit Food Protein, because it delivers that also.

The milk used in Fit Food Protein is 100 percent New Zealand protein that comes only from cows that graze on pesticide-free, chemical-free, natural grass pastures. These cows are never subjected to chemicals, hormones, antibiotics, genetically modified organisms, hyper-immunizations, injected pathogens, or any bovine growth hormones. This gives you peace of mind in addition to wellness. Plus, these cows are not from factory farms that feed their cows grains. Grain feeding can transform healthy milk proteins into allergens and carcinogens, which are caused by modern feeding methods that substitute high-protein, soy-based feeds for fresh green grass.

Grass-fed cow's milk has excellent levels of conjugated linoleic acid (CLA), which is transferred to you in the whey powder. CLA may be one of the most potent antioxidant substances in your diet. Additionally, it supports healthy weight, normal immune function, and helps promote normal insulin and cholesterol levels. Studies show that pasture-fed milking cows have 500 percent more CLA in their milk than cows fed silage.

Fit Food Protein, via grass-fed milking cows, provides you with a terrific source of CLA. This is good for you, because CLA can't be produced by your body. Instead, you must get it through foods like whole milk, butter, beef, and lamb.

But there's more to Fit Food Protein than just high-quality protein, lots more.

Only the Highest-Quality Minerals Are Used

While vitamins often take the spotlight in any discussion about dietary supplements, minerals are a vital part of Fit Food Protein. Most important, the minerals in Fit Food Protein are naturally chelated. Chelating is the process of binding the mineral ion by special bonds to one or two amino acids. Structurally, it works similar to two crab claws bound together, hence, *chelate* from the Greek word *chele*, meaning "claw."

From chelation, a mineral protein molecule complex is formed that:

- survives the acidity of the stomach and is nonionizing (like a mineral salt)
- readily assimilates into the intestine because of its neutral charge
- absorbs intact through your intestines due to its small molecule weight

But here is the catch: many manufacturers try to chelate minerals by simply mixing amino acids with minerals in a dry, powdered form. This does not allow the necessary covalent bonds to form, so it really isn't a chelate per the National Nutritional Foods Association's definition of a chelate.

Fit Food Protein uses chelated minerals from Albion, the top producers of high-quality minerals in the world. Look for the Albion logo or patent numbers on supplement bottles to be sure you are getting genuine chelated minerals. Albion's chelating process is so advanced, effective, and unique that it is patented. And the holder of the patent wrote a whole textbook on mineral absorption. When it comes to mineral supplements, they know what they are doing.

You not only get protein from the whey, you also get its synergistic impact from a link with chelated minerals for a blast of nutritional value.

Making Fit Food Protein Taste Delicious in Two Great Flavors

It would be one thing to take Fit Food Protein because it is quick and easy and provides a great protein supplement for your best health. But I know you probably wouldn't drink it if the taste wasn't good, even if you knew it was good for you.

Not to worry, though. Fit Food Protein is available in two of your favorite flavors and is, in fact, very tasty. What is not to like? You can enjoy it as a stand-alone beverage or dressed up a bit. Here are some ways people like to enjoy their Fit Food Protein:

- Vanilla is a great base for any fruit shake, creamy and smooth.
- Enjoy the smooth taste in breakfast almond strawberry drinks.
- The fructose-free vanilla is great for those wanting to reduce calories.
- Mix the powder with certified raw milk and farm fresh eggs with a pinch of banana, ten blueberries or three strawberries and enjoy.
- Put the Fit Food Protein in everything: pancake mix, smoothies...

- Feel free to experiment to discover your own favorite ways to enjoy Fit Food Protein.

Please realize that I am a huge advocate of controlling your blood sugar levels through diet. Adding more than a tiny amount of fruit to your Fit Food Protein can compromise your healthy blood sugar levels. So be conservative when piggybacking fruit into your Fit Food Protein drink.

MORE ENERGY FOR TODAY'S BUSY LIFESTYLE

Besides being quick, easy, tasty, and the world's most phenomenal source of protein, Fit Food Protein offers increased energy levels. Many of our customers tell us they like it for the sustained energy it gives them over a period of time. You can use it as an energy boost after working out, rebuilding your muscles after taxing them. Or feel satisfied longer, between meals, than with a carb-type meal.

Anyway you slice it, Fit Food Protein enhances your energy levels. What's more, with Fit Food Protein you get the peace of mind that you are taking a healthy protein supplement, even when life is hectic and crazy. Make it your go-to breakfast-time protein drink, postworkout snack, midmorning or midafternoon pick-me-up, or use any time life's demands have you running around. That's certainly not the time you should skimp on nutrients. Keep yourself healthy and fit for all the demands your lifestyle makes on you. After all, you don't want life to pass you by or to not feel you're at your peak.

Five Great Reasons to Use Fit Food Protein

1. **Convenience**: It fits easily into your busy lifestyle.
2. **Nutrition**: It is an exclusive, biologically active, 100 percent New Zealand whey protein that enhances your health and immune system.
3. **Taste**: Fit Food Protein is available in three scrumptious flavors for your enjoyment. It is never grainy or bitter.
4. **Energy**: It helps you maintain long-lasting, stabilized glucose levels so you can accomplish more.
5. **Cost**: Other, inferior protein drinks (or junk-food meals) cost more, sometimes much more.

Start Making Healthy Choices Today

When it comes to your health, why compromise by grabbing foods loaded with all kinds of subpar ingredients when you can choose Fit Food Protein and trust its nutritional support. Make a trade in your favor today: trade unhealthy junk-food choices for health-enhancing ones.

Take a can of Fit Food Protein and a shaker to the office to have on hand for a midmorning or midafternoon pick-me-up. Or use it to stave off hunger on days when you work late or stop at the gym on the way home. Your body and your energy levels will thank you many times over.

Discover today how to optimize your
I use it every day. I love it. My wife, Share
the kids ask for it every day. This is the best
supplement you have tasted. Try it today.

Fit Food Protein can be purchased by calling my office at 1-800-726-1834 or by ordering online at www. HealthMasters.com. My commitment to you is simple: if you are not 100 percent satisfied with your results, you don't need to send it back, just call our office for a full refund.

Indulge without sinning! Safeguard yourself and your loved ones by building your health with Fit Food Protein!

15

FLUSH THE FLUORIDE

Are you poisoning yourself with drugs added to your drinking water? I've already spent chapter 6 dealing with the importance of being water wise. This chapter, while again dealing with the importance of drinking plenty of pure water, puts the spotlight on the poison that literally attacks you every time you open the tap and fill a glass of sparkling, deadly tap water.

Flouride has quite a colorful and somewhat sinister history dating back to 1924. It seems that Interessen Gemeinschaft Farben (I. G. Farben), a German chemical manufacturing company, reportedly received a number of loans from American bankers that gradually led to the creation of the huge I. G. Farben cartel that included several well-known American corporate giants. In 1939, under a special agreement, the American Aluminum Company (Alcoa), then the world's largest producer of sodium fluoride, and the Dow Chemical Company offered that technology to Nazi Germany. Supposedly the German chemists devised a scheme during the war of attempting to control the population in any given area through the mass medication of drinking water with sodium fluoride. This tactic was apparently used in both German and Russian prisoner of war camps to make the prisoners "stupid and docile." The experiments were deemed successful enough to make plans during the war to fluoridate occupied countries, because it was found that fluoridation caused some slight damage to a specific part of the brain, causing the individual to become more passive.[1]

The Nazi Gestapo's reason for mass-medicating water with sodium fluoride was to see if it would sterilize humans and force the inmates in their concentration camps into calm, bovine submission.[2]

It gets even worse.

The following letter was received by the Lee Foundation for Nutritional Research in Milwaukee, Wisconsin, on October 2, 1954, from Charles E. Perkins, a research chemist:

> I have your letter of September 29 asking for further documentation regarding a statement made in my book, *The Truth about Water Fluoridation*, to the effect that the idea of water fluoridation was brought to England from Russia by the Russian Communist Kreminoff. In the 1930's Hitler and the German Nazis envisioned a world to be dominated and controlled by a Nazi philosophy of pan-Germanism. The German chemists worked out a very ingenious and far-reaching plan of mass-control which was

submitted to and adopted by the German General Staff. This plan was to control the population in any given area through mass medication of drinking water supplies. By this method they could control the population in whole areas, reduce population by water medication that would produce sterility in women, and so on. In this scheme of mass-control, sodium fluoride occupied a prominent place.

Repeated doses of infinitesimal amounts of fluoride will in time reduce an individual's power to resist domination, by slowly poisoning and narcotizing a certain area of the brain, thus making him submissive to the will of those who wish to govern him.

The real reason behind water fluoridation is not to benefit children's teeth. If this were the real reason there are many ways in which it could be done that are much easier, cheaper, and far more effective. The real purpose behind water fluoridation is to reduce the resistance of the masses to domination and control and loss of liberty.

When the Nazis under Hitler decided to go to Poland, both the German General Staff and the Russian General Staff exchanged scientific and military ideas, plans, and personnel, and the scheme of mass control through water medication was seized upon by the Russian Communists because it fitted ideally into their plans to communize the world.

I was told of this entire scheme by a German chemist who was an official of the great I.G. Farben chemical industries and was also prominent in the Nazi movement at the time. I say this with all the earnestness and sincerity of a scientist who has spent nearly 20 years' research into the chemistry, biochemistry, physiology and pathology of fluorine—any person who drinks artificially fluorinated water for a period of one year or more will never again be the same person mentally or physically.

Another letter corroborated Charles Perkins's testimony. Dr. E. H. Bronner, a nephew of Albert Einstein, had served time in a prison camp. After the war, he wrote the following letter, which was printed in the *Catholic Mirror* in January 1952:

> It appears that the citizens of Massachusetts are among the "next" on the agenda of the water poisoners. There is a sinister network of subversive agents, Godless intellectual parasites, working in our country today whose ramifications grow more extensive, more successful and more alarming each new year and whose true objective is to demoralize, paralyze and destroy our great Republic—from within if they can, according to their plan—for their own possession.
>
> The tragic success they have already attained in their long siege to destroy the moral fiber of American life is now one of their most potent footholds towards their own ultimate victory over us.
>
> Fluoridation of our community water systems can well become their most subtle weapon for our sure physical and mental deterioration. As a research chemist of established standing, I built within the past 22 years 3 American chemical plants and licensed 6 of my 53 patents. Based on my years of practical experience in the health food and chemical field, let me warn: fluoridation of drinking water is criminal insanity, sure national suicide. DON'T DO IT!!
>
> Even in very small quantities, sodium fluoride is a deadly poison to which no effective antidote has been found. Every exterminator knows that it is the most effective rat-killer. Sodium fluoride is entirely different from organic calcium-fluoro-phosphate needed by our bodies and provided by nature, in God's great providence and love, to build and strengthen our bones and our teeth. This organic calcium-

fluoro-phosphate, derived from proper foods, is an edible organic salt, insoluble in water and assimilable by the human body; whereas the non-organic sodium fluoride used in fluoridating water is instant poison to the body and fully water soluble. The body refuses to assimilate it.

Careful, bonafide laboratory experimentation by conscientious, patriotic research chemists, and actual medical experience, have both revealed that instead of preserving or promoting "dental health," fluoridated drinking water destroys teeth before adulthood and after, by the destructive mottling and other pathological conditions it actually causes in them, and also creates many other very grave pathological conditions in the internal organisms of bodies consuming it. How then can it be called a "health plan"? What's behind it?

That any so-called "Doctors" would persuade a civilized nation to add voluntarily a deadly poison to its drinking water systems is unbelievable. It is the height of criminal insanity!

No wonder Hitler and Stalin fully believed and agreed from 1939 to 1941 that, quoting from both Lenin's *Last Will* and Hitler's *Mein Kampf*: "America we shall demoralize, divide, and destroy from within."

Are our Civil Defense organizations and agencies awake to the perils of water poisoning by fluoridation? Its use has been recorded in other countries. Sodium fluoride water solutions are the cheapest and most effective rat killers known to chemists: colorless, odorless, tasteless; no antidote, no remedy, no hope: Instant and complete extermination of rats.

Fluoridation of water systems can be slow national suicide, or quick national liquidation. It is criminal insanity— treason!

Meanwhile, American education and research on fluoride, once considered a toxic, hazardous waste, continued to be funded by various aluminum, manufacturing, fertilizer, and weapons industries that were seeking to turn increasing amounts of fluoride industrial waste into a profit. Perhaps not too surprisingly, that research culminated in 1939 when Gerald J. Cox, a scientist employed by Alcoa, fluoridated lab rats and "proved" that the fluoride reduced dental cavities and claimed that it should be added to the nation's water supplies.[3]

Also, not surprisingly (considering the fact that in 1947 Oscar R. Ewing, a longtime Alcoa lawyer, was appointed head of the Federal Security Agency, a position that placed him in charge of the Public Health Service), during the late 1940s and early 1950s, most American cities began fluoridating their water, primarily to promote better dental health.[4]

In addition, this product, once considered a hazardous waste, quickly became the active ingredient in many pesticides, fungicides, rodenticides, anesthetics, tranquilizers, and pharmaceuticals, as well as dental gels, rinses, and toothpastes.

Today, it has become a multibillion-dollar industrial and pharmaceutical boon, even though it has been proven to be one of the strongest antipsychotic substances known and is contained in 25 percent of the major tranquilizers. It may not seem surprising that Hitler's regime practiced the concept of mind control through chemical means, but the American military continued the Nazis' research, exploring techniques to incapacitate an enemy or medicate an entire nation, as reported in the 1975 Rockerfeller Commission Report, a presidential briefing on CIA activities.[5]

LOOKING BACK, LOOKING AHEAD

Few survivors of the Nazi concentration camps are still living today—either the prisoners or those who conducted the tests. Therefore, we cannot be sure what happened or the motives involved. However, we can test fluoridated water today, and we do know that it can be poisonous, just as it was in those concentration camps.

What I can't understand is why we still drink fluoride? What does it do to our brain? Is it reversible?

Also, what we do know is that the substance referred to as fluoride is misnamed, since there is nothing like it mentioned in the periodic table. Neither is fluoride mentioned in the CRC handbook or the *Merck Index.*

Instead, there is a gas called fluorine. This gas has been used in various industries, such as aluminum manufacturing and the nuclear industry, and there are toxic by-products, including sodium fluoride. According to the *Merck Index*, and as mentioned earlier, sodium fluoride is primarily used as poison to kill rats and cockroaches. Ironically, sodium fluouride is also the active ingredient in most toothpastes and an additive to drinking water.

Sodium fluoride is also one of the basic ingredients in both Prozac (fluoxetene hydrochloride) and sarin nerve gas (isopropyl-methyl-phosphoryl fluoride). That same sarin nerve gas is what the members of Aum Shinrikyo released on a crowded Japanese subway train on March 20, 1995. It is still referred to in the Japanese media as "the subway sarin incident." In five separate, coordinated attacks, terrorists released sarin on several lines of the Tokyo Metro, killing twelve people, severely injuring fifty, and causing temporary vision problems for nearly a thousand others. This was (and remains) the most serious attack to occur in Japan since the end of World War II.

The American public needs to understand the fact that sodium fluoride is nothing more (or less) than a hazardous waste by-product of the nuclear and aluminum industries. In addition to being the primary ingredient in rat and cockroach poisons, it is also a main ingredient in anesthetic, hypnotic, and psychiatric drugs, as well as military nerve gas!

Why then is it still added to toothpastes and the drinking water of the American people?

It Gets Worse

As mentioned, historically, this substance was quite expensive for the world's premier chemical companies to dispose of, but as the 1950s and 1960s progressed, Alcoa and the entire aluminum industry, with a growing abundance of the toxic waste, somehow sold (and continues selling) the FDA and our government on the insane (albeit vastly profitable) idea of buying this poison at a 20,000 percent markup and then injecting it into our water supply as well as into the nation's toothpastes and dental rinses.

It is important to note that when sodium fluoride is injected into our drinking water, its level is approximately one part per million (ppm). However, since we only drink a small percentage of the total water supply, the hazardous chemical literally goes down the drain. In short, the chemical industry has a free hazardous waste disposal system, paid for by us!

Reports from independent scientists during the past half century have shown that sodium fluoride has many tragic results, including:

- shortening life spans
- promoting various cancers
- contributing to mental disturbances
- causing docility
- leading to subservience

Any scientist who dares to stand up against the widespread use of sodium fluoride or the industry's propaganda campaigns is routinely derided. As a result, when the subject of fluoridation arises, anyone on any level who questions the industry or the argumentatively dubious science behind the use of sodium fluoride is quickly ridiculed as a knuckle-dragging Neanderthal.

Remember that old adage: Follow the money!

Better yet, why not determine to flush the fluoride and sodium chloride poisons while providing your loved ones and yourself with plenty of pure water.

The Answer

In chapter 6 I detailed how to obtain pure water for your family. I won't go through all the points again. Hopefully, however, this chapter gives an even more urgent reason for providing plenty of nonpoisonous water for you and your loved ones.

What I am recommending is exactly what my family uses: the Health Masters Water Distiller Model 8800. Let me detail to you what my criteria are when evaluating a distiller:

1. It has to be easy to use. If it is complicated, I am not interested. I get aggravated when I use my DVD player. So if it's a hassle, I'm not signing up. Our distiller is simple to use: just fill it up with tap water and push start. It automatically turns off when the cycle is done. It couldn't be easier. And what a wonderful feeling it is to know what those simple steps can mean for you and your family!

2. It must be a good investment. If you want to spend a hundred dollars on a filter, that is exactly what you will get: a cheap product that is useless. Why waste your money? It's like buying something

you know you don't want because it's cheaper than something you want. All that will do is frustrate you. You'll always be thinking, *Why didn't I just wait and buy what I wanted?* Also, when you look at your long-term health investment, a water purifier is a great investment for you and your family. It only costs about twenty-five cents per gallon for pure water using the Health Masters Water Distiller Model 8800. If you're buying bottled water at over a dollar (or more) per gallon and you use thirty gallons a week, that's over two thousand dollars per year, which is over five times the one-time cost of a distiller that will last for many, many years.

3. It must produce plenty of pure water. This incredible unit can make up to six gallons a day of the purest water possible. One of the first things that friends do when they come over to our house is to ask for a glass of water. Our four children drink water constantly. The reason most kids don't drink water is because it tastes bad. Tap water tastes horrible! My college-age son even brings his water jugs home on the weekend so he can have great tasting, healthy water to drink. This unit even comes with a one-gallon Lexan polycarbonate collector bottle that is the highest quality plastic in the industry. I mentioned in chapter 6 that storing water in cheap plastic doesn't work well, because contaminants leach into the water.

4. It must be easy to maintain and clean. Every so often, because of the scale that builds up in the boiling tank, it will be necessary to clean the tank. This is a very easy process, and you can use some vinegar for very hard water. I use Health Masters Kleanwise Cleaner. Kleanwise is a biodegradable, phosphate-free product that dissolves scale without scrubbing. Also the boil tank is made from high-quality stainless steel to ensure many years of excellent service.

5. It must provide postfiltration protection. Sometimes water quality is so bad that organic chemicals can convert into gas when boiled. However, the Health Masters Water Distiller Model 8800 uses a coconut-shell carbon filter, which removes any gases that may form. After the steam has been converted into water, this is the final treatment. The coconut-shell carbon is the highest grade available. Many other types of carbon filters add silver, which can recontaminate your water.

6. It must have an ironclad guarantee. I have known the manufacturer of our distillation systems for twenty years. He and his wife actually came to me for nutritional counseling back in the 1980s. This man practices what he preaches. His commitment to you is simple: each unit comes with a one-year warranty and a one-hundred-day money-back guarantee. Missionaries and science labs all over the

world use these distillers. In fact, the Peace Corps uses these distillers. If the Peace Corps trusts our distillers to purify sewage-, bacteria-, and disease-ridden water to get crystal-clear drinking water, I'm sure it can do an incredible job on your tap water, no matter where you live.

Recently in Polk County, Florida, where I live, three hurricanes hit us within six weeks. I have a backup generator, which easily runs my distiller. Had I not had a distiller, I would not have had purified water to drink. We lost our power for over a week. So when it comes to disaster preparedness, enough said!

It seems that every time I pick up the paper, read a magazine, or watch the news, there are articles about the quality of water getting worse and the drugs that are being added to our drinking water. There is simply no better time to invest in a high-quality distiller. I have spent the last twenty years using Health Masters products. I have continued to research and never found anything any better or even close. That is why I use this product for my family. I highly recommend it for you and your family also.

Discover today how to optimize your health each day by getting plenty of pure, nonfluoridated water. I use my distiller every day. You can purchase yours by calling my office at 1-800-726-1834 or by ordering online at www. HealthMasters.com.

16

THREE SECRETS TO BURNING FAT AND CELLULITE

My wife and I have been married for over twenty-five years. We have four children. When I turned fifty, my wife gave me the best birthday party anyone could ever imagine. Passing the half-century mark was actually a very painless and enjoyable experience.

I have begun to realize that aging doesn't have to be a horrible, debilitating experience, which is so regularly seen by the standard medical model. When my mother was in a nursing home, her aging process was horrible. Someone else had power of attorney over my mother, and he allowed my mother to receive drugs that destroyed her memory and finally led to her death. That is the standard medical model.

That experience made me even more committed to read and research as much as possible in order to help people age well. It is my goal to share much of this information with you.

HGH

One of the most exciting breakthroughs on the subject of aging and longevity focuses on the buildup of body fat and cellulite through the reduction of the human growth hormone (HGH).

Perhaps you have heard of it, especially since more and more attention is being focused on it every day. It is a powerful product produced by the body's pituitary gland throughout life. The problem is, as you get older, it declines significantly. HGH is what keeps you young. Many doctors, especially in Hollywood, are injecting HGH into their patients over forty years old with amazing results. It has been clinically shown to increase lean muscle mass, increase bone density, lower body fat, strengthen the immune system, tighten up the skin, and even increase brain function.

Your next question should be, Why isn't everyone injecting this substance? Well, before you sign up for the injections, it is important to mention that there can be serious side effects, including arthritis, gynecomastia in men, enlargement of the forehead, high blood pressure, and increased insulin resistance.

Not appealing?

Well, I do have some good news for you. Seeing the benefits of HGH, yet deploring the possible side effects of the injections, I began doing extensive research on different types of supplements that were supposed to increase

HGH. Most did not, but I finally found a combination of products that have only positive side effects. These results have been incredible. Since I started using this combination of products, my skin has tightened dramatically, my body fat has gone down, my mental acuity has gone up, my workouts have become more intense, and my lean muscle weight and strength have gone through the roof!

And you should see my wife, Sharon. No one believes that she is over fifty. Not only has she experienced all the good results that I have enjoyed, but her cellulite is gone!

It may not be the fountain of youth, but it sure seems close. (Go to www.bodybyted.com to see some recent photos!)

OBSERVATIONS

It is one thing for my wife and me to enjoy these results, but we work out more than most and do everything possible to maximize our health. Therefore, my next step was to try this product using clinical observations. Here's what the people using my formulation have experienced:

- improved memory
- reduced wrinkles
- improved bone density
- lower blood pressure
- increased exercise performance
- lower body fat
- reduction of cellulite among women
- increased energy

I especially remember one young man, Chase, who began using this product. Within several months he lost sixty pounds and dropped eight inches off his waist! I don't have to tell you how excited Chase is about this product. He tells everyone he meets!

HEALTH MASTERS HGH STIMULATE

The research and development was completed several years ago. Now the results continue to speak for themselves. However, let me explain why this product works so well.

One of the key principles of the product is to release nitric oxide into the system. Several years ago the Nobel Prize was awarded to three scientists for demonstrating that nitric oxide relaxes smooth muscle. The smooth muscles are those that work with the arteries in helping to pump blood into the body. This relaxation effect allows for dilation of blood vessels and optimum delivery of oxygen and nutrients to the brain, heart, reproduction organs, other organs, and throughout the body, including the skin. This is also why this product may help to normalize blood pressure. By the way, this product also has an incredible effect for increasing sexual drive in men.

More than eighteen thousand research papers have been published regarding the beneficial effects of nitric oxide to date. Nitric oxide was even declared molecule of the year by the esteemed *Scientific Journal of Science.*

The way our stimulate increases HGH is by using the amino acids arginine and citruline. These amino acids signal the pituitary gland to release HGH. The reason that our Health Masters formula works so well is because all other HGH products that I have researched don't use citruline due to the high cost. If they were to use it, they probably would not list the amount, because only a trace amount would be used to maintain profitability.

We use it because citruline is six times as effective in HGH and nitric oxide production as arginine. Also, because our product is classified as a nutraceutical, we use 2000 mcg of folate to also facilitate HGH production (without folate, the body cannot produce HGH from citruline and arginine). I know of no other product that does this. Plus our manufacturing facility is an FDA drug-registered laboratory.

What all this means is simply that the product does what it is supposed to do, and you can be assured of the highest nutraceutical quality possible.

By the way, one important note, you should never take arginine and citruline by themselves. They are very powerful and must be taken with antioxidants. That is why my formula is balanced with vitamin C and E, as well as quercetin and polyphenols, the most potent antioxidants known.

BENEFITS NOW

When I am talking to my clients, I can tell by this time in the discussion that they want to stop talking about the technical stuff and get it so all the benefits begin.

"How do I get the product?" they usually ask.

Health Masters HGH Stimulate can be purchased by calling my office at 1-800-726-1834 or by ordering online at www.HealthMasters.com. My commitment to you is simple. I have been in business for three decades. If you are not 100 percent satisfied with your results on our HGH Stimulate, just return the product to our office for a full refund.

Judging by the results we have seen—and look no farther than my wife—you will be pleasantly surprised at all the benefits. I look forward to hearing great reports from each of you as you achieve maximum health with Health Masters HGH Stimulate.

17

Drop Over-the-Counter Drugs

It seems that for the past thirty years I have been preaching the same message, a message of hope and health through better nutrition. However, I do realize that my message has been smothered for the most part by the big pharmaceutical companies.

Let's be realistic. Big pharma owns the advertising time on all of the major networks and national newscasts. They spend hundreds of millions of dollars a year convincing the American public that toxic drugs are good. I find it hard to believe that these people can even sleep at night.

Several years ago the news broke that acetaminophen (the most popular brand-name is Tylenol) was toxic to the liver. Imagine that! I have been shouting it from the rooftops for over twenty years. Tylenol shouldn't even be on the market. It's poisonous. Two shots of Jack Daniels and four extra-strength Tylenol, and your liver is toast. You will probably need a liver transplant.

Here is where it gets even more crazy: NyQuil contains both alcohol and Tylenol. Read the label. I am not making this stuff up. The label even warns you about the possibility of serious liver damage.

And these are two examples of a virtual tidal wave of reasons for you to drop those over-the-counter drugs.

How Big Is the Over-the-Counter Problem?

In the United States alone there are more than one hundred thousand over-the-counter (OTC) medicines available to treat everything from an upset stomach to a sprained ankle. Yes, they do offer comfort, but they also come with risks.

More than five hundred thousand Americans end up in hospitals every year because of *unintentional* over-the-counter drug overdoses or reactions. Many of these half-million emergency hospital visits are due to an interaction between over-the-counter remedies and other medications.

Much of the risk relates to a tendency (and desire) for people to assume that over-the-counter medicines are absolutely, positively safe. "If they sell it in the local pharmacy and at Walmart, how dangerous could it be?"

The answer is as close as the print on the over-the-counter bottle. Many, if not all, of these easy-to-buy medicines carry potential side effects. Some of these side effects are very serious. Let me list several that you should avoid, if possible.

Acetaminophen (Tylenol)

Here is a quick look at recent developments concerning the documented negative impact of acetaminophen on the public:

- An FDA panel urges a ban on some prescription acetaminophen drugs.
- FDA advisers seek lower nonprescription doses.
- A U.S. advisory panel calls for greater restrictions on the widely used pain reliever acetaminophen, even recommending the banning of some medications that contain it, in a bid to prevent potentially fatal overdoses.
- An FDA panel of outside experts recommended the agency should take steps to curb the public's exposure to acetaminophen in both over-the-counter and prescription products that include the ingredient.
- Overdoses of acetaminophen have long been known to cause liver failure and even death.

Still, despite the warnings, FDA officials continue to be concerned that consumers are not heeding the warnings. In fact, acetaminophen-containing products had overall sales of $2.6 billion in 2008, according to IMS Health. Nearly 80 percent of that is from combination products sold directly to consumers.

Worse, acetaminophen is also included in more than two hundred over-the-counter cold and flu remedies and other medications. In fact, it has become the most widely used painkiller in the United States. Up to one hundred million Americans take acetaminophen every year.

Is it any wonder why acetaminophen is now the leading cause of acute liver failure in sixteen hundred cases in the United States, according to the Centers for Disease Control and Prevention.

When taken at the highest recommended dose, experts say acetaminophen is generally safe, but they acknowledge that the margin of error is very small.

Avoid it at all costs!

ASPIRIN

Anti-inflammatory painkillers, also known as NSAIDs, which include aspirin and ibuprofen, are known to cause stomach bleeding. The FDA earlier this year called for stronger warnings for both NSAIDS and acetaminophen products to highlight the stomach and liver risks.

Children and teenagers should never be given aspirin, because it could lead to a rare and sometimes fatal illness known as Reye's syndrome (RS). RS can quickly cause life-threatening damage to the liver and brain. It typically occurs in children or teens given aspirin while they are battling a viral illness.

If you notice your child or teen vomiting or having

diarrhea (in toddlers) three to six days after a viral illness, particularly if they've been given aspirin, get to an emergency room immediately.

Again, avoid aspirin at all costs, especially for use by children or teenagers!

Cough and Cold Medicines Containing Dextromethorphan (DXM)

Dextromethorphan (DXM), a synthetically produced ingredient found in many over-the-counter cough and cold remedies, is widely available and has replaced codeine as the most widely used cough suppressant in the United States. In fact, according to a National Youth Anti-Drug media campaign, over half of the over-the-counter drugs on the market (more than 125 products, and that number continues to rise) contain DXM.

The FDA says, "Although DXM, when formulated properly and used in small amounts, can be safely used in cough suppressant medicines, abuse of the drug can cause death as well as other serious adverse events such as brain damage, seizure, loss of consciousness, and irregular heart beat."

Avoid it!

Cough and Cold Medicines for Children

Each year, according to the Centers for Disease Control and Prevention, approximately seven thousand preteen children go to emergency rooms after taking cough and cold medicines. The risks, combined with a lack of evidence proving effectiveness, has led the FDA to recommend that cough and cold remedies not be used by children under the age of six. I believe that warning should apply to all young people.

Avoid these too!

Who Is Regulating the Regulators?

What is wrong with the FDA? They want to regulate vitamins and take your rights away to buy health-giving supplements. That's because the FDA and the drug companies know that high-quality nutraceuticals work. They don't want you to use them. The drug companies realize that treating you with drugs is much more profitable than keeping you healthy.

A few years ago, *60 Minutes* did a program on the revolving door at the FDA. It specifically said that many FDA members, after helping to get toxic drugs passed, left the FDA to work for the toxic drug companies they helped! Unbelievable! No wonder we have seen Washington become more and more corrupt throughout our lifetimes.

What Can I Do?

Aches and pains are a part of life. Taking over-the-counter medicines has become a way of life for too many people. So how can you reduce or completely drop your reliance on over-the-counter drugs?

The best way to reduce your risk of having reaction to a drug is to limit your exposure to it in the first place. This is something that can (and should) be done as a matter of course throughout your life.

In addition to all the other ways of achieving maximum health that I have already shared with you during the course of this book, here are five basics to develop a lifestyle that doesn't need over-the-counter drugs:

1. Drink plenty of pure water. You won't believe how much this simple step will relieve headaches, heal your body faster, and remove your dependence upon medicines.
2. Reduce or completely avoid sugary, carb-, and fat-filled foods. Instead, eat health-building foods.
3. Exercise regularly. Be sure to include stretching, aerobics, and strength training. You will quickly discover higher energy levels and a greater sense of well-being.
4. Keep stress to a minimum.
5. Get plenty of sleep every night.

It is so important and so easy to have proper brain health and good brain chemistry that will help you avoid over-the-counter medications, but there are certain things you need to eliminate from your diet. Avoid the Top Ten Foods Not to Eat (see pages 17–19). And make sure you take the supplements we talked about.

Thirteen Critical Supplements for the Healthy Brain Program

Here are my recommended Health Masters supplements:

1. HGH Stimulate
2. Fit Food Protein
3. Ultimate Multiple
4. Cod Liver Oil—Blue Ice Pure
5. B Complex
6. Norwegian Omega-3
7. Excellent C
8. Cortico B5-B6
9. Zinc Glycinate
10. Super Potent E
11. Memory Support
12. Ultimate D3-5000
13. 5-HTP

If you take all of these products every day, you will need fewer and fewer over-the-counter medications. You will also feel great and have greater energy if you start on this program!

If you have questions, please call us at 1-800-726-1834 or order online at www.HealthMasters.com.

18

GET YOUR DAILY DOSE
OF ESSENTIAL FATS

Fats? A daily dose? How could there be a chapter in a book titled *Maximum Health* that encourages getting your daily dose of fats?

The operative word is "essential." Not all fat is the same. Essential fats are necessary for human health. In fact, every cell in your body depends upon fats for survival and proper function. Your body, especially your brain, is made up of essential fats, and they are responsible for supporting the cardiovascular, reproductive, immune, and nervous systems. In addition, the human body needs essential fatty acids to manufacture and repair cell membranes.

Moreover, the good fats actually help burn the bad ones! Good fats compete with bad fats, so it's important to minimize the intake of trans fats and cholesterol (animal fat) while consuming enough good fats. Also, good fats raise your HDL (good cholesterol). Good fats attack some of the damage already done by the bad fats. This is very important in an age when so many Americans are struggling to get their cholesterol down and fighting heart disease and obesity.

Essential Fatty Acids

Essential fatty acids (EFAs) are necessary fats. Humans cannot make them (although our bodies can manufacture fat for storage from bad fats, such as excess carbohydrates and dietary fat), so EFAs must be obtained through diet. There are two families of EFAs (omega-3 and omega-6). Both are long-chain polyunsaturated fatty acids derived from linolenic acid. There is another fatty acid, omega-9, derived from oleic acid, and although it is necessary, it is not considered an EFA since the body can manufacture modest amounts on its own when essential EFAs are present.

Essential fatty acids are necessary for many specific reasons:

- The human body needs EFAs to manufacture and repair cell membranes, enabling the cells to obtain optimum nutrition and expel harmful waste products.
- A primary function of EFAs is the production of prostaglandins, which regulate body functions such as heart rate, blood pressure, blood clotting, fertility, and conception, as well as play a role in immune function by regulating inflammation and encouraging the body to fight infection.

- EFAs are also needed for proper growth in children, particularly for neural development and maturation of sensory systems, with male children having greater needs than females.
- Fetuses and breast-fed infants also require an adequate supply of EFAs through the mother's dietary intake.

Likewise, a deficiency of EFAs in the body can lead to numerous health conditions, such as:

- skin problems
- impaired vision
- hair loss
- depression
- diabetes and insulin resistance
- obesity
- slow or retarded growth
- learning difficulties, especially among children
- neurobehavioral developmental disorder such as attention deficit hyperactivity disorder (ADHD)
- dyslexia
- slow healing or failure of wounds to heal
- behavioral changes
- schizophrenia
- heart attacks
- stroke
- arthritic conditions
- miscarriages
- cancer

- asthma
- lupus
- accelerated aging
- Alzheimer's disease

EFA deficiency is common in the United States, particularly a deficiency in omega-3. Correcting that deficiency is possible since healthy adult dietary intake for both omega-3 and omega-6 is 1.5 grams of each. Once omega-3 and omega-6 are sufficient, the human body can manufacture modest amounts of omega-9 on its own.

Let's talk about each.

OMEGA-3 (LINOLENIC ACID)

Specifically, alpha linolenic acid (ALA) is the principal omega-3 fatty acid, which a healthy human will convert into eicosapentaenoic acid (EPA) and later into docosahexaenoic acid (DHA). EPA and the gamma linolenic acid (GLA) synthesized from linoleic (omega-6) acid are later converted into hormonelike compounds known as eicosanoids, which aid in many bodily functions, including vital organ function and intracellular activity.

Omega-3s are primarily used in the formation of cell walls, making them supple and flexible, and improving circulation and oxygen uptake with proper red blood cell flexibility and function.

Omega-3 deficiencies are linked to decreased memory and mental abilities, tingling nerve sensations, poor vision, increased tendency to form blood clots, diminished immune function, increased triglycerides and bad cholesterol (LDL) levels, impaired membrane function, hyper-tension, irregular heart beat, learning disorders, menopausal discomfort, itchiness on the front of the lower leg(s), and growth retardation in infants, children, and pregnant women.

Omega-3 is found in these foods:

- flaxseed oil (flaxseed oil has the highest linolenic content of any food)
- flaxseeds
- flaxseed meal
- hempseed oil
- hempseeds
- walnuts
- pumpkin seeds
- Brazil nuts
- sesame seeds
- avocados
- many leafy dark green vegetables (such as spinach, kale, purslane, mustard greens, and collards)
- wheat germ oil
- salmon
- mackerel
- sardines
- anchovies

One tablespoon of flaxseed oil daily by itself can provide the recommended daily adult portion of linolenic acid, although the time-released effects of consuming nuts and other linolenic-rich foods are considered more beneficial than a once-daily oil intake.

Omega-6 (Linoleic Acid)

Linoleic acid is the primary omega-6 fatty acid. A healthy human with good nutrition will convert linoleic acid into gamma linolenic acid (GLA), which will later by synthesized with EPA from the omega-3 group into eicosanoids. Some omega-6s improve diabetic neuropathy, rheumatoid arthritis, PMS, skin disorders (for example, psoriasis and eczema), and aid in cancer treatment.

Although most Americans obtain an excess of linoleic acid, often it is not converted to GLA because of metabolic problems caused by diets rich in sugar, alcohol, or trans fats from processed foods, as well as smoking, pollution, stress, aging, viral infections, and other illnesses such as diabetes. It is best to eliminate these factors when possible, but some prefer to supplement with GLA-rich foods such as borage oil, black currant seed oil, or evening primrose oil.

Omega-6 is found in many foods:

- flaxseed oil
- flaxseeds
- flaxseed meal
- hempseed oil
- hempseeds

- grapeseed oil
- pumpkin seeds
- pine nuts
- pistachio nuts
- sunflower seeds (preferably raw)
- olive oil
- olives
- borage oil
- evening primrose oil
- black currant seed oil
- chestnut oil
- chicken

Don't use corn, safflower, sunflower, soybean, canola, and cottonseed oils. They are nutrient-deficient when sold in many stores. Above all, avoid refined and hydrogenated versions of any of these foods.

OMEGA-9 (OLEIC ACID)

Again, this is necessary to the human body, but it is technically not considered to be an EFA because the human body can manufacture a limited amount, provided essential EFAs are present. Monounsaturated oleic acid lowers heart attack risk and arteriosclerosis and has been found to support cancer prevention.

Omega-9 is found in these foods:

- avocados
- olive oil (preferably extra virgin)

- olives
- almonds
- peanuts
- sesame oil
- pistachio nuts
- cashews
- pecans
- macadamia nuts
- hazelnuts

One to two tablespoons of extra virgin or virgin olive oil per day should provide sufficient omega-9 for adults, but the effects of obtaining these nutrients from nuts and other whole foods is thought to be more beneficial than consuming the entire daily amount via a single oil dose.

Maximizing Your EFAs

High heat, light, and oxygen destroy EFAs, so when consuming foods for their EFA content, try to avoid cooked or heated forms. For example, raw nuts are a better source than roasted nuts. Extra virgin olive oil or grapeseed oil are best to use for cooking oil, as they withstand high heat well. Don't use flaxseed oil for cooking, and never reuse any type of oil.

It is important to replace hydrogenated fats (such as margarine), cholesterol-based fats (butter and other dairy products), and poly-saturated fats (common cooking oils) with healthy EFA-based fats when possible.

Here are a few additional ways to use EFA
in creative ways:

- After every morning's workout, my wife, Sharon, and I mix Health Masters Fit Food Protein, adding a little flaxseed oil (don't use flaxseed oil if you are trying to lose weight). We also take Health Masters Cod Liver Oil in capsule or liquid form. This helps facilitate the burning of bad fats in your body by supplying plenty of EFAs.
- I recommend that you take three to four cod liver oil capsules (or one teaspoon of liquid) with every meal.
- When recipes call for vegetable shortening, replace the shortening with half as much virgin olive oil and a very small pinch of extra salt. You won't believe the tasty and healthy result.
- Sprinkle flaxseed meal on vegetables to add a slightly nutty taste.
- Add flaxseed and virgin olive oil to salads instead of supermarket salad oil.
- Replace oily snack foods (potato chips and corn chips) with nuts and seeds.

Undoubtedly you can find many more creative ways to add EFAs to your diet. For more information, I recommend that you order my wife Sharon's bestselling book, *The Maximum Energy Cookbook*. I also have a muchmore detailed chapter on EFAs in my book *Maximum Energy*.

Essential fats play such an important role in maximum health, but they are only part of an overall program of eliminating excess saturated fat from your daily diet, developing wise dietary habits, drinking plenty of pure water, taking supplements, and exercising consistently.

If you want more information about how to implement a healthy eating program that includes EFAs or if you have questions, call my office at 1-800-726-1834 or go online at www.HealthMasters.com.

19

REDUCE HYPERTENSION

Heart disease, hypertension, and cardiovascular diseases are the leading causes of death in the United States, claiming more than a million lives each year! It is no wonder that we have been hearing more and more about high blood pressure, or hypertension, and its effects on the body over the last few years.

All of us in the health field and most laymen now realize that high blood pressure is almost always a precursor to stroke and heart attack. In fact, hypertension (HTN) is the number-one reason adults visit their physicians, and the treatment of hypertension (HTN) is the single highest use of prescription drugs.

Patient awareness of HTN is on the rise with 85 percent of the adult U.S. population having their blood pressure taken on a regular basis. In this chapter I want to hopefully unlock the mystery of hypertension and explain in detail what HTN is and what to do about it. I pray that this information helps save your life or the life of someone you love.

HYPERTENSION

Blood pressure refers to the pressure your arteries place on the blood flowing through your venous system. Your heart has to overcome any resistance that happens as it pushes blood through your arteries. Think of a garden-variety hose. If the hose is larger than the amount of water flowing through it, there is no problem and no backup. But if the hose is small, the water cannot move through as freely, and there is a back pressure of water going in a reverse direction to the faucet. In the case of your heart, when the vascular resistance increases, the heart must beat harder to overcome this resistance, and there can be a backup of blood, which is the beginning of hypertension.

Over the years, there have been many arguments as to exactly how high does blood pressure have to be in order to be considered high. The 1988 report of the Joint National Committee on Detection, Evaluation and Treatment of High Blood Pressure reported that blood pressure above or equal to 140/90 should be considered high. Now this does not mean that if your blood pressure is 139/89 you are in the clear. Arbitrary cutoffs are necessary because scientists generally have an innate need to classify things.

So, what does 140/90 mean? What is it actually measuring? Let's start with examining the beating cycle of the heart. The heart has two basic phases: systole and diastole. Diastole is when the heart relaxes and fills with blood. This corresponds to the number on the bottom, or in this case, 90. Systole is when the heart squeezes and pumps the blood into the arteries. This corresponds to the number at the top, or 140. So when the blood is being forced through the venous system, the measurement is 140. Between beats the pressure is 90. The numbers refer to how much pressure is required to move water up a standardized glass tube, which is why you may see blood pressure measures as 140/90 mm H_2O.

EFFECTS OF HYPERTENSION

There are several factors that are associated with HTN and the common sequel, or after effects of the disorder. Standard medical texts divide hypertension into two major categories: primary of essential hypertension and secondary hypertension. Up to 94 percent of all hypertension is considered essential or has an unknown etiology or cause. Most likely, essential hypertension arises from a so-called genetic predisposition combined with environmental factors, such as stress, diet, sedentary lifestyle, and pollution. Secondary hypertension is high blood pressure arising as a symptom from a distinct disease process somewhere in the body. The major causes of secondary hypertension are renal (kidney) disease, endocrine (steroid hormones produced by the body), and oral contraceptives.

One of the most important aspects of essential hypertension that medical texts do not teach is that HTN is one of many diseases that is associated with the Western diet. People who live in the remote areas of Asia, the Pacific islands, Central and South America, and Africa do not suffer from HTN. Nor do they experience a rise in blood pressure that is associated with advancing age in the United States. The evidence that diet is actually a more important factor than genetics is demonstrated by the fact that racially identical members of these societies who seem exempt from HTN have a significant increase in the incidence of HTN when they move to a Western culture and adopt a Western diet. It is astounding to realize that in the United States approximately sixty million people suffer from HTN. That is 40 percent of the adult population!

GOOD NEWS!

The good news is that most of these risk factors can be mitigated with simple changes in diet and lifestyle. It has been my experience that the most common denominator of all hypertensive patients I come into contact with is their being overweight. This goes back to the Western diet (high in rich foods and low in fresh fruits and vegetables) and our sedate lifestyle. This is not to say that all people with high blood pressure are overweight, but in my experience the majority are.

One group of scientists has been studying the effects of hypertension at Harvard for over thirty years. The product, called the Framingham Study, clearly demonstrated a direct link between obesity and blood pressure. In subsequent studies of the children of those in the original research, the Framingham Offspring Study, up to 78 percent of HTN in men and 64 percent of HTN in women was directly attributable to obesity. Studies indicate that the distribution of body fat is also an important variable, because blood pressure and triglycerides (blood fats), as well as plasma glucose (blood sugar) levels, are highest in patients with trunk obesity, or obesity with the weight carried around the chest and abdomen. Adults who were obese as children are at particular risk to the ravages of hypertension. This is particularly concerning because of the dramatic rise in childhood obesity.

If you ever wonder if American children eat too much, visit your local mall and look around. It is obvious that we are setting our children up for a lifetime of health problems. In school, one of my professors expressed that if his hypertensive patients would maintain just 120 percent of their ideal body weight, he believed that 70 percent could come off of their hypertensive medications. Using the 1983 metropolitan height and weight table, this means that a medium-framed five-foot-ten-inch male whose ideal body weight is 151 to 163 pounds could weigh from 181 to 196 pounds and still have only minimal increases in blood pressure due to his obesity.

The average five-foot-six-inch woman, whose ideal body weight is 130 to 144 pounds could weigh from 156–173 pounds. The problem is that people do not stop at 120 percent of their ideal body weight. Many keep going and going and going. So the first line of defense in one's personal war against hypertension is weight reduction and institution of a fitness program specifically designed to meet the individual's needs.

This is one of the reasons I developed my Eat, Drink, and Be Healthy! exercise workout. I cannot stress to you enough the importance of exercise. In our sedentary Western culture, it is no longer an option. The videos we developed are designed to give you personal instruction in the privacy of your own home.

My second undergraduate degree from Florida State University is in exercise physiology and psychology. I have over twenty-five years' experience in this field and was a competitive athlete throughout my undergraduate and graduate years. In these tapes, I will teach you how to have maximum results in the shortest period of time possible and how to balance your program with eating and proper lifestyle. For information on this tape series, call my office at 1-800-726-1834. Many people simply do not know where to begin their personal weight reduction and weight maintenance lifestyle. Remember, diets don't work, but the Eat, Drink, and Be Healthy! program is a lifestyle you can live with!

Obesity is but one of the many dietary and environmental factors leading to hypertension. Other factors that correlate with high blood pressure include the ratio of sodium to potassium in one's diet, the percentage of polyunsaturated fats as well as total fats and cholesterol, how much fiber is on one's diet and the amount of simple carbohydrates and sugars.

SODIUM

The role of sodium in the pathogenesis of high blood pressure has been studied extensively and the results are decisive. There is a pressure inside the cell, which maintains the liquid inside and outside the cell in a state of equilibrium. This pressure is maintained by sodium in the cell and potassium outside of the cell. (The actual mechanism is simplified here. A complete discussion of cellular physiology will be available in a later report.) The excessive consumption of sodium in our Western diet produces an influx of water into the cells and causes swelling. This in turn produces an increased pressure around the walls of the arteries.

RISK FACTORS FOR HYPERTENSION

Of the following fifteen risk factors, all except gender and race can actually be reduced or eliminated with lifestyle changes:

1. Male gender
2. Black race

3. Obesity
4. Smoking
5. Hyperglycemia
6. Diabetes Mellitus
7. Family history of HTM
8. Physical inactivity
9. Stress
10. Type A personality
11. Caffeine abuse
12. Alchol consumption
13. Hypercholesterolemia
14. Hyperlipidemia
15. Hypertriglyceridemia

The last three risk factors collectively are referred to as hyperlipoproteinemia, or elevation of bad lipids and cholesterol with decreases in good lipids. These are also amenable to change through modification of lifestyle.

Potassium works outside the cell to offset the effects of the sodium on the inside. The fact that we do not consume sufficient potassium is compounded by the fact that the body does not conserve potassium as it does sodium. Although the body excretes sodium, it maintains more sodium than it does potassium, perhaps because of the levels of sodium we consume.

So if we just cut down on our sodium, will that help reduce our blood pressure? No, unfortunately it is not that easy. You see, it is not the absolute sodium content that is the problem; the problem is the ratio of sodium to potassium. When sodium is far in excess of potassium, susceptible individuals may become hypertensive. Therefore, sodium restriction alone may not reduce blood pressure, but it should be accompanied with potassium supplementation.

Three separate studies confirm the benefits of increasing potassium in the diet. In one study, ten thousand adults had their dietary intake of seventeen nutrients monitored. The results demonstrate an inverse relationship between the amount of potassium consumed and the mean systolic blood pressure.

The *American Journal of Clinical Nutrition* reported a comparison of ninety-eight vegetarians and a matched group of nonvegetarians. The average blood pressure for the vegetarians was 126/77; the non-vegetarians average was 147/88. Both groups had similar sodium intake and excretion, however, the vegetarian group had significantly higher levels of potassium. The British medical journal *Lancet* reported in 1982 that, during a trial with potassium supplementation, subjects who received potassium supplementation had, on the average, significantly lower blood pressures.

If you or someone you know is on anti-hypertensive medications, there is one thing of which you and your doctor should be aware. Many of the diuretics used to combat high blood pressure can rapidly deplete the body's stores of potassium. With the information we have seen above, it is not hard to extrapolate the fact that the anti-hypertensive medications can actually exacerbate hypertension in the long term. If this applies to you, do not stop taking your medicine without first discussing it with your physician! Show him this chapter and discuss it with him or her. You may actually enhance your physician's knowledge and understanding and get better healthcare.

A word of personal advice: If your physician does not want to discuss your current treatment and treatment options, shop around and find a physician who is more open minded and oriented to natural treatments.

Fiber

The recommended daily allowance of fiber is thirty grams a day. If you think you get even half of that, calculate how much you actually consume, and you will most likely be shocked. The Western diet is woefully deficient in fiber. Yet experimental studies show that people who increase their dietary fiber demonstrate a decrease in blood pressure. One study took three hundred health food store customers, people who are already at least health conscious by virtue of where they were found, and increased their dietary fiber one hundred grams per week. The results showed a decrease in blood pressure of 4mm Hg systolic and 3mm diastolic. Individuals suffering from diabetes often have hypertension (classified as secondary hypertension).

In a research program, twelve diabetic men were placed on a special diet for two weeks. The diet contained three times their normal dietary intake of fiber and a 50 percent increase in potassium. In just two weeks, subjects' average blood pressure dropped 10 percent. Raw fruits and especially vegetables contain an abundance of fiber, but they also have numerous other benefits. Researchers took thirty-two subjects and changed their diet so that 62 percent of their caloric intake came from raw foods. In 6.7 months, the average diastolic blood pressure of the group dropped 17.8mm Hg. The participants also dropped an average of 8.5 pounds. The weight loss could conceivably be responsible for the drop in blood pressure. Regardless, both are a significant decrease. It is also noteworthy that 80 percent of those who smoked or consumed alcohol spontaneously ceased that activity.

ESSENTIAL FATTY ACIDS

I discussed essential fatty acids (EFAs) in chapter 18. Let me add to that discussion here. You hear about saturated fat, unsaturated fat, and polyunsaturated fat. What do these terms mean? Let's reduce the complexity of this topic. Fat is a long chain of molecules, which can be thought of like a train with lots of cars. If all the cars are full, then it is saturated. If one of the cars is empty, then it is unsaturated. If two or more of the cars are empty, then it is polyunsaturated. Pretty easy isn't it?

Well, now that we know the difference, what does it mean for us? When the body breaks down fat into its smaller parts, the saturated fat makes more low density lipoprotein (LDL). These are the fats that clog arteries. Saturated fats are found primarily in red meat, dairy products, and some vegetable oils, such as cottonseed and coconut seed. Polyunsaturated fats make more high density lipoprotein (HDL), also known as good cholesterol. These bring the fats that can clog arteries back to the liver to be processed for other uses. Polyunsaturated fats are most of the vegetable oils and fish oils. These are often referred to as omega-3 (from fish and cod liver oil) and omega-6 (from sources such as evening primrose or flaxseed oil) fatty acids.

Polyunsaturated fats may actually lower blood pressure, because they are metabolized into prostaglandin. One of the actions of prostaglandin is to dilate the blood vessels, which will reduce pressure. Prostaglandin also enhances sodium and water excretion.

However, this effect is inhibited when aspirin or other nonsteroid anti-inflammatory medications are taken, because these medicines block the enzymatic activity that leads to the production of prostaglandin. Interestingly, standard medical procedure is to promote the use of aspirin to reduce the risk of heart disease.

Finland has done considerable research on the beneficial effects of increasing polyunsaturated fat while decreasing saturated fats. They have consistently found that the higher the ratio of saturated fats to polyunsaturated, the higher the individual's blood pressure, and the opposite is equally true. One study fed subjects a diet low in fats but high in polyunsaturated and saw blood pressure drop from an average of 139/89 to 129/81. This is significant for two reasons. First, it dropped the relative category of the patient from hypertensive to normotensive. Second, it only took six weeks. Other studies demonstrated similar benefits in a short time frame.

NUTRIENTS, SUPPLEMENTS, AND THERAPEUTIC CONSIDERATIONS

Studies have shown that hypertensive patients have lower intake levels of vitamins A and C and potassium. Supplementation with vitamin B complex, including 50 mg thiamine, 40 mg riboflavin, 200 mg pantothenate, cod liver oil, 200 mg nicotinic acid, and 50 mg lipoic acid was shown to lower blood levels of saturated fatty acids, while increasing polyunsaturated fatty acids in just ten days.

Several studies indicate that alterations in calcium metabolism have been implicated as a primary factor in the development of hypertension. Some have plainly demonstrated an inverse relationship between dietary calcium and blood calcium levels and blood pressure. It also seems that hypertensive persons actually secrete more calcium in their urine, thus increasing their dietary need.

Magnesium is a very potent vasodilator, and hypertension is a symptom of its deficiency. Magnesium helps to regulate contractility of smooth muscle, like those surrounding arteries, at the cellular level. Studies have found consistently low levels of magnesium in hypertensive patients, and the greater the level of hypomagnesemia, the higher doses of antihypertensive medications patients tend to be taking. The *British Medical Journal* reported a study that gave twenty hypertensive patients magnesium supplementation for six months. The average blood pressure of the group dropped 12/8 mm Hg.

Coenzyme Q_{10} (CoQ_{10}), also known as ubiquinone, is a little known nutrient. It is an essential component of the mitochondria, or the organelle, that produces cellular energy. CoQ_{10} can be synthesized in the body, but deficiencies have been reported. Cardiovascular disorders, such as hypertension, are body states that require increased tissue levels of CoQ_{10}, and heart tissue biopsies of patients with various heart diseases at death demonstrated deficiency in up to 75 percent of cases. In patients with documented hypertension, administration of 100 mg of CoQ_{10} daily for eight weeks was found to significantly reduce blood pressure, with 54 percent of the participants achieving greater than a 10 percent drop in their blood pressure

RECOMMENDATIONS

First and foremost, if you are currently being treated for hypertension or have high blood pressure, discuss with your physician the changes you wish to make to control your blood pressure naturally, before instituting a new program. If your physician does not wish to discuss natural options to your healthcare, I recommend finding a more open-minded physician who is experienced in natural medicine. Any doctor who believes that he or she has all the answers is a scary thought and is most likely not interested in your personal concerns.

Second, if needed, we recommend a weight reduction program along with an exercise program. We strongly recommend exercise, regardless of whether or not you are overweight. The reduction of stress alone may help reduce your blood pressure in a very short time. Dietary fiber should be increased to the recommended level of thirty grams per day. This can be accomplished by using high-fiber cereals or natural fiber supplements. Finally, many nutritional supplements have been proven to help reduce blood pressure, and I recommend the following as a minimal daily supplementation:

- **HGH Stimulate** improves circulatory, immune, and nervous system function, memory, reduces wrinkles, increases bone density, and decreases blood pressure. (Go to www.bodybyted.com to see the results!)
- **Ultimate Multiple** gives foundation nutrition for wellness and disease protection.
- **Cod Liver Oil** offers more vitamin A and D than any other product on the market.

- **Ossomag** provides superior calcium, magnesium, and vitamin D_3 formula to reduce and replace bone loss.
- **Excellent C** helps protect and support healthy connective tissue.
- **Magnesium and Malate Acid** (500 mg per day)
- **CoQ$_{10}$Max** (200 mg per day)
- **Zinc Glycinate** (15 to 30 mg per day)
- **Flax Seed Oil** (four capsules daily, 4000 mg)
- **Evening Primrose Oil** (four capsules daily)
- **Vascular Relaxant SR** helps protect and support healthy connective tissue.
- **Super Potent E** is excellent for the heart, circulation, and cancer prevention.

Avoid the following to guard against hypertension:

- No caffeine.
- No margarine or hydrogenated oils. Read product labels carefully. Hydrogenated oils are hidden in many products.
- Keep your fat intake to no more than 10 to 15 percent of your daily calorie intake. You can measure this by taking your total calorie intake, say 1,800 calories, and dividing that by 10, which equals 180. Each gram of fat contains 9 calories, which means that on a 1,800-calorie diet, a person could consume 180 calories, or 20 grams of fat.
- No pork or shellfish.

- No luncheon meat. These typically contain sodium nitrate, a known cause of colon cancer.
- No dairy products.
- No alcohol. Alcohol decreases the body's ability to burn fat by almost 35 percent.
- Cut bread consumption to one slice per day (use only whole grain bread).
- Use olive, grape seed, or macadamia nut for your oil needs. However, use these products sparingly, because they are 100 percent fat.
- No aspartame or NutraSweet, which interferes with the blood sugar regulation in your body. Researchers also theorize that use of aspartame can cause people to gain weight. Plus, aspartame is extremely toxic.
- No monosodium glutamate (MSG). Besides being loaded with excess sodium, MSG damages brain cells, just like its cousin NutraSweet (both are called excito toxins in neurochemistry).

RESULTS

Matt came to see me several years ago. He was thirty-three years old, ten pounds overweight, with a blood pressure of 180/120. Matt's mother had informed him that his father had been receiving treatment for hypertension since he was forty years old, which was fifteen years earlier. She told Matt that his father had been impotent for the past fifteen years due to his blood pressure medication.

Obviously, Matt was extremely motivated. Within one month of following my Eat, Drink, and Be Healthy! program and taking the supplements I recommended, his blood pressure dropped to 120/70 with no drugs!

If high blood pressure can be lowered by changing your diet, doesn't it make sense that if you had been eating correctly to begin with, you never would have developed hypertension?

For more information about reducing hypertension or any of the products mentioned, call my office at 1-800-726-1834 or go online at www.HealthMasters.com. My commitment to you is simple. I have been in business for three decades. If you are not 100 percent satisfied with your results with any of the products, simply return the product to our office for a full refund.

Judging by the results we have seen—and Matt is just one of many, many examples—you will be pleasantly surprised at all the benefits you will see and feel as you achieve maximum health!

20

BOOST YOUR IMMUNE SYSTEM

As we move into this final chapter, it should be evident that I am serious about getting you and your loved ones healthy, keeping you and your family healthy, and safeguarding you against all the diseases and illnesses around you. The problem is that too many people are often confused and massively misinformed. That is why I am ending this book with a recommendation for you to supercharge your immune system with technology that incorporates the latest science.

While there are no cure-alls, this new ingredient is designed for both specific health conditions and overall wellness. I am introducing a product called Immune Support DF.

Immune Support DF contains high concentrations of immunoglobulins. It can be used by people of all ages who face challenges to their health. Immune Support DF is low fat and free of lactose and other milk proteins. It has no known side effects except better health. Research has demonstrated that oral immunoglobulins (defined later in this chapter) survive stomach acid and remain active in the digestive tract. Immune Support DF has been shown to increase immunity, lower cholesterol, improve moods, improve muscle and connective tissue, improve growth, and support gastrointestinal health. Additionally, there are studies that show its relevance related to irritable bowel syndrome, inflammatory bowel disease, HIV, cancer, and sports recovery. I take this product daily, as do my wife and children. Once you finish reading this chapter you will know why!

What Is Immune Support DF?

Immune Support DF is a patented composition that contains several proteins. It is derived from no-bovine-growth-hormone cattle specifically raised for food. Just as consumers use colostrums supplements, originating from cattle, Immune Support DF comes from cattle as well.

I focus primarily on nutritional supplements and nutraceuticals from all sources. Some are derived from plants, rocks, fish, and in this case, mammals. Cattle raised as food animals produce specific immunity against a broad range of organisms because they are routinely exposed to common environmental pathogens (disease-causing microbes) to a much greater degree than humans.

As a result, the immunoglobulin of bovine origin contains antibodies that help kill human pathogens. This includes such pathogens as E. coli (linked to diarrhea), rotavirus (associated with digestive distress), H. pylori (produces ulcers), salmonella (brings about food poisoning), candida (triggers yeast infection), streptococcus (causes strep throat and other health issues), and staphylococcus (sets off infections).

Immune Support DF is particularly rich in the immunoglobulins IgG, IgM, and IgA. It contains approximately 45 percent IgG. It also contains transferrin, cytokines, interleukins, interferons, and lymphokines. In addition, Immune Support DF is rich in growth factors such as insulin-like growth factor I and II (IGF-I and IGF-II) and transforming growth factors (TGF).

These are the amazing ingredients in Immune Support DF:

Component
- Total Protein 89%
- IgG 46–53%
- Others present .... IgM, IgE, IgD, IgA
- Total Immunoglobulin 51–58%

Other proteins
- Casein 0%
- (b-lactoglobulin) 0%
- Bovine serum albumin 10%
- Cysteine$_2$ 3.3

Iron-binding capacity

- Transferrin/Lactoferrin   7.50%
- Protease inhibitors   Present
- IGF-I (ng/g protein)3   3,820
- TGFb-1 (ng/g protein)   127
- Fat   0.20%
- Lactose   0
- Moisture   4%

Before you start to fuss at me for all the scientific jargon, remember this material is being taught all over the world. So let me explain to you what this means in English.

IMMUNOGLOBULINS

Immunoglobulins are one of the most important products of the immune system. Also known as antibodies, they are substances in your blood that are produced by the body's immune system. The basic function of immunoglobulins is to find and tag foreign substances (antigens) such as bacteria, viruses, and other environmental pathogens. When an immunoglobulin attaches to an antigen, this prevents the antigen from finding its target, rendering it inactive. For example, if the antigen bound by an antibody is a virus, the antibody can prevent the attachment of the virus to your cells. Likewise, binding of an antibody to a toxin prevents the uptake of the toxin by the body. In both examples, the antibody has effectively neutralized the foreign invader. Immunoglobulins can also tag the foreign substance with a coating so that it can be recognized as foreign, ingested by specialized white blood cells, destroyed, and presented on the surface of the white blood cells for recognition by other cells of the immune system. Unlike antibiotics, immunoglobulins allow the immune system to specifically recognize foreign invaders while ignoring good bacteria that are part of the body's natural environment. What this means is that it can help stop a problem before it starts.

So why should any of us care?

A person experiencing decreased immune function is at an increased risk of developing frequent colds, flus, and cancer. With a compromised immune system, initially mild infections may become more serious. A person may be born with an immune system that produces low levels of antibodies in general, or the immune system may produce low levels of antibodies in response to certain diseases (like cancer). This is why the Immune Support DF is great to knock out colds or sore throats before they get a foothold in your body.

The five major types of immunoglobulins are:

1. **IgA antibodies** are found mainly in the nose, breathing passages, the digestive tract, ears, eyes, and vagina. IgA antibodies protect body surfaces that are exposed to the outside from foreign organisms and substances. This type of antibody is also found in saliva and tears. About 10–15 percent of

the antibodies usually present in the body are IgA antibodies. A small percentage of people do not make IgA antibodies.

2. **IgG antibodies** are found in all body fluids. They are the smallest but most abundant of the antibodies, normally comprising about 75 percent to 80 percent of all the antibodies in the body. IgG antibodies are considered the most important antibodies for fighting bacterial and viral infections. IgG antibodies are the only type of antibody that can cross the placenta. Therefore, the IgG antibodies of a pregnant woman can also help protect her baby.

3. **IgM antibodies** are the largest type of antibody. They are found in blood and lymph fluid and are the first type of antibody produced in response to an infection. They also cause other immune system cells to produce compounds that can destroy invading cells. IgM antibodies normally comprise about 5–10 percent of all the antibodies in the body.

4. **IgD antibodies** are found in small amounts in the tissues that line the abdominal or chest cavity of the body. The function of IgD antibodies is not well understood. They appear to play a role in allergic reactions to some substances such as milk, some medications, and some poisons.

5. **IgE antibodies** are found in the lungs, skin, and mucous membranes. They cause the body to react

against foreign substances such as pollen, fungus spores, and animal dander. IgE antibody levels are often high in people with allergies.

Immunoglobulins are plentiful in the human body. In fact, one-third of the proteins found in blood are immunoglobulins. The body's mucous membranes (the protective barrier that runs from the tip of the sinuses to the bottom of the intestinal tract), tears, lungs, and other orifices all have immunoglobulins coating them. Immunoglobulins can be thought of as extra reinforcements to help defend the body. This is particularly important in the digestive system. All that enters the body through the mouth and the nose goes into the digestive system, so it is a major site of invasion by microbes. While the body has many defenses, immunoglobulins are a critical component of the defense network. Immunoglobulin is the specific protein used by the body to flush foreign organisms from the intestinal tract.

TRANSFERRINS

Transferrin is a term that describes a family of iron-binding protein with antiviral, antibacterial, anti-inflammatory properties. Transferrin has been implicated in the treatment of such diseases as cancer, HIV, herpes, chronic fatigue, candida albicans, and other infections. In the intestinal tract, a specific transferrin called lactoferrin may help by stimulating intestinal cell growth and enhancing the growth of good intestinal microflora. (Intestines contain both good and bad bacteria. Maintaining these in the right balance is important for digestive health.)

A strong antioxidant, lactoferrin scavenges free iron, which prevents uncontrolled iron-based free radical reactions. Additionally, lactoferrin has positive immune modulating effects. It gives the immune system the tools it needs to operate at the appropriate level. An immune system that is overstimulated leads to autoimmune conditions, while an immune system that is underactive leads to illness and disease.

Cytokines

Cytokines are small protein molecules at the core of communication between immune system cells and between these cells and cells belonging to other tissue types. Poor cellular communication leads to abnormal cell growth (cancer) or autoimmune conditions (rheumatoid arthritis). They are involved in antiviral and anti-tumor activity and regulation and intensity of immune responses.

Elevations in inflammatory cytokines (a certain type of cytokine) are often involved in involuntary weight loss and loss of lean body mass. Cytokine modulation may offer tremendous benefits to individuals affected by immune deficiencies, chronic diarrhea, and inflammatory disease.

Interleukins

Interleukins are the cytokines that act specifically as mediators between leucocytes (white blood cells). The function of the immune system depends in a large part on interleukins, and deficiencies of a number of them can lead to autoimmune diseases (such as lupus, multiple sclerosis, and rheumatoid arthritis) or general immune deficiency.

Interferons

One of the first cytokines to be discovered was interferon. Interferon is produced by T cells (small white blood cells that orchestrate the immune defense and macrophages, a type of white blood that ingests foreign material). They are a family of proteins with antiviral properties.

Presently, interferons are being used as a drug treatment program for those with certain types of cancer and viral infections.

Lymphokines

Lymphokines, another type of cytokine, are powerful chemical substances secreted by lymphocytes (small white blood cells produced in the lymphoid organs and paramount in the immune defenses). These soluble molecules help direct and regulate the immune responses. This is a key for all of us who wish to have a properly functioning immune system.

Insulin-Like Growth Factor I and II (IGF-I and IGF-II)

IGF I and II affect how the body uses fat, protein, and sugar. IGF-I is one of the only substances known to stimulate the repair and growth of DNA and RNA, making it one of the most powerful antiaging substances. IGF-I has been clinically proven to help increase lean muscle mass and may help regulate blood sugar and cholesterol levels.

Transforming Growth Factor (TGF)

Transforming growth factor (TGF) stimulates the proliferation of cells in connective tissue and assists in the formation of bone and cartilage. It is also showing promise as a therapeutic agent in bone and wound healing. TGF can help repair tissue and may support the development of growth and the lining of the intestinal system. If you have arthritis or joint problems, this is a must!

Applications

So now that we know what's in Immune Support DF, how does it work? The immune system is the body's means of protecting us from foreign organisms or substances such as germs, toxins, and allergens. Because people encounter these things every moment of every day, it is essential to maintain a healthy immune system. In addition, common everyday psychological and physical factors such as stress, poor nutrition, dieting, travel, and strenuous athletic training may tax a person's immune system and cause it to function at less than optimal levels.

Immune studies are very difficult and expensive to perform on humans, so many of these studies must use animals as subjects. Immunoglobulins have been given by mouth to successfully improve immune function, growth, and the health of young animals since the 1990s. More than one hundred million young animals per year are fed diets supplemented with immunoglobulin as a natural means to improve their health status.

As detailed through the content list above, Immune Support DF assists the immune system naturally and thus reduces the burden on the immune system so that nutrients in the body can be used for productive functions elsewhere. This data indicates that antibodies against common pathogens are found in high concentrations in Immune Support DF.

Best of all, Immune Support DF kills multiple types of pathogens and germs. The antibodies found in Immune Support DF help kill and protect us from such common pathogens as anti-listeria, anti-campylobacter, anti-e. coli (0157), anti-salmonella.

For more information about Immune Support DF or any of the products mentioned, call my office at 1-800-726-1834 or go online at www.HealthMasters.com.

Maximum Health

Immune Support DF is a major breakthrough, but as with all of the steps detailed in this book, you are the crucial factor.

I have spent decades developing my Eat, Drink, and Be Heathy! program (go to www.bodybyted.com to see the results!). Again and again, people's lives have been changed as they have learned how to develop great habits and how to eliminate bad habits. Armed with decades of research and development, I have written this book specifically to offer the very best strategies that I have gleaned and utilized by offering twenty steps to a power-packed immune system to safeguard you and your loved ones with these twenty chapters filled with proven, practical principles, beginning at the top by maximizing your brain.

I have devoted my career to blasting away the barriers that tend to keep people of all ages and backgrounds from achieving their goals, and this book was born from my overwhelming desire—as someone who has spent most of his life motivating people toward maximum health, energy, fitness—that you have a life of adventure and wellness, no matter what happens around you or how others respond to always-present challenges.

But with every aspect of maximum health, everything depends upon how you take responsibility for you!

Earlier in the book I mentioned the old adage, "Life is God's gift to you. What you do with it is your gift back to

Him." I also pointed to the fact that God gave you quite a gift: "I will praise You, for I am fearfully and wonderfully made; marvelous are Your works, and that my soul knows very well" (Psalm 139:14), and I mentioned that the Bible also makes this fact very clear: "Each of you should know how to possess his own vessel in sanctification and honor" (1 Thessalonians 4:4). Another translation of that passage reads, "Learn to appreciate and give dignity to your body, not abusing it, as is so common among those who know nothing of God" (1 Thessalonians 4:4–5, msg).

Self-responsibility lies at the center of health and wellness. Your life and health depend upon factors largely under your own control. You hold the key to tomorrow's doors. Your actions and decisions affect all the next steps. In fact, you are the key!

Clearly, God desires the best for you: "The thief does not come except to steal, and to kill, and to destroy. I have come that they may have life, and that they may have it more abundantly" (John 10:10). He is the key to abundant life, and it is up to us to discover how to eat as He teaches and live life to the max while in obedience to His will.

Maximum health is up to you as your receive wisdom to use the tools and principles available to you. It is my prayer that you will achieve every goal that you set. And what better time than right now to get started?

Feel free to call my office with any questions: 1-800-726-1834.

NOTES

INTRODUCTION

1. "WHO Declares Swine Flu Pandemic," BBC News, June 11, 2009.
2. "Avian Influenza Frequently Asked Questions," World Health Organization, December 5, 2005. http://www.who.int/csr/disease/avian_influenza/avian_faqs/en/.
3. "Ancient Athenian Plague Proves to Be Typhoid," *Scientific American*, January 25, 2006, www.scientificamerican.com.
4. "Past Pandemics That Ravaged Europe," BBC News, November 7, 2005.
5. Lester K. Little, ed., *Plague and the End of Antiquity: The Pandemic of 541–750* (New York: Cambridge University Press, 2006); see also "Plague: The Black Death," http://science.nationalgeographic.com/

science/health-and-human-body/human-diseases/
plague-article.html.

6. Stéphane Barry and Norbert Gualde, "The Biggest Epidemic in History," *L'Histoire*, June 2006, 45–46; Robert S. Gottfried, *The Black Death: Natural and Human Disaster in Medieval Europe* (New York: Free Press, 1983); "Black Death," in *Dictionary of the Middle Ages*, ed. Joseph R. Strayer, 13 vols. (New York: Scribner, 1982–89), 2:257–67.

7. "Bubonic Plague Hits San Francisco, 1900–1909," A Science Odyssey, Public Broadcasting Service (PBS), www.pbs.org; E. G. Pryor, "The Great Plague of Hong Kong," *Journal of the Hong Kong Branch of the Royal Asiatic Society* (Hong Kong: Royal Asiatic Society of Great Britain and Ireland, 1975), 69.

8. Colette Flight, "Smallpox: Eradicating the Scourge," BBC, bbc.co.uk.

9. Greg Lange, "Smallpox Epidemic Ravages Native Americans," *Online Encyclopedia of Washington State History*, January 23, 2003, HistoryLink.org; "The Story of Smallpox and Other Deadly Eurasian Germs," BBC, bbc.co.uk.

10. F. J. Palella Jr., K. M. Delaney, and A. C. Moorman, "Declining Morbidity and Mortality Among Patients with Advanced Human Immunodeficiency Virus Infection: HIV Outpatient Study Investigators," *New England Journal of Medicine* 338, no. 13 (1998): 853–60.

11. K. A. Sepkowitz, "AIDS—The First 20 Years," *New England Journal of Medicine* 344, no. 23 (June 2001): 1764–72.

12. C. Bell, S. Devarajan, and H. Gersbach, "The Long-Run Economic Costs of AIDS: Theory and an Application to South Africa," World Bank Policy Research Working Paper No. 3152, www1.worldbank. org/hiv_aids.

13. C. W. Potter, "A History of Influenza," *Journal of Applied Microbiology*, October 2001, 572–79; Mike Adams, "A History of Influenza from 412 BC–AD 2006," www.naturalnews.com.

14. Jonathan Dushoff, "Mortality Due to Influenza in the United States—An Annualized Regression Approach Using Multiple-Cause Mortality Data," *American Journal of Epidemiology* 163, no. 2 (2006): 181–87, www.aje.oxfordjournals.org.

CHAPTER 2: EAT FOR MAXIMUM HEALTH

1. *Associated Press*, "Decade's Health Goals Unmet," *Dallas Morning News*, January 1, 2010.

2. Dawn Thorpe Jarvis, RD, LDN, "Why Are Americans So Overweight?" *Extraordinary Health* 1 (2007): 12.

3. Jarvis, "Why Are Americans So Overweight?" 12.

4. Wellness International Network, www.winltd.com.

5. Daniel Yee, Associated Press, March 15, 2007.

6. ABC News, September 6, 2007.

CHAPTER 3: BE WARY OF IMMUNIZATIONS

1. Shari Roan, "Swine Flu 'Debacle' of 1976 Is Recalled," *Los Angeles Times*, April 27, 2009, www.latimes.com.

2. Roan, "Swine Flu 'Debacle' of 1976 Is Recalled."

3. Robert S. Mendelsohn, MD, *How to Raise a Healthy Child…in Spite of Your Doctor* (New York: Random House, 1984), 232.

4. Mendelsohn, *How to Raise a Healthy Child*, 233.

5. "UNICEF: The State of the World's Children: Focus on Nutrition," www.unicef.org.

6. "Vaccination Refusal May Cause NY to Take Children," *Health Keepers* (Spring–Summer 2001), 10.

7. "Vaccination Refusal May Cause NY to Take Children," 10.

8. "Vaccination Refusal May Cause NY to Take Children," 10.

9. James Murphy, *What Every Parent Should Know About Childhood Immunization* (Boston: Earth Healing Products, 1998), 63, citing Louis Dublin and Alfred Lotka, *Twenty-Five Years of Health Progress* (New York: Metropolitan Life Insurance Company, 1973), 48.

10. Murphy, *What Every Parent Should Know About Childhood Immunization*, 45.

11. Mendelsohn, *How to Raise a Healthy Child*, 236–37.

12. Murphy, *What Every Parent Should Know About Childhood Immunization*, 111.

13. Murphy, *What Every Parent Should Know About Childhood Immunization*, 111–12.

14. Neil Z. Miller, *Vaccines: Are They Really Safe and Effective?* (Santa Fe, NM: New Atlantean Press, 1998), 25.

15. Murphy, *What Every Parent Should Know About Childhood Immunization*, 39.

16. Vijendra K. Singh, PhD, testimony, Government Reform Committee, U.S. House of Representatives, April 6, 2000.

17. Mendelsohn, *How to Raise a Healthy Child*, 239.

18. Miller, *Vaccines*, 30.

19. Miller, *Vaccines*, 30, citing "Rubella Vaccine and Susceptible Hospital Employees: Poor Physician Participation," *Journal of the American Medical Association*, February 20, 1981.

20. Miller, *Vaccines*, 10.

21. Miller, *Vaccines*, 10.

22. Murphy, *What Every Parent Should Know About Childhood Immunization*, 87–91.

23. Harris L. Coulter, PhD, and Barbara Loe Fisher, *A Shot in the Dark: Why the P in the DPT May Be Hazardous to Your Child's Health* (Garden City, NY: Avery Publishing Group, 1991), 74–75.

24. Coulter and Fisher, *A Shot in the Dark*, 72.

25. Murphy, *What Every Parent Should Know About Childhood Immunization*, 76.

26. Murphy, *What Every Parent Should Know About Childhood Immunization*, 75.

27. Coulter and Fisher, *A Shot in the Dark*, 217.

28. Coulter and Fisher, *A Shot in the Dark*, 212.

29. Miller, *Vaccines*, 32.

30. Miller, *Vaccines*, 18–21; citing Michael Anderson, *International Mortality Statistics* (Washington DC: Facts on File, 1981), 177–78.

31. Leon Chaitow, *Vaccination and Immunisation: Dangers, Delusions and Alternatives* (Saffron Walden, Essex: C. W. Daniel Co., 1998), 141.

32. Coulter and Fisher, *A Shot in the Dark*, 215.

33. Coulter and Fisher, *A Shot in the Dark*, 204.

34. Coulter and Fisher, *A Shot in the Dark*, 185.

35. Coulter and Fisher, *A Shot in the Dark*, 219.

36. Michael J. Goldberg, MD, "A New Definition," www.neuroimmunedr.com; Dorothea Carney, "The Autism Epidemic," www.the-autism-epidemic.com.

37. Goldberg, "A New Definition."

38. *60 Minutes*, CBS Television, November 12, 2000.

39. Congressman Dan Barton, "Autism: Present Challenges, Future Needs," U.S. House of Representatives, April 6, 2000.

40. Autism-PDD Network, www.autism-pdd.net.

41. Mary N. Megson, "Is Autism a G-Alpha Protein Defect Reversible with Natural Vitamin A?" www. autism.com.

42. Cited in Megson, "Is Autism a G-Alpha Protein Defect Reversible with Natural Vitamin A?"

43. "UNICEF: The State of the World's Children," www. unicef.org; accessed February 29, 2001.

44. "Diagnosing Autism," www.autism-pdd.net/ Diagnosing-autism.html.

45. Robert S. Mendelsohn, *Confessions of a Medical Heretic* (Chicago: Contemporary Books, 1979), 132.

46. Bernard Rimland, PhD, "Background and Introduction to the Position Paper of the Consensus Conference on the Mercury Detoxification of Autistic Children," Autism Research Institute, Kirkman Laboratories, Lake Oswego, OR.

47. Jack Challem, "Gut Feeling and the Origins of Autism," *Let's Live Magazine*, May 2001, 48.

48. Challem, "Gut Feeling and the Origins of Autism," 46.

49. Challem, "Gut Feeling and the Origins of Autism," 48.

50. "Tox FAQs for Formaldehyde," Agency for Toxic Substances and Disease Registry, Centers for Disease Control, www.atsdr.cdc.gov.

51. William G. Crook, MD, and Laura J. Stevens, *Solving the Puzzle of Your Hard-to-Raise Child* (New York: Random House, 1987), 35.

52. Ben F. Feingold, MD, *Why Your Child Is Hyperactive* (New York: Random House, 1975), 161.
53. Murphy, *What Every Parent Should Know About Childhood Immunization*, 55.
54. Murphy, *What Every Parent Should Know About Childhood Immunization*, 53.
55. Murphy, *What Every Parent Should Know About Childhood Immunization*, 55.
56. Murphy, *What Every Parent Should Know About Childhood Immunization*, 56–57.
57. Chaitow, *Vaccination and Immunisation*, 62.
58. Feingold, *Why Your Child Is Hyperactive*, 163–64.

CHAPTER 5: USE THE VIRUS KILLER

1. L. Y. Matsuoka, J. Wortsman, J. G. Haddad, P. Kolm, and B. W. Hollis, "Racial Pigmentation and the Cutaneous Synthesis of Vitamin D," *Archives of Dermatology* 127 (1991): 536–38.
2. H. Glerup, K. Mikkelsen, and L. Poulsen, "Commonly Recommended Daily Intake of Vitamin D Is Not Sufficient If Sunlight Exposure Is Limited," *Journal of Internal Medicine* 247 (2000): 260–68; H. Glerup and E. F. Eriksen, "Vitamin D Deficiency, Easy to Diagnose, Often Overlooked," *Ugeskr Laeger* 161 (1999): 2515–21.
3. B. L. Diffey, "Solar Ultraviolet Radiation Effects on Biological Systems," *Physics in Medicine and Biology* 36 (1991): 299–328.

4. J. Moan, A. Dahlback, and R. B. Setlow, "Epidemiological Support for an Hypothesis for Melanoma Induction Indicating a Role for UVA Radiation," *Photochemistry and Photobiology Journal* 70 (1999): 243–47.

5. M. Ranson, S. Posen, and R. S. Mason, "Human Melanocytes as a Target Tissue for Hormones: In Vitro Studies with 1 Alpha-25, Dihydroxyvitamin D3, Alpha-Melanocyte Stimulating Hormone, and Beta-Estradiol," *Journal of Investigative Dermatology* 91 (1988): 593–98.

6. L. Y. Matsuoka, J. Wortsman, J. G. Haddad, and B. W. Hollis, "In Vivo Threshold for Cutaneous Synthesis of Vitamin D3," *Journal of Laboratory and Clinical Medicine* 114 (1989): 301–5.

7. R. M. Sayre, J. C. Dowdy, J. Shepherd, I. Sadig, A. Bager, and N. Kollias, "Vitamin D Production by Natural and Artificial Sources," Photo Medical Society Meeting Presentation, March, 1, 1998.

8. J. M. Pettifor, G. P. Moodley, and F. S. Hough, "The Effect of Season and Latitude on In Vitro Vitamin D Formation by Sunlight in South Africa," *South Africa Medical Journal* 86 (1996): 1270–72; A. R. Webb, L. Kline, and M. F. Holick, "Influence of Season and Latitude on the Cutaneous Synthesis of Vitamin D3: Exposure to Winter Sunlight in Boston and Edmonton Will Not Promote Vitamin D_3 Synthesis in Human Skin," *Journal of Clinical*

Endocrinology and Metabolism 67 (1988): 373–78.

9. *Current Opinion in Lipidology* 18 (February 2007): 41–46; A. Zittermann, "Vitamin D and Disease Prevention with Special Reference to Cardiovascular Disease," *Progress in Biophysics and Molecular Biology* 92 (2006): 39–48; A. Zittermann, S. S. Schleithoff, G. Tenderich, H. K. Berthold, R. Korfre, and P. Stehle, "Low Vitamin D Status: A Contributing Factor in the Pathogenesis of Congestive Heart Failure?" *Journal of the American College of Cardiology* 41 (2003): 105–12.

10. S. Hahn, "Low Serum 25-HydroxyVitamin D Concentrations Are Associated with Insulin Resistance and Obesity in Women with Polycystic Ovary Syndrome," *Experimental and Clinical Endocrinology and Diabetes* 114, no. 10 (November 2006): 577–83.

11. *The Spine Journal* 15, no. 2 (January 2003): 177–79.

12. K. M. Dixon, S. S. Deo, A. W. Norman, J. E. Bishop, G. M. Halliday, V. E. Reeve, and R. S. Mason, "*In Vivo* Relevance for Photoprotection by the Vitamin D Rapid Response Pathway," *Journal of Steroid Biochemistry and Molecular* Biology 103, nos. 3–5 (March 2007): 451–56.

13. H. A. Bischoff, H. B. Stahelin, N. Urscheler, R. Ehrsam, R. Vonthein, P. Perrig-Chiello, A. Tyndall, and R. Theiler, "Muscle Strength in the Elderly: Its Relation to Vitamin D Metabolites," *Archives*

of Physical Medicine and Rehabilitation 80, no. 1
(January 1999): 54–58.

14. Yoshihiro Sato, MD, Munetsugu Kikuyama, PhD,
and Kotaro Oizumi, MD, "High Prevalence of
Vitamin D Deficiency and Reduced Bone Mass in
Parkinson's Disease," *Neurology* 49 (1997): 1273–78.

CHAPTER 6: BECOME WATER WISE

1. "Dehydration Definition," www.mayoclinic.
2. "Dehydration Definition," www.mayoclinic.
3. Sally Squires, "Soft Drinks, Hard Facts," *Washington Post*, February 27, 2001.
4. "Drinking Even Diet Soda May Be Harmful to Your
Health," University of Rochester Medical Center,
July 25, 2007, www.urmc.rochester.edu.
5. "Bottled Water: Pure Drink or Pure Hype?" National
Resources Defense Council, www.nrdc.org.
6. "Bottled Water: Pure Drink or Pure Hype?" National
Resources Defense Council, www.nrdc.org.
7. "Bottled Water: Pure Drink or Pure Hype?" National
Resources Defense Council, www.nrdc.org.

CHAPTER 8: EXERCISE YOUR WAY TO HEALTH

1. "Exercise Stimulates, Satisfies Appetite," *American
Journal of Clinical Nutrition*, October 2009;
reported by Reuters on November 25, 2009.

2. "Exercise Stimulates, Satisfies Appetite," *American Journal of Clinical Nutrition*, October 2009; reported by Reuters on November 25, 2009.

Chapter 9:
Safeguard Your Health with Sleep

1. "Importance of Sleep," Harvard Women's Health Watch, www.health.harvard.edu/press_releases/importance_of_sleep_and_health.
2. Cherie Calbom with John Calbom, *Sleep Away the Pounds* (New York: Warner Wellness, 2007), xiii.
3. National Sleep Foundation, http://www.apa.org/topics/sleep/why.aspx#.
4. "Sleep Medicine Alert," National Sleep Foundation, http://www.apa.org/topics/sleep/why.aspx#.
5. National Sleep Foundation, http://www.apa.org/topics/sleep/why.aspx#.
6. "Importance of Sleep," Harvard Women's Health Watch, www.health.harvard.edu/press_releases/importance_of_sleep_and_health.
7. F. W. Turek and M. U. Gillette, "Melatonin, Sleep, and Circadian Rhythms: Rationale for Development of Specific Melatonin Agonists," *Journal of Clinical Sleep Medicine* 6 (November 2004): 523–32; A. G. Wade, I. Ford, and G. Crawford, "Efficacy of Prolonged Release Melatonin in Insomnia Patients

Aged 55–80 Years," *Current Medical Research and Opinion* 23, no. 10 (October 2007): 2597–605.

CHAPTER 11: CLEAN OUT YOUR ARTERIES

1. D. Karunasagar, M. V. Krishna, S. V. Rao, and J. Arunachalam, "Removal and Preconcentration of Inorganic and Methyl Mercury from Aqueous Media Using a Sorbent Prepared from the Plant Coriandrum Sativum," *Journal of Hazardous Materials* 118, nos. 1–3 (February 2005): 133–39.

2. H. Gurer and N. Ercal, "Can Antioxidants Be Beneficial in the Treatment of Lead Poisoning?" *Free Radical Biology and Medicine* 29, no. 10 (2000): 927–45; M. Aga, "Preventive Effect of Coriandrum Sativum (Chinese Parsley) on Localized Lead Deposition in ICR Mice," *Journal of Ethnopharmacology* 77, nos. 2–3 (October 2001): 203–8.

3. M. L. Queiroz, "Protective Effects of Chlorella Vulgaris in Lead-Exposed Mice Infected with Listeria Monocytogenes," *International Immunopharmacology* 3, no. 6 (June 2003): 889–900.

4. W. Jiang, D. Liu, and W. Hou, "Hyper Accumulation of Cadmium by Roots, Bulbs and Shoots of Garlic," *Bioresource Technology* 76, no. 1 (January 2001): 9–13.

5. J. H. Lee, H. S. Kang, and J. Roh, "Protective Effects of Garlic Juice Against Embryo Toxicity of Methyl Mercuric Chloride Administered to Pregnant Fischer 344 Rats," *Yonsei Medical Journal* 40, no. 5 (October 1999): 483–89; S. J. James, W. Slikker, S. Melnyk, E. New, M. Pogribna, and S. Jernigan, "Thimerosal Neurotoxicity Is Associated with Glutathione Depletion: Protection with Glutathione Precursors," *NeuroToxicology Journal* 26, no. 1 (January 2005): 1–8; L. M. Gaetke and C. K. Chow, "Copper Toxicity, Oxidative Stress, and Antioxidant Nutrients," *Toxicology* 189, nos. 1–2 (July 2003): 147–63.

6. R. N. das Neves, F. Carvalho, M. Carvalho, E. Fernandes, E. Soares, M.L. de Bastos, and M.L. de Pereira, "Protective activity of Hesperidin and Lipoic Acid Against Sodium Arsenite Acute Toxicity in Mice," *Toxicologic Pathology* 32, no. 5 (September–October 2004): 527–35.

7. M. Bludovska, D. Kotyzova, and J. Koutensky, "The Influence of Alpha-Lipoic Acid on the Toxicity of Cadmium," *General Physiology and Biophysics* 18, special no. (October 1999): 28–32; R. L. Keith, I. Setiarahardjo, Q. Fernando, H. V. Aposhian, and A. J. Gandolfi, "Utilization of Renal Slices to Evaluate the Efficacy of Chelating Agents for Removing Mercury from the Kidney," *Toxicology* 116, nos. 1–3 (January 15, 1997): 67–75.

CHAPTER 12:
BUILD HEALTH WITH SUPPLEMENTS

1. Linus Pauling, "Vitamin C and Cancer," *Linus Pauling Institute of Science and Medicine Newsletter* 1, no. 2.

2. *British Journal of Cancer* 49 (1988): 321–24; *International Journal of Epidemiology* 17 (1988): 281–88).

3. L. C. Clark, "Effects of Selenium Supplementation for Cancer Prevention in Patients with Carcinoma of the Skin," *Journal of the American Medical Association* 276, no. 24 (1996): 1957–85.

4. L. Packer and Y. Suzuki, "Alpa-Lipoic Acid and Inhibition of Gene Activating Transcription of HIV," Biological Oxidants and Antioxidants: New Developments in Research and Health Effects Conference, Pasadena, CA, 1993.

5. R. Passwater, *Lipoic Acid: The Metabolic Antioxidant* (New Canaan, CT: Keats Publishing, 1995), 1–47; L. Packer, E. H. Witt, H. J. Tritschler, "Lipoic Acid as a Biological Antioxidant," *Free-Radical Biological Medicine* 19, no. 2 (1995): 226–50.

6. K. Folker, *Biomedical and Clinical Aspects of Coenzyme Q,* vol. 6 (New York: Elsevier, 1990); K. Folker, *Clinical Investigator* 71 (1993): supplement, 51–54.

7. K. Lockwood, *Biochemical and Biophysical Research and Communications* 212 (1995): 172–77.

8. *Linus Pauling Institute of Science and Medicine Newsletter*, Palo Alto, CA.

9. Eric Braverman, MD, and C. C. Pfeiffer, *The Healing Nutrients Within* (New Canaan, CT: Keats Publishing, 1988), 99; D. P. Jones, *Nutrition and Cancer* 17, no. 1 (1992): 57–75.

10. S. S. Hendler, *Doctor's Vitamin and Mineral Encyclopedia* (1990): 42; *Journal of the National Cancer Institute* 73 (1984): 1463–68; and M. Michsche et al., *Oncology* 34 (1977): 234–38.

11. G. Block, "The Data Support for a Role for Antioxidants in Reducing Cancer Risk," *Nutrition Reviews* 50 (1992): 207–13; G. Block, "Fruit, Vegetables, and Cancer Prevention: A Review of the Epidemiologic Evidence," *Nutrition and Cancer* 18 (1992): 1–29; B. E. Cohen and I. K. Cohen, "Vitamin A: Ajunvant and Steroid Antagonist in the Immune Response," *Journal of Immunology* 3 (1073): 1376–80.

12. Linus Pauling, "Vitamin C and Cancer," *Linus Pauling Institute of Science and Medicine Newsletter* 1, no. 2; G. Block, "Beyond Deficiency: New Views on the Function and Health Effects of Vitamins," New York Academy of Sciences, February 1992; and E. Cameron and L. Pauling, *Cancer and Vitamin C* (New York: Warner Books, 1981).

13. M. T. Murray, "PCO Cources: Grape Seed vs.

Pine Bark: A Review and Comparison" *Botanical Report, Health Counselor* 7:1; R. Passwater and C. Kandaswami, *Phycogenol: The Super Protector Nutrient* (New Cannan, CT: Keats Publishing, 1994), 7–8; and J Masquelier, "Pycnogenols: Recent Advances in the Therapeutic Activity of Procyanidins," in *Natural Products as Medicinal Agents*, ed. J. L. Beal and E. Reinhard (Stuttgart: Hippokrates Verlag, 1991), 343–56.

14. L. C. Clark, "Effects of Selenium Supplementation in Cancer Prevention in Patients with Carcinoma of the Skin," *Journal of the American Medical Association* 276, no. 24 (1996): 1957–85.

15. J. Shabert and N. Erlich, *The Ultimate Nutrient: Glutamine* (New York: Avery Publishing, 1994).

16. *Cancer* 52 (1983): 70–73.

17. P. N. Steinberg, "A Wondrous Herb from the Peruvian Rainforest," Townsend Letter for Doctors (1994): 130; B. W. Davis, "A New World Class Herb for AK Pratgice" (1992); "Phytochemical and Biological Research on Uncaria Tomentosa," *Bollettino-Societa Italiana Biologia Sperimentale* 65, no. 6 (1989): 517–20.

18. J. Richardson, *The Little Herb Encyclopedia*, 146.

19. W. Boericke, *Manual of Homeopathic Materia Medica* (New Delhi: B. Jain Publishers, 1927).

20. H. Schroeder, "Scandium, Chromium, Gallium.

Yttrium, Rhodium, Palladium, Indium in Mice: Effects on Growth and Life Span," *Journal of Nutrition* 101 (1971): 1431–38.

21. I. Smith, *Trace Metals in the Environment, Volume 5—Indium* (Ann Arbor: Ann Arbor Science Publishers, 1978).

22. G. Bonadio, "Methods for Administering Nutritional Indium," U.S. Patent, Washington DC, December 1999.

23. Bonadio, "Methods for Administering Nutritional Indium."

CHAPTER 15: FLUSH THE FLUORIDE

1. "The Fluoride Conspiracy," Information Liberation, www.informationliberation.com/?id=14949.

2. For additional research, see Joseph Borkin, *The Crime and Punishment of I. G. Farben* (New York: Free Press, 1978).

3. "The Fluoride Conspiracy," Information Liberation, www.informationliberation.com/?id=14949.

4. "The Fluoride Conspiracy," Information Liberation, www.informationliberation.com/?id=14949.

5. "The Fluoride Conspiracy," Information Liberation, www.informationliberation.com/?id=14949.